ML 3506 .S39 1996

Setting the tempo

D0046889

DATE DUE

SETTING THE TEMPO

*Fifty Years
of Great Jazz
Liner Notes*

SETTING

the TEM

Fifty Years
of Great **JAZZ**
Liner Notes

Anchor Books Doubleday New York London Toronto Sydney Auckland

Edited and with an Introduction by **TOM PIAZZA**

AN ANCHOR BOOK
PUBLISHED BY DOUBLEDAY
a division of Bantam Doubleday Dell Publishing Group, Inc.
1540 Broadway, New York, New York 10036

ANCHOR BOOKS, DOUBLEDAY, *and the portrayal of an anchor*
are trademarks of Doubleday, a division of
Bantam Doubleday Dell Publishing Group, Inc.

Book design by Terry Karydes

Photo Credits
Title page ii: Art Blakey performing at Carnegie Hall. Undated photograph.
Carole & Florence Reiff/Corbis-Bettmann.
Title page iii: Ornette Coleman blowing on a plastic saxophone at the
Music Inn. Photograph, June 1959.
Carole & Florence Reiff/Corbis-Bettmann.

Library of Congress Cataloging-in-Publication Data
Setting the tempo : fifty years of great jazz liner notes / edited and
with an introduction by Tom Piazza.
p.   cm.
1. Jazz—History and criticism.   I. Piazza, Tom, 1955–
ML3506.S39   1996
781.65' 015—dc20   *96-15569*
CIP
MN

ISBN 0-385-48000-8
Introduction, selection, and headnotes copyright © 1996 by Tom Piazza
All Rights Reserved
Printed in the United States of America
First Anchor Books Trade Paperback Edition: September 1996

1   3   5   7   9   10   8   6   4   2

CONTENTS

v

ACKNOWLEDGMENTS

The editor and publisher are grateful for permission to include the following copyrighted material in this volume.

George Avakian
Liner notes to *Chicago Jazz* (Decca) reprinted by permission of George Avakian. Copyright © 1940 by George Avakian. Liner notes to *Ellington at Newport* by Duke Ellington (Columbia) reprinted by permission of Columbia records. Copyright © 1956 by Columbia Records.

Whitney Balliett
Liner notes to *The Boss of the Blues* by Joe Turner (Atlantic) reprinted by permission of Whitney Balliett. Copyright © 1956 by Whitney Balliett. Liner notes to *Pacific Jazz* by the Gerry Mulligan Quartet reprinted by permission of Whitney Balliett. Copyright © 1955 by Whitney Balliett.

Amiri Baraka (LeRoi Jones)
Liner notes to *LadyLove* by Billie Holiday (United Artists) reprinted by permission of Amiri Baraka. Copyright © 1963 by Amiri Baraka. Liner notes to *Coltrane Live at Birdland* by the John Coltrane Quartet (Impulse) reprinted by permission of Amiri Baraka. Copyright © 1962 by Amiri Baraka.

Danny Barker
Liner notes to *Chu Berry and His Stompy Stevedores* by Chu Berry (Epic) reprinted by permission of Louisa Barker. Copyright © 1969 by Danny Barker.

Michael Brooks
Liner notes to *The Lester Young Story Vol. 1* by Lester Young (Columbia) reprinted by permission of Michael Brooks. Copyright © 1976 by Michael Brooks.

Ornette Coleman
Liner notes to *Change of the Century* by Ornette Coleman (Atlantic) reprinted by permission of Ornette Coleman. Copyright © 1996 by Ornette Coleman.

Stanley Crouch
Liner notes to *At the Five Spot* by Thelonious Monk (Milestone) reprinted by permission of Stanley Crouch. Copyright © 1977 by Stanley Crouch. Liner notes to *The Freedom and Space Sessions* by Booker Ervin (Prestige) reprinted by permission of Stanley Crouch. Copyright © 1979 by Stanley Crouch.

Andrew White
Liner notes to *On a Misty Night* by John Coltrane (Prestige) reprinted by permission of Andrew White. Copyright © 1973 by Andrew White.

Every effort has been made to trace and contact copyright holders prior to publication. However, in some instances this has proved impossible. If notified, the publisher will be pleased to rectify any omissions at the earliest opportunity.

INTRODUCTION

The back of a record album might seem an unlikely birthplace for even a minor literary genre. At first glance, the text on the albums' back sleeves—or liners (hence the term *liner notes*)—appears to promise little more than glorified promotional copy for the enclosed record. It is striking how often this writing contains much more: background on the musicians and the recordings, historical context, musical analysis, a window into the recording process, intimate anecdotes and personal views of the musicians that have an immediacy and warmth rarely found in other jazz writing—setting the tempo, in a sense, for the listener's appreciation of the music.

Liner notes play a special role in a jazz fan's development. They have often been the place where a new fan first begins to learn about the musicians and the repertoire of jazz. There is always that moment, which any jazz fan recognizes, of unwrapping the record, putting it on, and settling in to read the notes, to *get the word*, on the music from an expert. Good liner notes stick in the listener's mind and attach themselves to the experience of listening to the record; the best, in fact, like David Himmelstein's notes to Booker Ervin's *Setting the Pace*, or Amiri Baraka's to *Coltrane Live at Birdland*, have themselves become classics, touchstones of the music.

Of course, liner notes provide factual information and are in fact the main source of printed factual data for some artists. But the best liner notes, whether historical, musicological, narrative, or impressionistic, have always provided something beyond facts; they tell the listener, in many subtle ways, what it means to be a jazz fan. They embody styles of appreciating the music, a range of possible attitudes toward it. It is in this extra dimension that the liner note as a form really distinguishes itself.

The present collection is my selection of forty-nine of the best liner notes ever written. Included are at least one set apiece by most of the best writers in the field, along with as many notes as I could find by musicians themselves. I tried as much as possible to use notes that addressed a broad stylistic panorama of the music, from Bunk Johnson to Ornette Coleman, and to make sure there was a mixture of writing about such lesser-known players as Warne Marsh and Jess Stacy, as well as about the music's better-known players.

But ultimately, the determining factor in almost every case was whether the notes stand on their own and make good reading apart from the record they were originally meant to accompany. Ideally, *Setting the Tempo* will be read as a collection of voices, of writing by people with distinctive attitudes toward the music they write about, people who convey some of their own personalities and sensibilities along with a true love for the music. The best jazz writers, like all good writers, have individual *sounds*.

In the late 1930s, the 78-rpm record was the dominant commercial record format. Double-sided recordings, pressed on shellac, were usually issued one by one, not in sets, and contained two tunes for anywhere between thirty-five and seventy-five cents. At that time—the height of the big band era—the overwhelming popularity of swing music had stimulated interest in the 1920s' "hot jazz," out of which swing had grown. But the records from ten or fifteen years before could be hard to find; then, as now, recordings went in and out of print quickly.

As the originals became scarce and the demand obvious, record companies began reissuing the old recordings in booklike "albums" with pockets that would contain anywhere from four to six 78-rpm reissues of material by Bessie Smith, Bix Beiderbecke, Louis Armstrong, Duke Ellington, and other musicians and bands that had blazed the jazz trail. The earliest example of such reissuing that I know of was brought to my attention by California collector George Hocutt: a 1936 album of recordings by Bix Beiderbecke on Victor, issued only five years after the cornetist's early death and including several previously unissued items.

Sometimes the packages centered around themes instead of star performers, as with Columbia's *Hot Trombones* or Brunswick's *Riverboat Jazz* albums, which collected recordings by a number of different artists. Already, such collections were encouraging a kind of historical perspective on jazz music that bordered, at times, on mythologizing, and that was unusual for such a young art. The earliest examples of jazz album annotations accompanied these sets, as booklets, and were instrumental in setting the tone—epic/heroic, for the most part, with elegiac and even tragic overtones when discussing those who died young—in which writers would address jazz music for decades to come.

Jazz liner notes began to come into their own in a more modern sense with the first sets of multiple new recordings issued together in multipocket albums. Dan Morgenstern, of the Institute of Jazz Studies at Rutgers University in Newark, New Jersey, believes the first of these to be Decca's *Chicago Jazz* album, of 1940, for which musicians identified with the late-1920s Chicago school, like Eddie Condon, Bud Freeman, and Jimmy McPartland, gathered together for new sessions to recreate the style of fifteen years before.

This was followed by Decca's *New Orleans Jazz* album, organized along the same lines and including musicians of the stature of Louis Armstrong, Sidney Bechet, and Henry (Red) Allen. Both were organized by producer George Avakian, one of the heroes of jazz recording. He annotated the Chicago set, and Charles Edward Smith annotated *New Orleans Jazz;* both sets of notes are included in this book's first section, called "The Early Years." That section also includes a stylish set of notes by the infallibly patrician newspaper columnist and commentator George Frazier for Brunswick's 1945 album of reissues of recordings by the short-lived clarinetist Frank Teschemacher.

Throughout the 1940s, record companies continued to issue both kinds of albums—reissues and newly recorded performances organized around a theme or, occasionally, a star performer. In the process, the act of assembling or recording the album itself became a subject of interest, and the recording circumstances themselves sometimes became the subject of an album's annotations.

This collection's second section, called "A Moment's Notice," contains examples of this approach. One of the best known is producer Dave Stuart's story of finding and recording the legendary New Orleans horn man Bunk Johnson. Composer and writer Gunther Schuller's tale of tracking down and, finally, recording the great Kansas City alto man Buster Smith, best known as Charlie Parker's teacher, follows it, along with George Avakian's notes on the Duke Ellington band's historic performance at the 1956 Newport Jazz Festival. One of this collection's gems, David Himmelstein's notes to Booker Ervin's *Setting the Pace,* is a harrowing odyssey describing the events surrounding the recording session, which took place in Germany. The section ends with a set of my own notes describing a trio session led by pianist Barry Harris.

In the 1950s and 1960s, jazz liner notes entered a golden age. Companies like Prestige, Blue Note, Atlantic, Columbia, and RCA/Victor gave copious space on the liner for extended essays on the music and musicians involved. This was the era of Nat Hentoff, Martin Williams, Dan Morgenstern, Ira Gitler, Whitney Balliett, Leonard Feather, and Orrin Keepnews. Notes by working jazz writers from this period comprise most of this collection, and are collected, by author, in the section called "Straight Ahead," which also documents subsequent decades.

In fact, the 1970s gave new life to the liner note as a form with the proliferation of *twofers,* which were two-for-the-price-of-one LP sets of reissues of classic LP material from the 1950s and 1960s, much as the early multipocket 78 albums reissued earlier 78s. During this period, younger writers such as Stanley Crouch and Robert Palmer hit their stride. The collection continues up to the present, with fine contributions by some excellent contemporaries like Loren Schoenberg and Felicity Howlett, both of whom are musicians as well as historians and fans.

As most jazz fans know, some of the best and most memorable liner notes have been written by musicians; pianist Bill Evans and composer and bassist Charles Mingus were two of the best-known liner notes writers among musicians. Mingus, especially, liked to annotate his own recordings; of all jazz musicians he was the most outspoken about the inadequacies of jazz writers. Other musicians have also taken to the form with great success, as the other notes in the section entitled "The Musicians Themselves" demonstrate.

As recordings slide out of print, much fine writing has gone with them; rescuing these few, at least, from limbo has been a happy task. My thanks go to the many people who recommended favorite notes or who suggested leads, and especially to Dan Morgenstern of the Institute of Jazz Studies at Rutgers, Dr. Bruce Boyd Raeburn of the Tulane Jazz Archive, Jerry Brock of the Louisiana Music Factory, George Hocutt, Ed Newman, Stanley Crouch, Loren Schoenberg, Esther Smith of Rutgers, Charlie Conrad and Jennie Guilfoyle of Anchor Books, and my agent, Gail Hochman. And, of course—and most importantly—to all those who gave permission for notes to be used in this collection.

—Tom Piazza
New Orleans, 1996

PART ONE

The Early Years

GEORGE AVAKIAN

Chicago Jazz

Various Artists
(Decca 121)

The purpose of this album is to set down on wax once more a type of music played in the twenties by a small group of young white musicians in Chicago. What they played has come to be known as Chicago style and is recognized as the greatest advance of white musicians in the essentially colored art of hot jazz.

Their music drew mainly from three sources, of which New Orleans jazz, as they heard it played by New Orleans Negroes in Chicago, is the most important—for behind all jazz is the history of New Orleans music. Earlier by-products of this music included the Friar's Society Orchestra (later called the New Orleans Rhythm Kings), a group of white Chicago and New Orleans men, and the Wolverines Orchestra, which was built around the late Bix Beiderbecke of Davenport.

As high school boys with their first instruments, the Chicagoans were attracted by the Friar's Society Orchestra. Six boys attending Austin High School formed the nucleus of a youthful jazz band known as the Austin

Blue Friars. Jimmy McPartland (cornet), Frank Teschemacher (clarinet), Bud Freeman (tenor sax), Dave North (piano), Jim Lannigan (bass), and Dick McPartland (banjo) all attended Austin. Dave Tough on drums and Floyd O'Brien with his trombone rounded out the personnel. Teschemacher, destined to become the greatest white musician in the annals of jazz, started out on violin and banjo, but switched to clarinet after hearing Leon Rapollo of the Friar's Society band. Listening to Johnny Dodds and Jimmy Noone made it stick.

About the same time, the Austin gang heard of King Oliver for the first time. Then in 1923 along came the Wolverines, and Louis Armstrong left Oliver to strike out on his own. The Austin boys were not alone in their respect for the New Orleans men and their followers. Other youngsters, friends of theirs, were eagerly taking in all they could of this music—Eddie Condon, Muggsy Spanier, and Milt Mezzrow were among the first.

In trying to emulate the music they heard, the Chicagoans produced music peculiar to themselves. The most striking aspect of Chicago style jazz is its powerful drive. The middle and end of each chorus particularly arouses in the musicians a reaction like Pepper Martin diving for home plate. They play hard, with never a letup, but these two concentration points plus the four beats of the bar are always emphasized.

Ensembles are improvised; cornet lead with the other horns rounding out the harmony and filling in, always with the rhythmic drive in mind. The rhythm section, of course, plays an important part in creating this tension, principally through the judicious use of emphases and cross rhythms by drums and banjo. Today the guitar has replaced the banjo, and this less percussive instrument has proven more effective in ensembles, but not as striking for this particular purpose. When he played banjo, Eddie Condon would sometimes use a different rhythm pattern of each chorus of a record (*Friar's Point Shuffle*, 1927) and on *I've Found*

10

a New Baby (1928) he leads the rhythm section in four different patterns during one chorus. One of these is a shuffle effect which has been grotesquely exaggerated into a commercial attraction by Jan Savitt and Henry Busse.

To further sustain this driving tension, the Chicagoans use such devices as diminuendos and crescendos in ensemble passages, coming to a sudden stop on the last beat of the sixteenth bar of a tune and picking up again on the second beat of the seventeenth, and playing out endings of a solo chorus together so as to give the next chorus a rousing send-off.

One of the most repeated adages about the peculiarities of Chicago style has always been that the Chicagoans use few notes. It is true that they seem to avoid using any more than they have to, but Teschemacher, who was Chicago style personified, has recorded numerous solos built on eighth notes—although at the same time he frequently stretched two or three notes into an entire phrase. Boyce Brown, twenty-nine-year-old saxophonist who is classified as one of the Chicago gang, is even more extreme than Teschemacher. His is a fluid style of playing, in which the notes pour out in a perfect torrent for measures at a time. Yet he is as "Chicagoan" as Floyd O'Brien, who once made five notes in slow tempo seem perfectly natural for the first four bars of a solo (*Tennessee Twilight*, 1933). The "Chicago punch" is there in both of them, and that's what counts.

Despite the uncompromising nature of their music, the Chicagoans found jobs where they could play as they liked. The original Austin gang held an engagement at the White City Ballroom in 1925, followed by radio work over Chicago's WHT. But today Chicago style must be judged by its records, made by bands which never existed outside of the recording studio. *Friar's Point Shuffle* and *Darktown Strutters' Ball* (1927); *China Boy* and *Sugar, Nobody's Sweetheart* and *Liza, There'll Be Some Changes Made* and *I've Found a New Baby* (1928) are probably the most "Chicagoan."

After the Depression set in, the Chicago boys split up, many of them wandering to New York. In the past ten years, some have gained fame. Gene Krupa, for instance, has his own band. Others, like Bud Jacobson, have almost been forgotten. Teschemacher, the ringleader, was killed March 1, 1932, in an automobile accident, when he was only twenty-six years old. Dave North retired in 1931 and is now a maintenance engineer for the Tele-Register Corporation in Chicago. Jim Lannigan gave up hot music and is now finishing out his sixth year in the Chicago Symphony. Mezzrow is now in the publishing business.

So in some cases rounding up the boys again for these records was a problem—a problem accentuated by contractual obligations and engagements in distant parts of the country. The six records in this album represent eight months of arduous preparation. The results are well worth the effort: the first records in a decade by the Chicagoans, *playing as they did in the twenties*. Not copying, nor trying to improve, but recapturing the youthful spirit which produced the greatest hot records made by white musicians.

The Records

Eddie Condon's Chicagoans

PERSONNEL: *Max Kaminsky (cornet); Brad Gowans (valve trombone); Pee Wee Russell (clarinet); Bud Freeman (tenor sax); Joe Sullivan (piano); Eddie Condon (guitar); Clyde Newcomb (bass); Dave Tough (drums). (Recorded in New York, August 11, 1939.)*

With the exception of Sullivan and Tough, this personnel drew directly from Bud Freeman's Summa Cum Laude Orchestra. As the latter combination now records as a unit for Decca, an interesting comparison can be made between these efforts for the album and the band's usual style of playing. Brad Gowans is a veteran of fifteen years with jam bands, and Clyde Newcomb has played bass in small bands exclusively for several years. The rest of the men are of the old Chicago school.

These records are close to the New Orleans influence and emphasize the power and drive inherent in Chicago style music.

Nobody's Sweetheart

All the tunes recorded in this album are standards which the Chicagoans often played. This one was recorded twice before: by Teschemacher and Muggsy with Charles Pierce in 1927, and by Jimmy McPartland, Tesch, Freeman, Sullivan, Condon, Lannigan, and Krupa in 1928, under the name of McKenzie and Condon's Chicagoans.

Pee Wee Russell opens this side with a clarinet introduction which is at first reminiscent of Teschemacher's on the 1928 *Changes Made*. Kaminsky, Gowans, and Freeman then play the melody in three-part harmony—it almost sounds arranged—while Pee Wee floats off by himself in a counter-improvisation. This is one of the best bits of work Pee Wee has recorded in years. Brad Gowans and Bud Freeman share the next chorus, then Max Kaminsky contributes a tremendous cornet solo with the help of a deftly handed mute. Joe Sullivan finishes out his chorus until two bars from the end, when the whole band bursts in for the big push. The final chorus is pretty much a definition of Chicago ensemble playing. It is probably the high point of the album. The first climax comes halfway through, then Kaminsky's biting cornet brings the band up again into the last half of this grand finale. The boys had no right playing so well; this was something hoped for but not expected.

Much of the credit for the power generated by the band must go to Davey Tough (who, with Kaminsky and Sullivan, drew top honors on the session). Note especially the lift he gives the first and last choruses. This side, incidentally, was completely unrehearsed except for the introduction. The master used marks

13

the first playing of the tune; it was not even run through for timing.

The climax in the middle of the last chorus recalls the use of the more violent "stop-and-go" on the 1928 version of *Nobody's Sweetheart,* which is reproduced almost exactly by Bob Crosby's Bob Cats in *Stumblin'* (Decca 1593).

Friar's Point Shuffle

Frankly, there's no such tune as *Friar's Point Shuffle.* The name comes from the blues chorus Red McKenzie sang on the old Jungle Kings record by Muggsy, Tesch, Mezz, Sullivan, Condon, Lannigan, and Wettling. It has been said that Friar's Point is a town in Missouri with a handful of inhabitants—all colored.

With the old *Friar's Point Shuffle* as a basis, the boys played the blues with the same thought in mind—not to produce an orthodox, nostalgic blues, but to apply the power technique to the twelve-bar theme. So once again we have the emphasis on drive. As before, this number was recorded immediately, without any rehearsal. Six choruses was estimated as the proper length and off they went. A subsequent master of this side turned out almost as well, and on the whole there is little to choose between the two, but the solos on the master finally picked are considerably better.

Between each chorus, the band fills in the eleventh and twelfth bars, which is an important factor in keeping up the constant drive of this record. Joe Sullivan plays a marvelous chorus in the colored blues piano tradition, followed by Pee Wee's fine dirty-toned clarinet. Then Davey Tough threw away his brushes, grabbed the sticks, and he and Max Kaminsky led the band through the final choruses.

There'll Be Some Changes Made

A classic among the Chicagoans' efforts has always been the Chicago Rhythm Kings record of 1928, with Mugs, Tesch, Mezz, Sullivan, Condon, Krupa, and Red McKenzie's famous vocal. This is a somewhat different treatment, but the "explosions" in the middle and end of the ensembles are based on the earlier record. The boys lived for those spots.

After an opening ensemble, Bud Freeman takes his best chorus of the date, with Maxie, Pee Wee, and Brad rigging up a spontaneous background in the last sixteen bars. Sullivan and Russell split the next chorus, and then there's another of those hell-for-leather free-for-alls with a sudden diminuendo at the halfway mark, picking up again to a full-blast finish.

Some Day Sweetheart

Here's a record with the all-time shortest first chorus! *Some Day Sweetheart* was the last side of the session and the band tried as before to make a master without timing the number. But they ran far over the three-minute mark when they used the customary ensemble-solos-ensemble routine, losing a great second chorus by Joe Sullivan. So Eddie Condon had the masterful idea of cutting down that first ensemble to one bar and going right into Joe's solo. The record will show you how it was done.

Sullivan, Russell, and Freeman play a series of half-choruses and then comes another fine ensemble, starring that remarkable combination of Kaminsky and Tough. These two boys had it that day and their ensemble work was an invaluable aid to the success of the session.

Jimmy McPartland and His Orchestra

PERSONNEL: *Jimmy McPartland (cornet); Bud Jacobson (clarinet); Boyce Brown (alto sax); Floyd Bean (piano); Dick McPartland (guitar); Jim Lannigan (bass); Hank Isaacs (drums). (Recorded in Chicago, October 10, 1939.)*

This combination is unique in that it brings to records men who have been conspicuously absent. Bud Jacobson and Boyce Brown had appeared only once on records, the McPartlands were last heard from in a 1936 session, and Jim Lannigan had recorded only with the Jungle Kings and the McKenzie–Condon gang, twelve years ago. Bean and Isaacs, who were with Jimmy McPartland at the Off-Beat Club in Chicago, had never been in a studio before.

With a soloist of McPartland's caliber and two remarkable ensemble men in Jacobson and Brown, one cannot help but draw a parallel to Bix and the Wolverines.

China Boy

The first record by the Chicagoans was *China Boy* and *Bull Frog Blues,* made by Muggsy and Tesch in 1926. The McKenzie–Condon band recorded *China Boy* again in 1928.

To most, this record will serve as an introduction to Boyce Brown's alto sax. He shares a chorus with Bud Jacobson and gives us a typical solo: perfectly executed, fast, full of notes, but completely logical and amazingly conceived. Boyce's personality is expressed in his music—a statement which has been worn thin, but here it is the cold truth. Boyce is unlike any musician you have ever met, and his is a completely individual and unorthodox style. Take warning that Boyce will need a lot of listening. His complexity makes a casual hearing worthless. Careful attention will be rewarded by an understanding of the subtleties of Boyce's ideas, which are distinctively his own.

A surprising contrast to the 1928 *China Boy* appears in the release of Floyd Bean's piano chorus in the form of a bass solo by Jim Lannigan. On the old record, Jim was given the same shot at the mike. In those days, when Jim slapped a string bass, it stayed slapped. He barged through his eight bars on the same note, beating his instrument to a pulp. Here, Jim plays softly and with a delicacy emphasized by Dick McPartland's guitar chording. (Special kick: Note how one of the guitar strings vibrates longer than the rest.) In the final chorus, Jimmy McPartland adds a distinctly Chicagoan touch with his clipped cornet work at the start of the final sixteen bars.

Jazz Me Blues

Long a standard jam number, *Jazz Me Blues* has been recorded twice by the Chicagoans, each time with different type of band. Fine ensembles and breaks mark the first part of this record, which also has the highest batting average for solos among these sides. Floyd Bean, Bud Jacobson, Boyce Brown, and Jimmy Mc-Partland are all heard, with Jacobson's brief effort taking the palm. The final choruses spotlight another version of the "stop-and-go," followed by a neatly prepared passage culminating in breaks by bass and guitar. Dick McPartland, by the way, is well recorded and his guitar work is the outstanding feature of the band's rhythm section.

Throughout the date, Bud Jacobson backs up all the cornet solos with unobtrusive sustained notes. This has never been done on record before, although Tesch backed up Muggsy's cornet solo on the first chorus of the 1928 *Changes Made* with an orthodox clarinet part, which is not at all what Jacobson is doing here. Bud rates four stars for this touch alone.

Sugar

McPartland's rendition is patterned somewhat after the McKenzie–Condon *Sugar*, with first chorus followed by verse. Jimmy himself is the star of this side, in which he is probably closest to Bix in tone, phrasing, and ideas. The two have often been compared and in several cases have been mistaken for one another on obscure records.

Once more, as on all the records in the album, the ensembles are excellent. Dick McPartland again heads the rhythm section, this time giving it a fine Chicago shuffle. Bud and Boyce contribute solos and back up Jimmy's lead more admirably than ever. Notice how Boyce rolls the band into the last half of the

17

sock chorus. The three of them are working together still—Jacobson is now rehearsing a small jazz band which includes Brown and McPartland.

The World Is Waiting for the Sunrise

Because the boys catch the old "Chicago jump" quality, this is probably the most successful side of the session. Chicagoans have been playing this tune since the Armstrong Sunset Cafe days. Recently it has been a favorite at Paul Mares' P&M Barbecue jam sessions and at the Monday night get-togethers in Squirrel Ashcraft's home, which almost invariably include Jimmy and Boyce.

The elaborate introduction is a great surprise, but it is steeped in tradition. The rigorous tension of their playing was probably behind the Chicagoans' early idea of getting all their pretty stuff out of their systems at once. The flowery opening, complete with bowed bass, reminds one of the concerto-style beginning to Louis Armstrong's 1926 *You're Next*, the rhapsodic ending of the old Charles Pierce *Sister Kate*, or the introduction to the 1928 *Liza*—which included four six-beat measures!

Hank Isaacs' drums break the spell and set the pace for Bud and Boyce, filling in again behind Jimmy's lead. Boyce's alto sax and Floyd Bean's powerful piano share solo honors this time. Hang on to Boyce or you'll be left behind. And don't overlook Bean—his choruses on this date stamp him a two-fisted discovery.

Final chorus...another stop...Bud Jacobson's grand clarinet behind that cornet lead...then it's all over.

George Wettling's Chicago Rhythm Kings

PERSONNEL: *Charlie Teagarden (trumpet); Floyd O'Brien (trombone); Danny Polo (clarinet); Joe Marsala (tenor sax); Jess Stacy (piano); Jack Bland (guitar); Artie Shapiro (bass); George Wettling (drums). (Recorded in New York, January 16, 1940.)*

18

Four of the "old men" of the Chicago school got together in this session with Floyd O'Brien of the Austin Blue Friars; Charlie Teagarden and Artie Shapiro, who have done their best with members of the Chicago gang; and Joe Marsala, youthful veteran of the jam band field.

Wettling, Stacy, Bland, and Polo were already established musicians in Chicago when the high school kids were starting out. But in spite of Bland's thinning red hair and the graying locks of the others, these four pack power to spare and the session produced driving music typical of the old days. As George Wettling said after hearing the tests, "That's really the Chicago style as I knew it."

An unusual aspect of this date lies in the fact that Danny Polo plays tenor sax in Joe Sullivan's orchestra and Joe Marsala plays clarinet with his own band, yet they switched instruments for these records and each turned in his best recorded work!

Bugle Call Rag

Just to make this version a little different from most renditions, the boys decided to use only three breaks throughout the side. Then, on the opening break, Teagarden stopped halfway and Wettling finished up—an idea suggested by the writer's thirteen-year-old brother! The tempo is also somewhat slower than the usual breakneck treatment accorded to *Bugle Call Rag.*

The rhythm section attains a fine rock, equally noticeable in ensembles and behind the solos. Marsala's tenor chorus is comparable to Bud Freeman at his best; O'Brien's trombone exhibits his usual restraint and completely hot tone. Note Charlie T's clipped work in the fill-ins before and after Jess Stacy's fine piano chorus.

This side was run over two or three times beforehand, and each time that Floyd came to his break he played something completely different—and so good that Wettling nearly lost his mind with every break. The splendid break on the master perked

19

up the whole band, and with Wettling socking it out in grand style, the boys go into a corking finale.

I Wish I Could Shimmy Like My Sister Kate

This just about takes the all-time cake for a slow drag. The band had to drop the intro and even then couldn't rely on much wax left over after the three eighteen-bar choruses. Most of the boys hadn't heard the tune since it was recorded by Muggsy and Tesch in 1927, but after a couple of trials around Stacy's piano, they couldn't wait to get going on this old classic.

The last two choruses make the record. Danny Polo plays a buoyantly light solo, effectively backed by Jess Stacy's sustained tremolos. Keep listening for Jess after O'Brien takes a staggering break and goes into an equally astonishing half-chorus. The writer would walk a mile for a Camel if he could trade it in on a Floyd O'Brien solo. For this sort of trombone, Floyd has no equal. Wettling's neatly timed cymbal flutter leads Jess into a half-chorus and then the gang piles in with everything but Otto Hess and his camera.

Darktown Strutters' Ball

Two beats by the Wettling–O'Brien team and that rolling ensemble is off again. Listen for Floyd's long notes. The highlight of a series of fine solos is Jess Stacy's. Jess really dug in on the last half, the back of his neck turning a slow crimson. And don't miss Floyd coming out of the fourth chorus like a surfboard into his own solo.

This whole session is beautifully recorded. Marsala, Polo, and O'Brien come out clearly in the ensembles under Charlie T's lead. In the solo choruses, Stacy's piano and Jack Bland's loosely rhythmic guitar are faithfully reproduced, adding much to the drive of Wettling's drums. Not many recording jobs bring out the piano and guitar so effectively. The rhythm behind Teagarden on this side is just one striking example.

The original Chicago Rhythm Kings recorded this number in 1928; this year's edition (with completely different personnel!) played it in the same key at a slightly slower tempo. As in *Bugle Call Rag*, Charlie Teagarden's trumpet lead-in is so brilliant that you can catch traces of an echo, despite the scientifically padded studio.

Listen for Floyd O'Brien's nearly New Orleans trombone in the opening bars of both the first and last choruses and catch George Wettling's buildup behind Danny Polo's release in the final chorus. All these sides finish up with double endings, but none so effectively as *I've Found a New Baby,* which closes with four completely Chicagoan "time-stands-still" bars.

The Chicagoans

Jimmy McPartland (cornet)—A rougher edition of Bix. Worked with Benny Goodman and Jack Teagarden in Ben Pollack's old band. More recently has been leading his own combination in Chicago. Looks like an All-American fullback—the kind coeds go for.

Max Kaminsky (cornet)—Maxie's a little guy from Boston with a broad "A" and a TNT horn. Lived with Tesch in Chicago and played with all the boys.

Floyd O'Brien (trombone)—One of the overlooked men in jazz. Never spectacular, always modest. The writer wanted Floyd to take two choruses on one of the Wettling sides, but Floyd protested: "Aw, shucks, I couldn't think nothin' up. Let Jess take two."

Pee Wee Russell (clarinet)—Long-faced St. Louis man with shoe button eyes. Many consider him the greatest clarinetist since Tesch. Has been playing in New York jam bands for five years: Louis Prima, Bobby Hackett, and now Bud Freeman.

Bud Jacobson (clarinet)—One of the boys who stayed around Chicago all along. Family man and a barrelhouse gent. First-rate composer on the side. Played piano exclusively for a while but returned to clarinet and tenor sax a few years ago. Like Pee Wee, he always looks worried.

Danny Polo (clarinet)—Worked with Floyd Town, Murph Steinberg, and the older crowd while the Austin boys were more or less attending classes. Took a trip to Europe with Freeman and Tough in 1927 and didn't get back until the war broke out last fall.

Bud Freeman (tenor sax)—Most critics call Bud the best white tenor saxophonist in jazz. Sports an Oxford accent some of the time and a mustache over a quiet smile all of the time. Got his first tenor sax at nineteen: "I started crying for one at seventeen and I cried two years."

Joe Marsala (tenor sax)—There was a time when Joe drove a truck in Chicago and played clarinet at night. Then he came to New York and gave up the truck. Has been a 52nd Street landmark for years, leading his own small jam band.

Boyce Brown (alto sax)—A unique phenomenon among jazz musicians—a serious thinker! Writes poetry, studies philosophy, and has his own theories on metaphysics and alto sax. Has been attracting much attention with Earl Wiley's Trio at the Liberty Inn in Chicago.

Joe Sullivan (piano)—Studied at the Chicago Conservatory of Music and played on nearly all the old Chicago style records. Just got over a long illness and formed his own band after a short stay with Bob Crosby. Hear his *Just Strolling* on Decca 600.

Jess Stacy (piano)—Up from the riverboats. His first records (with Paul Mares and Boyce Brown) won him a job with Benny Goodman in 1935. We were discussing the Wettling date after it was over when someone started a playback of *Found a New Baby* and Jess interrupted the conversation: "Say, what's that? Something new? Sounds good! Who's on it?"

Eddie Condon (guitar)—Probably the greatest rhythmic guitarist of all time. Has never taken a solo and swears he never will. A wiry little guy with an impressive personality. With his pal, Willie (Red) McKenzie, he set most of the record dates for the Chicagoans.

Dick McPartland (guitar)—Works with Floyd Town, old-time Chicago tenor sax man—job which took him down to Atlanta, Georgia, for the winter. Only recorded twice before, each time with his kid brother, Jimmy.

Jack Bland (guitar)—Was rediscovered working in a midtown club in New York when everyone thought he was still somewhere in Chicago. One of Red McKenzie's original Mound City Blue Blowers. He and Eddie Condon used to record together, using a guitar and banjo simultaneously.

Jim Lannigan (bass)—Getting Jim for the album was fairly easy. When his brother-in-law, Jimmy McPartland, told him about it, he ran out for a haircut and finessed the classics for the day. However, he's gone back to the Chicago Symphony to stay.

Dave Tough (drums)—Built on the general lines of a four-day fugitive from a funeral parlor. The Tough residence used to be a haven for Bud Freeman during his frequent terms in the parental doghouse. Davey's greatest gift is an amazing sense of timing, much in the manner of Baby Dodds.

George Wettling (drums)—Silver-thatched George is now with Paul Whiteman. A swell man for a small band. Writes a screwball column for drummers in *Down Beat*. Very much of a regular guy. Closely associated with Muggsy, Tesch, and "good ol' Jess."

Frank Teschemacher (clarinet)—Dave Dexter of *Down Beat* recently discovered that Tesch's name has been misspelled for years as "Teschmaker." Only Louis Armstrong ranks above Tesch among the great jazz soloists. Then, now, and always, Tesch is the idol of the Chicagoans.

Among those identified with the Chicago style who were unable to record for this album were Muggsy Spanier, Red McKenzie, Gene Krupa, Earl Wiley, Dave North, Rod Cless, and Milt Mezzrow.

(1940)

24

CHARLES
EDWARD SMITH

New Orleans Jazz

Various Artists
(Decca A-425)

You have often heard that instrumental jazz began in New Orleans, but this is the first time an album has been produced to support the thesis. An imposing number of New Orleans veterans and a few younger men, who got their musical apprenticeship sitting next to such men, ensure that this music is "the real thing," like Tom Anderson's cabaret, where so many of them played at one time or another. The titles in the album suggest a background flashing with the surface gaiety of Rampart Street cabaret and Basin Street palace, yet deep-rooted in New Orleans life: a coal cart rattling through the balconied byways of the Vieux Carré, a triple-tone piano playing behind the lace curtains of Basin Street, the invigorating jazz of the dance halls and the deep blues of the tonks, a brass band tune called *Down in Jungletown* for the Mardi Gras, and a great blues for one of the world's most expansive streets, Canal Street.

Jazz style is blues style adapted to brass band instruments. It is not ragtime grown up, as many people seem to believe. Ragtime was essentially a St. Louis piano style, drawing inspiration chiefly from Negro social dances and blues. By the 1890s, it had become a *written* music as well, and the Scott Joplin rags were familiar to every musician in New Orleans, whether or not he could read. The great ragtime band of the city was John Robichaux's group of Creole Negro musicians, who played at Antoine's Restaurant back in the gaslight era.

In contrast to this well-behaved orchestra, Buddy Bolden's band played blues—*219 Blues* was one—and stomps. The Bolden band played in dance halls where the men kept their hats on and in honky tonks where the pay of two to three dollars a night was supplemented by what Frankie Dusen could badger out of the girls and their escorts. It was this band to which George Baquet of the Robichaux orchestra (who helped Sidney Bechet on clarinet) went for inspiration. It was this band in which Willie (Bunk) Johnson (who was later to have such an influence on Louis Armstrong) played cornet next to King Bolden when he was still in knee pants. It was also this band that Jack Laine (grandpappy of white Dixieland style) singled out when he explained how early jazz came from the Negro section of uptown New Orleans.

The openings for Negro jazz musicians, as for the white men who adapted their music, were in Tom Anderson's "county"—Storyville. This was the honky-tonk part of town. It didn't create jazz, any more than did the brass band instruments on which it was played. But both were contributing factors, and important ones. Colored and white outfits were called *ragtime* bands, but this was only because the term was ready-made for them. Depending upon improvisational skill rather than written music, they soon transformed rags into stomps.

Such bands as that of Bolden got jobs playing for the funerals that were still part of New Orleans life. This local adaptation of a European custom contained in it both the sorrow and joy associated with death in early religious observance. Cornet, clarinet, and trombone, playing the sweet slow dirge on the way to the graveyard, came back to town playing bright tunes, such as the famous *High Society Rag*. Or, wearing the same aprons they wore at funerals, but the other side out, they would swing down Rampart Street in a parade, the "second line" of kids mimicking their rhythmic movements. On weekends they played on advertising wagons during the afternoon, for the cabarets at night. Listening to the trombone on *Honky Tonk Town*, one recalls that the term *tailgate* derives from the former jobs, the trombone's place being at the rear end of the wagon, where his slide on the long notes wouldn't get in the way of the other instruments.

To each of these outlets they brought their own peculiar instrumental style, influencing the Creole Negroes from downtown who contributed so many of the great clarinet, string bass, and piano players to early jazz. And from each of these several environments new elements entered their music, hence the stomps that hark back to marches, the rags that suggest quadrilles. By a careful selection of titles and choice of personnel for each of the five bands in this album, it is hoped to suggest some of the backgrounds that influenced New Orleans jazz in its formative period.

Characteristic of New Orleans jazz were its *free improvisational* rhythms within the confines of strict tempo, and its melodic improvisations that took the form of definite parts. Traditional limits and patterns gave it its own line of development, that was adhered to when the music moved north, despite differences in treatment between Negro bands, such as that of King Oliver, and white bands, such as the New Orleans Rhythm Kings.

The first Bolden band sometimes had two cornets and two clarinets, but basically its instrumentation was cornet, clarinet, trombone, guitar, string bass, and drums. This is also the basis for the instrumentation of the bands in this album, although a piano and a soprano sax have been added. (In early days, jazz bands did not include pianos, and though pianos of all descriptions could be found in honky tonks and sportin' houses, few dance halls were equipped with them. As for the saxophone, it was a late starter in hot jazz. When Luis Russell came up from Panama in 1920, his small band, which included Louis Armstrong on cornet, also had Barney Bigard, a pioneer reed man, on tenor sax... This group played at Tom Anderson's North Rampart Street place.)

In jazz the elements that assume primary importance are those that represent its development from folk music. Examples of such influence—some of which refer back to African sources—may be found in the improvisational rhythms and melodies of jazz, the parallels to folksinging technique in the use of individual (not conventionalized) vibrato as a functional part of instrumental style, as well as in the tonal freedom described as *hot intonation*. An important feature of New Orleans instrumental technique is that it combines *attack*—the precise definition of each note—with fluidity.

Now to summarize the ensemble of which the records in this album are illustrative. The rhythm section gives the music its solid rhythmic base, contributing as well to the melodic impact. The cornet, usually playing the melody or a variation of it, is the lead instrument. The clarinet (on some of these records, soprano sax) plays fast runs interspersed with sustained notes, and legato phrases as, for example, in Jimmy Noone's work on *Keystone Blues*. The third instrument in the melodic hierarchy, the trombone, supports the others with a kind of rhythmic bass, and occasionally supplies its own counter-melody. When these instruments are in action, handled by men who are capable of improvising parts, we may be sure there will be no gaps in the pattern.

In the halcyon days of Storyville, as many as two hundred musicians found either permanent or part-time employment playing a music that had no local, much less international, standing. By the time Storyville closed in 1917, many bands had already ventured north, east, and west. Sidney Bechet was one of the first of the hot jazzmen to play a Command Performance at Buckingham Palace, but the fact of his having played before royalty, a feat duplicated by other New Orleanians, is not so remarkable as is the impression this musician made on European critics and public. It was Ansermet, French music critic, who observed in 1919—twenty-one years ago!—that Bechet's "own way" of playing was "perhaps the highway the whole world will swing along tomorrow."

Today we can look back upon more than half a century of jazz development. Tracing the music's background, we can see how it followed the Mississippi and the Missouri, leaving its stamp on such cities as St. Louis and Kansas City. We can look back upon more than a decade of Chicago jazz—recreated in Decca's *Chicago Jazz* album—that found its public in the blowsy hideaways and noisy dance halls of the Prohibition era. And always, in every important band in jazz, we can point to the presence or influence of men from New Orleans. When Decca decided to produce an album illustrative of this process, it was natural that they should begin with a small band led by Louis Armstrong. His contribution to present-day jazz has been more varied and more influential than that of any other single individual. But this contribution has never been one of mere technical inventiveness. A feeling for melodic improvisation lends to every chorus he plays an unforgettable beauty of line. Sidney Bechet is also distinguished for his improvisational gift. That is one reason for bringing these two great musicians together. Another is that they played together on advertising wagons in New Orleans—a long, long time ago.

One further word concerning the personnel of this album. It consists largely of men who have helped to pioneer jazz, yet whose talents are now at ripe maturity. Johnny Dodds' clarinet never wailed out the blues with more sincerity than on *Red*

Onion Blues; Wellman Braud, Lil Hardin Armstrong, and Nat Dominique were good when they played at the De Luxe Cafe some twenty-odd years ago—they are right at the top today. And some of the men, too young to have participated in the early periods of jazz, are not too young to have grown up with it. Thus the album can properly claim to include definitive examples of New Orleans music.

Jazz was an outgrowth of folk music. If you think folk music rough and crude, you will quite likely think of jazz in the same way. From a purely descriptive point of view, this attitude might be justified . . . but for the delineation of sonorities, not the definition of the music itself. Like folk music, jazz in its earliest form—that is, New Orleans jazz, has its own traditions. If Igor Stravinsky, Shostakovich, and Maurice Ravel (among others) have been able to understand various phases of this process, there seems little reason why Americans, too, should not approach jazz on its own merits, at least in those periods where it is comparatively free of the influence of popular music as such. One of the widespread fallacies about it is the belief that jazz of more than fifteen years ago was necessarily backward and that the good things were added thereunto in the Broadway refineries! You don't find this belief very strong in New Orleans, and the orchestra leader who wisecracked, "I had a great success in New Orleans, Buddy Bolden notwithstanding," wasn't kidding anyone, unless perhaps himself.

The Records

Louis Armstrong and His Orchestra

PERSONNEL: *Louis Armstrong (trumpet); Sidney Bechet (clarinet and soprano sax); Claude Jones (trombone); Luis Russell (piano); Bernard Addison (guitar); Wellman Braud (string bass); Zutty Singleton (drums). (Decca Record No. 25099)*

One of the most popular myths in jazz is that all blues are alike. This is certainly not true of New Orleans, where each blues has a distinct melody, an assertion that every listener will be able to judge for himself, since there are no less than eight blues in this album.

To those whose jobs were in the sportin' world, trains assumed an unusual importance. Train number 219 went west to Dallas on the Texas and Pacific, number 217 making the return trip. An additional verse, supplied by the writer, is based on the fact that eastbound trains from New Orleans are routed over the tracks of the Louisville and Nashville.

219 is a slow blues and on the first ensemble chorus, with Bechet playing clarinet, we hear the overlapping phrases that typify this style. While Louis sings the vocals in a full husky voice, Russell plays tinkling honky-tonk piano and Bechet and Claude Jones interpolate short phrases. Then, after a powerful and very blue chorus by Sidney Bechet on soprano sax, Zutty thumps twice on the bass drum and Louis leads the band on the final chorus. Not the least part of the strong rhythm section is the string bass, the tonal beauty of which marks Wellman Braud as a distinguished interpreter of the blues.

Perdido Street Blues
Lil Hardin Armstrong

The Perdido Street of this blues composed by Lil Hardin Armstrong begins at the old Eagle Saloon, on the corner of South Rampart Street. Back of the saloon was the Masonic Hall where Buddy Bolden, first "King" of jazz, played blues and stomps. It's a vacant lot now and the friendly lights are missing from the corner where Dago Tony's used to be, where eleven-year-old Louis used to slip in, to try to play the blues on Willie (Bunk) Johnson's cornet. When night came to this drab neighborhood of unpainted frame houses, the yellow lights of the corner tonks created a world of its own for Negro dock wallopers, railroad firemen, day laborers, and, yes, even for Louis and his gang—Black Benny, Kid Rena, and the rest—who hung around to listen to the music.

A slashing clarinet break, marked off by stop-time, serves as an introduction to this highly successful attempt to recapture the essential qualities of New Orleans music. As the clarinet shifts to low register midway through the introduction, it is backed up by a shuffle rhythm and out of this comes the first ensemble chorus, led by trumpet. Notice the balance of the trombone. This is the true New Orleans ensemble that the old King Oliver discs could only hint at because of acoustical recording. (Don't mistake us, though, those Gennett Olivers are immortal wax, for anyone's money.)

One of the great improvisers in jazz, Bechet is also one of its foremost exponents of blues style on clarinet. A powerful reedy tone and the use of a growl give expression to his creative talent on the solo that follows the first chorus of *Perdido*. Then Luis Russell takes over for a few bars, succeeded by Addison on guitar and a haunting trombone chorus by Claude Jones, with Bechet's soprano sax backing him up. Harmonic phrases by the band give an intense pulse to the last two choruses, which are taken by Louis Armstrong on trumpet. The sureness of Louis' playing is always a joy to listen to, and never more so than here, where a beautiful glissando is reached not as a technical feat, but as the inevitable melodic climax. (Decca Record No. 25100)

Coal Cart Blues
Louis Armstrong and Lil Hardin

PERSONNEL: *Sidney Bechet (soprano saxophone); Louis Armstrong (trumpet); Bernard Addison (guitar); Wellman Braud (bass).*

With Sidney Bechet and Louis Armstrong recording together after more than fifteen years, the time seemed opportune to show these giants of jazz playing together as a duo, with the rhythm section confined to simply guitar and string bass. For this, nothing could have been more appropriate than *Coal Cart Blues,* which they first recorded with Clarence Williams' Blue Five. (The earlier wax is now available on an HRS reissue and listeners will want to compare the two.) The tune has an interesting history, in addition to this earlier version, for it recalls a period during Louis' childhood when he perched himself atop a coal cart drawn by a mule and sold charcoal to the lovers of Creole cuisine in Vieux Carré, croaking his wares in as hoarse a voice as he could muster.

A few years later, Louis was at the municipal boys' home, playing in a boys' brass band that was so good it got professional jobs. Captain Joseph Jones sat with me on the steps of the home, just a year ago, Louis' battered old cornet and bugle on his lap, and told me the two most impressive characteristics of the boy who was to be the next "King" after Oliver, in a direct musical line from King Bolden. One was Louis' inexhaustible fund of vitality and good nature—"He doesn't look natural to me when he's not smiling"—and the other was his matchless ambition—"He was twelve years old and wanted to sing bass!"

To those familiar with Louis Armstrong's vocal technique, it need not be explained that this is the natural complement of his trumpet style. And just as on trumpet he has never lost the instrumental style and intonation that derive from blues, so he bases his vocal technique upon that of blues singers. How marvelously he adapts this talent to his own unique gifts has been amply described by Panassie, William Russell, and others. In this vocal of *Coal Cart Blues,* all the points that have been mentioned—husky timbre, glissando, rhythmic accent, etc.—are employed for quite a simple and purposeful end: to express the material. Note how the use of the natural speaking voice charges with dramatic credibility the sentence beginning "Of course the cart was hard..."

An interesting parallel may be drawn between the ensemble passages on the HRS reissue and the instrumental duets played by Louis Armstrong and Sidney Bechet on this record. On the earlier record, there is a trombone and Bechet plays a traditional clarinet part. On the present disc, there are only two instruments and they must, perforce, keep the ensemble full and strong by themselves. Here is craftsmanship so easy that it's unobtrusive, harmonic phrases blending into interweaving parts with a naturalness that comes of long practice. With Addison on guitar and Wellman Braud on string bass, this is easily one of the most melodic records in jazz.

Down in Honky Tonk Town
Chris Smith and Chas. McCarron

PERSONNEL: *Louis Armstrong (trumpet); Sidney Bechet (clarinet and soprano sax); Claude Jones (trombone); Luis Russell (piano); Bernard Addison (guitar); Wellman Braud (string bass); Zutty Singleton (drums).*

This is a *go* record all the way from the vigorous introduction to the last bar of the all-in chorus that ends the record. The tune seemed so perfect for *tailgate* trombone that the verse section was given solely to trumpet and trombone. And Claude Jones turns in the long notes like a veteran. The chorus, with Sidney now in the ensemble, leads into his soprano sax solo, a striking variation that brings out Bechet's powerful tone and technique on this instrument. The trombone takes over, sliding into his chorus with a very definite bounce, and then Addison gives us a few bars of that rhythm guitar. Louis blasts a path for a short drum solo by Zutty, the melody instruments counting off in a sort of stop-time in reverse—and then it's all in for the last chorus.

The composer of *Honky Tonk Town* was in the studio while this number was being recorded. It's hard to believe when you look at him but Chris Smith, who also wrote *Ballin' the Jack,* is sixty-one years old! He was born in Charleston, South Carolina, and his ancestry is partly West Indian. He wrote *Honky Tonk Town* as a "good-time" number, not with any special city in mind. But New Orleans took it to heart, for where was there a honkytonk town such as fabulous Storyville? Louis was playing this tune when he got the job that first took him away from New Orleans. He was then a boy of eighteen, playing cornet at a dance in Cooperative Hall. Fate Marable dropped in, listened, and hired him for a riverboat job on the Strekfus Line. After two years on the Mississippi and in New Orleans, Louis came north to join King Oliver and to become America's number one jazz trumpeter.

Red Allen and His Orchestra

PERSONNEL: *Henry (Red) Allen, Jr., (trumpet); Edmond Hall (clarinet); Benny Morton (trombone); Lil Hardin Armstrong (piano); Bernard Addison (guitar); George (Pops) Foster (string bass); Zutty Singleton (drums).*

Canal Street Blues
Joseph Oliver

This composition by Joe (King) Oliver is a jazz tribute to one of the world's most beautiful streets, the wide and expansive boulevard known as Canal Street. It begins at the curve of the Mississippi where that famous river flows almost due north and where young Red Allen was wont to catch the ferry for Algiers, and it follows a slanting line to the suburbs, dividing uptown from downtown.

Naturally enough, this record is inspired by the King Oliver treatment on Gennett, a date on which Lil Hardin Armstrong also played piano. It's a moderately slow blues with overlapping phrases by clarinet through the first ensemble, which concludes with some dynamics in close harmony suggested by the Gennett. Henry Allen, Jr., contents himself with playing first-rate lead trumpet on this number, and the hot choruses are given to Edmond Hall on clarinet, Lil Hardin Armstrong on piano, Benny Morton on trombone, and Bernard Addison on guitar. Each of these choruses helps to recreate the nostalgic mood of this piece, with top billing for Lil's honky-tonk piano. Benny Morton's chorus is a full and rich melodic variation and Addison plays a clean guitar solo that will impress many listeners as his best job on the date.

Down in Jungletown
Edward Madden and Theodore Morse

Here is a brass band tune, accepted for years as the theme of the King of the Zulu's Parade, the famous Negro parade that kicks out with fun and satire for the climax of the New Orleans Mardi Gras. Edmond Hall, Red Allen, Pops Foster, and Zutty Singleton have played for so many parades that they immediately gave the proper lift to this number, even to the suggestion of singing clarinets. In those parades Pops Foster played bass horn, but he can, and does, thump out with the proper spirit on string bass. On this side again, we have to pause to praise the work of Red Allen, who knows how to give the appropriate interpretation to whatever he plays, and also to Benny Morton, who never marched in a Mardi Gras parade but who knows the New Orleans trombone style. The spirited ensemble sets the pace, is followed by excellent solo choruses by Edmond Hall on clarinet, Benny Morton on trombone, and Red Allen on trumpet. Clarinet and trombone come in to back up Allen and on the last chorus all three catch a ride.

Zutty Singleton and His Orchestra

PERSONNEL: *Henry (Red) Allen, Jr., (trumpet); Edmond Hall (clarinet); Benny Morton (trombone); Lil Hardin Armstrong (piano); Bernard Addison (guitar); George (Pops) Foster (string bass); Zutty Singleton (drums).*

King Porter Stomp
Ferd Morton

Jelly Roll Morton's *King Porter*, one of the oldest and best of the stomp tunes, is here given the first significant small band treatment it has had in years. Jelly Roll named this piece after Porter King, a friend of his from Florida, a piano player famous for his treatment of Joplin rags. Since Jelly's piano solo of the tune on Gennett, it has been a swing classic. He recorded it once more, early this year, but meanwhile—in the close to two decades between—it has become famous through its interpretation by big bands (notably Fletcher Henderson, Dorsey Brothers, Benny Goodman, and Count Basie). The present recording, on the other hand, employs almost the identical instrumentation used for playing stomps not two decades ago but three—when a Basin Street "Professor" also included this type of music in his vast repertoire.

A short introduction and ensemble chorus set the furious pace that is kept up throughout the record. The first solo, very much in the mood, is taken by Edmond Hall on clarinet. This is followed by a chorus by Red Allen in which he uses a triple-tongued effect to create suspense. After a short chorus by Benny Morton on trombone, Edmond Hall comes in again, more in the mood than before. A drum chorus by Zutty and an all-in ensemble complete the record. Zutty's powerhouse drumming is spotlighted here at its best—we get those crowded passages on the snares, a nicely shaded tonal transition on cymbals, and sultry undertones on the bass drum.

Shim-Me-Sha-Wabble
Spencer Williams

Here is one of the swing standards in an unusually "sultry" treatment that brings out great choruses by Red Allen, Edmond Hall, and Benny Morton. With this virtuoso talent harnessed to material of genuine melodic interest, the stature of Henry

Allen, Jr., is quite apparent. On the first chorus, he employs an expressive and very fitting intonation which is emphasized by the rhythm section, particularly the bass drum, and by the coordination of clarinet and trombone. This album, and of course this record, will also bring to the attention of a far wider public a clarinet player who deserves to be better known, Edmond Hall. The tone of his clarinet has a reedy timbre and he too gets "dirty" effects through the use of a growl. This chorus is typical New Orleans style in that it includes runs of short notes as well as slightly legato phrases, and employs both registers so naturally that one is only aware of the melodic impact. After another fine chorus by Red Allen and one of those *Shim-Me* drum breaks that belong to any proper interpretation of this number, Benny Morton gives out with a fine solo, the ample melodious tone topping off the disc. From there on it's New Orleans coda.

Down on that glittering and sinful thoroughfare known as Basin Street, the piano players were called "Professors." Each "palace" had a number of parlors, with a piano in every one! On these pianos the "Professor" played according to the whims of the guests, blues, stomps, snatches of opera, or even a dash of Chopin. Spencer Williams was a Basin Street "Professor" and *Shim-Me-Sha-Wabble* was composed by him perhaps in tribute to those "Entertainers from the East," mentioned in the old *Blue Book* "county" guide, "who do nothing but sing and dance!" He is also the composer of *Basin Street Blues* and *Mahogany Hall Stomp*. The latter named after a little four-story palace at Number 235 N. Basin Street, the cutglass transom of which read LULU WHITE.

Although it has nothing to do with this record, the following description from the *Blue Book* is a quaint and amusing bit of Americana and gives you an idea of the setting in which Spencer Williams and Clarence Williams, too, won professional status. (The implication that Lulu White was a great beauty has not been confirmed by anyone who knew her, though the rest of the story is accurate enough.)

Nowhere in this country will you find a more popular personage than Madam White, who is noted as being the handsomest Octoroon in America, and aside from her beauty, she has the distinction of possessing the largest collection of diamonds, pearls, and other rare gems in this part of the country.

To see her at night is like witnessing the electrical display on the Cascade at the St. Louis Exposition.

Her mansion possesses some of the most costly oil paintings in the Southern country. Her mirror parlor is also a dream.

Johnny Dodds and His Orchestra

PERSONNEL: *Nat Dominique (trumpet); Johnny Dodds (clarinet); Preston Jackson (trombone); Richard M. Jones (piano); Lonnie Johnson (guitar); Johnny Lindsay (string bass); Warren (Baby) Dodds (drums).*

Red Onion Blues
Clarence Williams

This is a great slow drag blues played by what is so obviously a great blues band that one needn't be afraid to use that adjective. Dodds and Dominique give us the undiluted blues, Preston Jackson plays hot *tailgate* to the last groove, and the rhythm section is every bit as effective as on *Gravier Street*. If this record had been made under difficult acoustic conditions circa 1923 and the master thrown away a few years later, it would now be a rare collectors' item, with duly constituted experts handing down learned opinions as to its personnel. But it was made in Chicago circa 1940 and since Decca is not making a first edition, or even using the wrong label, it's available to all who know, or want to know, the real New Orleans blues. We'd prefer to leave it at that, but it would be unfair not to indicate what happens. After a low blues introduction, Johnny Dodds and Nat Dominique share the first chorus. Then comes an ensemble passage that is true honky tonk, based upon blues piano. Then a long chorus by Johnny Dodds, very blue, the band building up tension by repeating chords. More honky-tonk ensemble and then Preston Jackson leading the last chorus in some of the hottest tromboning in the album.

The Red Onion itself was a low honky tonk on South Rampart Street, along the Basin (a term used even after the Basin was filled in). There was sawdust on the floor and during the summer a small fish-fry booth stood out front. In addition to the saloon, there was a cubbyhole for gambling and a "back room" where gambler-pianists and hard-up blues singers played and sang for what they could get. It was a work ticket and payoff place for railroad workers, section gangs, and so forth, and was therefore popular with gamblers and other denizens of the sportin' world. In those days—around 1910—a gambler wore striped pants, starched jumper, and a high-crowned black Stetson hat. Usually he had a twenty-dollar gold piece on his watch chain, and wore P.I. shoes—buttoned high-tops, extra-long and with the toe turned up. In summer the South Rampart Street gamblers wore silk undershirts and gold-buckled suspenders with diamonds in them. The life of the girls who frequented the tonks was hard, insecure, and unutterably lonely, yet blues singers like Ann Cook at the Red Onion managed to express it with dignity and moving simplicity. This depth of feeling is, I think, conveyed in this blues by Clarence Williams, who played piano at the Red Onion for a time. Among others who played there at one time or another were Frankie Dusen, who played trombone with Bolden, and Bob Frank, piccolo player of the Peerless band.

This blues is named for a street that has been associated with bawdy life ever since 1857, when the city fathers first began their attempts to "regulate" such life by geographical stratagem. By the early part of this century, Gravier Street was in a completely Negro part of predominantly white Storyville, and outside the limits of the "county" proper. Louis Armstrong played for Buddy Bottley, at the corner of Franklin, and Sidney Bechet also once played there with Willie (Bunk) Johnson. It was a honky tonk—in other words, a low-class cabaret. So was Spanola's, where it was said Negro dock workers were paid off (an old waterfront custom; in many cities where it was practiced, the boss of the docks also had an interest in the saloon!). Spanola's had a "back room" for gambling and little "wine rooms" for private parties. When they needed a piano player they'd simply phone the Big 25 on the party-line phone and one would be sent over.

From the opening bar this record is packed with wonderfully good examples of New Orleans ensemble. The first chorus is of special interest because here there are passages in which the trumpet seems almost a foil for the clarinet (as in some of the very early records made by the Original Dixieland Jazz Band). In the second chorus, the clarinet part is more traditional and the trumpet is nearer the melody. There is a splendid solo by Lonnie Johnson on guitar—in its economy of note and in the virility of its attack, this chorus is perhaps as near the old New Orleans guitar style as anything in the album. Then Johnny Dodds, the great blues clarinetist, takes it on down for two choruses. It's harmonic-rhythmic accompaniment through both, with the brass muted for the first and open for the second.

Listeners will observe differences in tonal balance that result from the choice of musicians for each band. This is most noticeable in the melodic section, though careful listening makes it easily discernible in the rhythm as well. The husky intonation of Preston Jackson's trombone makes it as distinctive in tone quality as Jack Teagarden's or Jimmy Harrison's. And Johnny Dodds' wailing blue clarinet, with its deep resonant tone, seems to get right down to the bedrock soul of all blues. Nat Dominique has a tendency to play slightly off the tone and in this, as well as in some of his melodic flights, he suggests comparison with the great Freddy Keppard. To this melodic balance so appropriate to blues playing, a good rhythm foundation is supplied by Richard M. Jones, veteran composer and blues pianist; Lonnie Johnson, acknowledged to be one of the finest guitar players in jazz; Johnny Lindsay, another alumnus of the King Oliver band, on string bass; and Baby Dodds, whose first licks were learned from Ma Rainey's drummer, a man nicknamed "The Rabbit."

Jimmy Noone and His Orchestra

PERSONNEL: *Nat Dominique (trumpet); Jimmy Noone (clarinet); Preston Jackson (trombone); Richard M. Jones (piano); Lonnie Johnson (guitar); Johnny Lindsay (string bass); Minor (Tubby) Hall (drums).*

Keystone Blues
Clarence Williams

The tempo of this blues suggests a relatively high-class tonk and such was the Keystone, on South Rampart Street across from the Red Onion. Downstairs was the saloon and the inevitable gambling room with its conch, blackjack, dice, and so forth. Upstairs, serviced by dumbwaiter from the bar, was the cabaret, and above this floor were the rooms of the girls who worked there as entertainers. Clarence Williams tells how piano players along South Rampart Street used various types of ground bass and, indeed, the title of another piece in this album, *New Orleans Hop Scop Blues,* is actually the name of such a bass.

When rural blues was adapted to the piano back in the last century, one of its earliest characteristics was the use of a ground bass. Its most successful outgrowth was a bass roll used by gin-mill and play-party pianists in Chicago, St. Louis, and Kansas City—a development coincidental with but not a part of the transitional phase of jazz as it came northward from, say, 1910 right through the 1920s. It took the name *boogie woogie* from a dance that is quite rhythmic and beautiful in its movement when not subjected to jive interpretation.

Boogie woogie piano certainly deserves a name of its own. Some of its exponents may be counted among our more gifted contemporaries. Nor need we remind listeners of its widespread influence. But before there could be *boogie woogie* piano, there had to be quite a varied and widespread tendency toward it in blues piano playing. Thus we had, in various places from Pensacola to Dallas and from St. Louis to Chicago, such interesting names for what the left hand does (and the right hand knows it!) as *walking bass, rolling bass, fast western, catch-up bass* (a *walk* and a chord), and, naturally enough, a New Orleans *hop scop*. On *Keystone,* the bass is somewhat like a *hop scop,* and it is accomplished with the help of string bass and trombone, in the harmonic-rhythmic manner we have mentioned elsewhere.

The number opens on the bass figure and repeats it as a four-bar break between choruses. Lonnie Johnson starts the solo work with eight exciting bars of his full-toned guitar, which will suggest to many listeners the bell-like tones of the flamenco players. Nat Dominique's long solo, with Noone in back of him, is a splendid performance. The mechanics of Dominique's style are generally uncomplicated and one might therefore say he comes close to a simple blues technique. But while his technical equipment does not appear so extensive as, for instance, that of Red Allen, his subtle tonality is an achievement comparable only to the vocal tone shading of folksingers. Preston Jackson comes in with a lot of gusto and stays there through eight bars—try counting bars on him and you'll come upon a wonderful example of "swinging around the beat." Then Dominique is in again for a short chorus, followed by Jimmy Noone, showing us once more how a beautiful melodic line is created. Tubby Hall breaks with the concentration on snares, we hear a few bars of Johnny Lindsay's string bass—enough to appreciate its fine tone—and then it's a few bars to tie in, with overlapping phrases from the ensemble clarinet of Jimmy Noone.

New Orleans Hop Scop Blues
George W. Thomas

Played in a bright tempo, this old New Orleans tune strikes the ear again with its rich melody, and it could hardly have had more adequate treatment. A hot trombone break opens the record, then clarinet and trumpet strains emerge from the blue chords of the ensemble. This sequence is repeated to introduce an explosive trombone chorus by Preston Jackson. Lonnie Johnson takes a chorus on guitar, playing with a fine economy of notes and climaxing his solo with incisive rhythmic chords. Nat Dominique plays a muted trumpet chorus and Jimmy Noone turns in a solo that makes one understand why he is considered one of the foremost exponents of jazz style on clarinet. His breathless attack in which notes are phrased with a definition that is absolutely sure, the legato phrases varying the more staccato runs— these and a beautiful limpid tone express a forthright melodic line which, it need hardly be added, is also a characteristic of New Orleans music. The final ensemble maintains this high quality, and the most prominent trombone lick in this chorus is an old favorite from "down yonder."

The Musicians

Louis Armstrong (trumpet)—Jobs in brass bands, on wagons, and in Storyville cabarets; two years on Strekfus Line. North, 1922, to join King Oliver. Then—Fletcher Henderson; Lil's Dreamland Syncopators; Erskine Tate's Vendome "Little Symphony"; Carroll Dickerson; and, for more than a decade, Louis Armstrong and His Orchestra. He is universally acknowledged the greatest figure in jazz and the one chiefly responsible for modern jazz trumpet style. Born New Orleans, 1900.

Henry (Red) Allen, Jr. (trumpet)—Served apprenticeship chiefly with Allen Brass Band led by his father, and Sidney Desvigne's Syncopators. North to join Oliver, 1927; Strekfus Line, 1928; Luis Russell, 1929. In 1930s Redman; Waller; Henderson; Mills' Blue Rhythm; and is still with Louis Armstrong. A favorite with musicians and followers of jazz. Born Algiers, across the river from New Orleans, 1908.

Anatole (Nat) Dominique (trumpet)—An authentic blues trumpet player rediscovered! One of his early influences was Manuel Perez, one of first jobs at Astoria Roof. Strekfus Line, 1921. Toured with Jelly Roll Morton. With Dodds Brothers at Kelly's Stables, Chicago. Born New Orleans, 1892.

Claude Jones (trombone)—His talented New Orleans style tromboning has been featured with many leading bands, including Fletcher Henderson; Cab Calloway; Don Redman. Is now with Coleman Hawkins. Born in Boley, Oklahoma, 1900, in a family of musicians, he deserted law course at Ohio's Wilberforce College, 1921, to become charter member of the band that swung the Midwest, McKinney's Cotton Pickers.

Benny Morton (trombone)—Just to prove that musicians are made as well as born, here's another "foreigner" who plays New Orleans trombone. Born in New York City, 1907, he got his first jobs around Harlem when that was about the only place in town aware that a new music was on its way. Joined Fletcher Henderson in the 1920s. More recently was Count Basie's star slide man.

Preston Jackson (trombone)—Helped Louis keep the brasses bright in many of those Chicago bands mentioned ... born New Orleans, 1902, he came north about 1917. Wrote about New Orleans music for English and Continental magazines before most American fans knew what it was about.

Sidney Bechet (clarinet and soprano saxophone)—Played on wagons, in brass bands, in cabarets, in many historic bands. North to Chicago, 1918; at De Luxe with Lil Hardin and Wellman Braud; at Pekin with Tony Jackson, the sportin' house piano player who composed *Pretty Baby;* to Europe with Will Marion Cook. Between 1922–24, vaudeville and for a short time with Duke Ellington; again Europe, featured with Lord Douglas revue; joined Noble Sissle about 1928; in 1932, organized a band with Tommy Ladnier. Since then has been starred with own band at many nightspots. "Pops" Bechet, often called "The Grand Old Man of Jazz," is grand but not old ... born on St. Anthony Street, New Orleans, 1897.

Edmond Hall (clarinet)—Although he has been featured for years with such bands as Claude Hopkins and Lucky Millinder, Hall's fine talent reached the ears of hot fans when he took to the hot nightspots. He was born in New Orleans, 1901, played with Bud Russell and in a band led by the son of Joseph Petit, old-time valve trombonist. Is now with Joe Sullivan.

Johnny Dodds (clarinet)—Johnny Dodds was born in uptown New Orleans, April 12, 1892, names as his first important influence Sidney Bechet, who was phenomenal on clarinet at a very young age. Before Dodds came north, he played in Storyville and in the cabarets along South Rampart Street. Best known for the period in which he played with King Oliver, Johnny is also identified with Kelly's Stables, Chicago, where he played for six years. A short part of this time, "King" Keppard was on trumpet; during the remainder of the stay, it was Nat Dominique. Dodds' style profoundly influenced many clarinet players, including the late Frank Teschemacher, and it is possible to say of him that he never played a "commercial" note in his life. This is not the same thing as saying Johnny was always perfect, for he wasn't, but it is a clue to the deep personal quality one feels in his work. When Johnny Dodds came into Decca's Chicago studio, to make the two sides for this album, he was returning to New Orleans, helping to recreate a music that grew out of the lives of people like himself. This was his last job, for he died of a paralytic stroke on August 8, 1940. This album becomes, therefore, not merely a sampling of authentic New Orleans jazz, but a tribute to a fine musician who helped make it.

Jimmy Noone (clarinet)—Another powerful influence upon Chicago, the fine stylist who was one of Benny Goodman's teachers. Born New Orleans, 1894, he remembers being inspired in 1911, by Fred Keppard and Richard M. Jones. Storyville jobs with Ory, Oliver, Petit, Keppard, Clarence Williams, etc. With John Robichaux, 1915. A year or so later he replaced George Baquet in the Original Creole

Band that became Oliver's famous orchestra. Also played with Charlie Cook, Dave Peyton, and others, and had own band with Earl Hines.

Luis Russell (piano)—First job, 1918, in a Colon (Panama) bistro. Up to New Orleans, 1920. North to Chicago, about 1924, with Cook; then with King Oliver. His own fine orchestra grew out of Oliver band, at the Nest (Harlem), which was for years a musicians' hangout. That band had Omer Simeon, Barney Bigard, Jay C. Higginbotham, Paul Barbarin, and, later, Red Allen, Pops Foster. Played two weeks with Louis Armstrong and about five years later (1935) he and several of his men helped to form Louis' present orchestra. Born Bocas del Toro, Panama, 1902.

Lil Hardin Armstrong (piano)—Has been playing New Orleans piano since 1917, when trying out for Sugar Johnny's De Luxe Cafe band, she asked, "What key is it in?" Sugar Johnny said, "Hit it, gal," and the music student from Fisk University has been hitting it ever since. With King Oliver and as leader of Lil's Dreamland Syncopators, she has helped make jazz history. Has a fine technical understanding of what constitutes New Orleans music, is a talented composer and arranger. Born Memphis, Tennessee, 1901.

Richard M. Jones (piano)—A onetime Basin Street "Professor," a veteran of Claiborne Williams' band (when in knee pants), he played solo piano at Storyville saloon the Annex, 1906, played at Lulu White's, at Countess Piazza's, cabaret jobs with Piron, Oliver, Keppard, etc. A fine blues pianist and composer, he has played and toured with many great blues singers, including Ma Rainey show (1918), and has had own orchestra. Born New Orleans, 1889.

Bernard Addison (guitar)—One of our leading guitar players, he was with Armstrong in 1929; Fletcher Henderson in 1933; Fats Waller in 1934; Mills Bros., 1935–37. A native of Annapolis, Maryland, he did jobs with Claude Hopkins in 1921, when still in his teens. Born 1907.

Lonnie Johnson (guitar)—One of the foremost guitar players in jazz, made duets with the late Eddie Lang, played in New Orleans at the Red Onion, at the Big 25, then with Creath (St. Louis, 1923); with Louis Armstrong, Chicago and New York; with Lil Hardin Armstrong, Chicago. Well known for his solo guitar, this album presents Lonnie Johnson as he has long deserved to be known, playing guitar in a New Orleans band. Born New Orleans, 1898.

Wellman Braud (string bass)—This fine musician played in New Orleans for several years before coming north, 1917, to Chicago. Played in band that opened Pekin. Played with Lil Hardin at De Luxe, with Bechet at Royal Garden. To London with Elgar's Creole Band, 1922; with Vaughn's Orchestra, 1923–27. Early 1927, toured New England with Duke Ellington, with Duke for that long Cotton Club run and until 1935. Works now chiefly on recordings, special band dates, etc. Born outside New Orleans, 1891.

George (Pops) Foster (string bass)—Played with so many jazz bands and brass bands in New Orleans that he can't remember all of them. Played at Billy Phillips' Franklin Street Cabaret with King Oliver; in Tuxedo Band with Zutty and others. About 1918, Strekfus Line. Joined Charlie Creath's band, 1920, working out of St. Louis. Toured West Coast with Liberty Syncopators. Joined King Oliver, 1927, in New York City. Later joined Russell's band that joined forces with Armstrong. Born New Orleans, 1892.

Johnny Lindsay (string bass)—One of first jobs was at the old Grunewald Hotel in New Orleans with John Robichaux. Came north in 1920s and played with Oliver, Armstrong, Richard M. Jones. Born New Orleans, 1892.

Arthur (Zutty) Singleton (drums)—Among early jobs were Orchard Cabaret with Louis Armstrong, Caddilac with Luis Russell, etc. Zutty also played on Strekfus Line and with Charlie Creath. North to Chicago, 1925, with Charlie Cook; with Noone; with Dave Peyton; with Carroll Dickerson; and to New York with Louis Armstrong, 1929. Has played with Waller, Eldridge, and many others, has been spotlighted in front of other bands (Bud Freeman's, Bobby Hackett's) for his superb drumming. Now has his own small band at a New York nightspot. Born New Orleans, 1898.

Warren (Baby) Dodds (drums)—The man behind the drums on most of those King Oliver Gennetts. Played Storyville jobs with Bob Lyons (bassist of Buddy Bolden band) in 1914. Came north early 1920s, played with King Oliver, Johnny Dodds. Gives band a solid pulse and the tone of his drumming blends perfectly into ensemble. Born New Orleans, 1898.

Minor (Tubby) Hall (drums)—Inspired by Buddy Bolden's drummer, "Zino," first played drums more than thirty years ago. Played Storyville jobs with Perez and other old-timers. His Chicago period dates from the De Luxe Cafe days and he's played with Oliver, Dickerson, Armstrong, and others. Born New Orleans, 1892.

(1940)

GEORGE FRAZIER

Frank Teschemacher
(Brunswick B-1017)

Frank Teschemacher was just shy of his twenty-seventh birthday when the Packard in which he was riding along a Chicago street hit the rear end of a taxicab, careened wildly over the curb, and crashed into a tree with such momentum that his body was catapulted onto the hard pavement. He never recovered consciousness. In the years that have slipped by since that morning in 1932, Frank Teschemacher has come to occupy a lofty niche in jazz.

Teschemacher played clarinet. Whether he was the greatest hot clarinetist of all time—or merely the second-greatest, or even the third- or the fourth- or the fifth-greatest—is not important. What is important is that he "played good." Just how good is for each of you to determine when you hear him on the records in this album.

Notes are not the only improvisations in hot jazz. More often than not the anecdotes are improvised, too. This is doubly true when the subject meets an untimely end. What there is about early death that should inspire tall tales I do not know. But I do know that there must be something. A man—especially a man of not inconsiderable jazz endowments—perishes young; and all of a sudden the tales about his life and death begin to incorporate the misty qualities of folklore. It was true of Beiderbecke and of Berigan, and it was certainly true of Frank Teschemacher. For everywhere that jazz musicians gather—on a bus roaring through the everlasting night, in smoke-drenched bars in the hours before dawn, in back rooms the length and breadth of the land—everywhere that jazz musicians gather to smoke or to drink or merely to talk small talk, the apocrypha grow. So presently what you have is not the accredited facts about Leon Bismarck Beiderbecke or Bernard Berigan or Frank Teschemacher, but a gossipy fugue on the accredited facts. You have a theme and variations in which the variations are so elaborate, so fanciful, that the theme is all but obscured. If Tesch seems a little less fantastic, a little less incredible than several others among the departed, it is simply because he was too studious, too self-conscious, to be readily molded into the fabulous patterns which imaginative jazz musicians like to invent for their colleagues *post mortem*. The facts about the life and death of Frank Teschemacher (1905–1932) are these.

He was born into a middle-class Kansas City family on March 13, 1905. By 1912, when his family moved to Chicago, he had already begun piano lessons. A few months later he gave them up to study banjo. At fourteen he switched to violin, an instrument he was to play from time to time during his brief life. He was a quiet, moody boy, whose natural shyness was magnified by the fact that he had crossed eyes and a bad case of acne.

Austin High School in Chicago has acquired an imposing reputation as an incubator for hot musicians. It was while he was a student there that Teschemacher became acquainted with a group of boys who shared his deep devotion to a kind of fresh and exciting music that was called, for want of a better name, jazz. They were Jimmy and Dick McPartland, Jim Lannigan, Dave North, and Bud Freeman. They were regarded, at that time, as inordinantly irresponsible kids who cared little for book learning. The years, however, have bathed them in the glow of recognition, and in jazz their names are big and splendid. After school they used to gather at Teschemacher's house and play their kind of music. Even then, Frank, who had decided to cast his lot with the clarinet, bore the unmistakable stamp of genius.

In June 1925, he left Austin, and for the next few years he played with Husk O'Hare's Wolverines. During the winter of 1925, this group was the house band at radio station WHT; the uninhibited music that they produced marked one of the pioneer series of jazz broadcasts. Across the street from WHT was Kelly's Stables, where Johnny Dodds, the fine Negro clarinetist, used to play nightly. Johnny's influence on the way Tesch plays on some of the records in this album can be traced back to the nights when the Wolverines frequented Kelly's Stables.

The Chicago of those innocent years was a fine, toddlin' town. Jazz was everywhere, and it was the best—free and shining and incorruptible. Over at the Sunset a magnificent young trumpeter named Louis Armstrong was making jazz history. In his band was a sharply dressed kid named Earl Hines, whose piano work in that period has yet to be surpassed. It was such a barrelhouse environment that conditioned Teschemacher. And it was this environment that produced two records by McKenzie–Condon's Chicagoans which appeared in 1928. When Bee Palmer, an enormously popular singer of that era, heard them, she became so enthusiastic that she arranged for a New York job for the youngsters who had made them. So Tesch, Joe Sullivan, Gene Krupa, Jimmy McPartland, Bud Freeman, Jim Lannigan, Eddie Condon, and Red McKenzie started for Manhattan. But the prospective job folded before they ever reached there. After a week at the Palace accompanying a ballroom team, they split up. Teschemacher joined Red Nichols. Three months later he returned to Chicago, where for the rest of his life he worked with a succession of stultifyingly sweet bands.

In the spring of 1932, he was rehearsing with a group formed by Bill Davison, the cornetist, for an engagement at Guyon's Paradise. He never got to play the job. On the morning of February 29, he was riding in Davison's Packard when it hit a taxi. Five hours later, he was dead.

So Frank Teschemacher died, and in one way it was a terrible thing. But in another way it wasn't. For he died before jazz had a chance to become swing and before the age of the latter-day saints of the clarinet (who shall go unmentioned here). He never had a chance to be pursued by the autograph hounds, and he never had a chance to be terrific on West 52nd Street.

I realize that he played with some very sad bands, but I realize too that when he played hot he wasn't doing so because he was conforming to a vogue. He was doing so because he wanted to. I think you should remember that when you come to play the records in this album.

The Records

Frank Teschemacher never played "pretty" in the accepted sense, and he was never the technical wizard a lot of boys are, but he had it in his heart and he sounded fine. He played a feverish, strangulated style with colossal drive, and in the all-in ensembles his notes seemed like sparks flying from a blacksmith's anvil. He plays that way on these records.

Chicago Rhythm Kings

I've Found a New Baby
There'll Be Some Changes Made
PERSONNEL: *Muggsy Spanier (cornet); Frank Teschemacher (clarinet); Milt Mezzrow (tenor sax); Joe Sullivan (piano);*

54

Eddie Condon (banjo); Jim Lannigan (tuba); Gene Krupa (drums). (Recorded April 1928)

It would be patently absurd to maintain that all the items in this album are of uniform quality. They are not. But their one unifying characteristic is the Teschemacher clarinet. The best of the recordings is, to me anyway, *There'll Be Some Changes Made.* That's a wonderful job—possibly the finest record ever made. The legend has it that Tesch's lips were bleeding by the time he finished the date. That was more than sixteen years ago, and in the meantime the people who were there (in the studio at the time) have lost their sharp memory of what happened. No matter, for the significant thing is that the record approaches perfection. The beat throughout is wonderful. You should notice, though, that it is Tesch who gives the band its drive. Muggsy's cornet is marvelous as it punches out the lead, and Krupa's percussion has variety and enormous life. But it is Tesch who makes the record the breathless affair it is.

I've Found a New Baby, a product of the same date, has the same fever as its backing. Even the plunk of the banjo is not disturbing. The lovely thing about these two sides is the fact that the band is coordinated. Everyone works for a common interest. I am especially fond of the way Krupa shades Mezzrow's tenor saxophone solo. Mezzrow, by the way, plays superbly—with thinner tone than Bud Freeman's, but with the same feeling and style. As for Joe Sullivan, he is full and rocking and really a quite wonderful pianist.

To go back to *Changes* for a moment: When the record was made, Muggsy missed the last note and was so furious with himself that he ran to the window and tried to throw his horn out. This, by the way, is the model for an incident in Dorothy Baker's novel *Young Man with a Horn.*

Chicago Rhythm Kings

Baby, Won't You Please Come Home

PERSONNEL: *Muggsy Spanier (cornet); Frank Teschemacher (clarinet); Milt Mezzrow (tenor sax); Joe Sullivan (piano); Eddie Condon (banjo); Jim Lannigan (tuba); Gene Krupa (drums). (Recorded April 1928)*

Baby, Won't You Please Come Home has never been issued before. It was accidentally discovered while research was being done on an entirely different orchestra. Aside from Teschemacher's playing, it is notable for one of the worst vocal choruses in the history of recording. It is by Eddie Condon, ordinarily an astute man, and he ends it with a fanciful flourish that is strictly out of a happily vanished era.

Joe "Wingy" Manone and His Club Royale Orchestra

Trying to Stop My Crying

PERSONNEL: *"Wingy" Manone (trumpet); Frank Teschemacher (clarinet); George Snurpus (tenor sax); Art Hodes (piano); Ray Biondi (guitar); Augie Schellange (drums). (Recorded December 1928)*

The Cellar Boys

Wailin' Blues
Barrel House Stomp

PERSONNEL: *"Wingy" Manone (trumpet); Frank Teschemacher (clarinet); Bud Freeman (tenor sax); Charlie Melrose (piano and accordion); George Wettling (drums). (Recorded January 1930)*

I don't like people who write about pear-shaped tone, etc., any more than Eddie Condon does, and I don't think your listening to these records should be burdened by any such diagnoses. But

I would like to point out several things that may escape the jazz uninitiated. "Wingy" Manone, for example, is very good in *Trying to Stop My Crying, Wailin' Blues,* and *Barrel House Stomp.* He has a big tone and a good beat. He would have made better records if he had used a bass. As they are, they sound empty. Their merit lies in the performances by Manone, Freeman, and, of course, Tesch. Listen especially to the Teschemacher clarinet behind Manone's vocal in *Crying.*

Elmer Schoebel and His Friar's Society Orchestra

Copenhagen
Prince of Wails

PERSONNEL: *Dick Feigie (cornet); Jack Read (trombone); Frank Teschemacher (clarinet); Floyd Town (tenor sax); Elmer Schoebel (piano); Charlie Barger (guitar); John Kuhn (tuba); George Wettling (drums). (Recorded October 1929)*

Copenhagen and *Prince of Wails* are a good deal less than the records perfect. They have certain almost mechanical ensemble effects, and the general impression is too often that of a band playing at a country club dance. But Teschemacher is consistently wonderful. Notice in *Prince of Wails,* for example, how things perk up when he takes a solo. Considering the company he kept on that record, this is a magnificent achievement.

Just one more thing: The two best recordings in the album— *Changes* and *New Baby*—are not easy listening for novices. But they are more than worth the effort you are willing to put into them.

(1945)

PART TWO

A Moment's Notice

DAVID STUART

*Bunk
Johnson
and His
Superior
Jazz
Band*

Bunk Johnson
*(Good Time Jazz
M 12048)*

How We Recorded Bunk!!

In the early summer of 1942, Willie Bunk Johnson wrote in one of his remarkable letters—he put a period between each word—that he had worked sufficiently with his new trumpet and was now ready to record. At that time he sent a six-inch "homemade" acetate of unaccompanied trumpet. The record is lost and I cannot recall the tune. But I do recall that the solo was no great shakes of a thing, and that it momentarily gave me the blues.

Nevertheless, we all knew he must be recorded, as soon as possible; time was running out on the New Orleans originals, and the Second World War was about to grab most of us. So I got in touch with Bill Colburn (true jazz lover) and Hal McIntyre (then a fig-type disc jockey) in San Francisco to ask if they'd drive with me to Louisiana the first of June to see Bunk and help record him. They were hot for the idea. Then I called William Russell (top authority on N.O. jazz) in Pittsburgh and Gene Williams (then editor and publisher of *Jazz Information*) in New York, and both agreed to meet us in Bunk's hometown, New Iberia.

The three of us from the West arrived in New Iberia on Thursday, June 4, 1942, and immediately rented in the center of town a vast home that I like to believe was the Shadows. After showering to cool off—the weather was red-hot and sticky—and cleaning up generally, we had dinner, with grits, of course, then drove across town to Bunk's house. Although we all thought of Bunk as an old friend, and I had corresponded with him for several years, none of us had ever met him. So we were a pretty excited crew, indeed.

Bunk was sitting on his porch, waiting for us. He waved as we pulled up and jumped out of the car and raced across the yard to greet him. It was marvelous and went off like fireworks, and all at once we were as thick as thieves. And Bunk, who had the most remarkable memory of anyone I've ever known—even more remarkable than Jelly Roll Morton's—was quietly answering a salvo of questions fired by three history-hungry greed-heads. In the end it was Bunk who suggested we might like to hear him play a tune or two.

This was what we'd come two thousand miles for, yet we followed him into the house with a certain trepidation. After all, he hadn't really played horn for a good number of years, and it was only recently that he'd been fitted with workable false teeth and a new trumpet. His cornet had been destroyed in 1932, and his teeth went soon after. Since then he had worked the rice fields, hauled cane, and taught music on rare occasions.

But it was bootless worry, chicken skepticism. Bunk took his horn from the case and rubbed the gold finish lovingly as he held it out for our inspection. He whipped the valves several times. Then he opened up on a slow blues that put tears in my eyes. Broke me up! Just thinking about it now makes my spine tingle all over again. He played his "head music" exactly as we'd dreamed he would. Rhetoric aside, it was altogether an amazing performance. Bunk played several more tunes and we talked for a couple of hours before he finally said, "I rise mighty early for work," and sent us off elated and limp.

Bill Russell and Gene Williams arrived the following day. That evening we were back at Bunk's for more music and talk of the session. It was decided that the five of us would go on to New Orleans the next day to get together a band, and Bunk would follow on the bus Monday. Any missing instrument he would see to then.

The one-hundred-fifty-mile drive into New Orleans was pleasant, especially the fifty miles along the Bayou Teche. Saturday evening we went to see Johnny St. Cyr, banjoist of Hot Five fame. He was playing in a dime-dance joint, a squalid dive, making a dollar fifty for eight hours' work. We took a table, gave the hustlers the brush, and dug the band. When I think back on it, it seems they played *High Society* every other number, and not well. But it afforded the girls the opportunity to bounce the tricks around, shaking, from time to time, a coin from their trousers. The band was only so-so, but St. Cyr was fine. And so was the bass player who none of us knew. His name was Austin Young, and he would be happy to record with Bunk Johnson.

Unfortunately, St. Cyr said he couldn't make the session. It was a blow to lose St. Cyr, but we did have a discovery in Austin Young. From St. Cyr we found where Louis de Lisle Nelson was working: "Big Eye" Louis, who in 1905 was playing clarinet with the Golden Rule Orchestra at Fewclothes' Cabaret in the District. In 1941 I had heard him and he was playing fine. Alas! Now he wasn't; time was telling all too rapidly. A second disappointment. But in the band was a good solid drummer, Ernest Rogers, another man unknown to us. He too would be happy to record with Bunk.

About then we called it a night, and Sunday we slept late, accomplishing little. Monday Bunk arrived—his first appearance in the city in nearly twenty years! We told him about "Big Eye," and that Sunday we'd seen Alphonse Picou, and that he wasn't playing well, either.

"Do you remember a man you especially liked?"

"Yes," he said immediately. "George Lewis. Believe he lives at 827 St. Phillip Street."

"You know his playing well?"

"Yes, indeed. I was playing with him in Evan Thomas' band the night Evan was murdered. It was in Rayne, thirty-five miles out of New Iberia. We were playing in a hall, and this bastard John Gilbey came in with a big knife. He was drunk and swearing he'd kill Evan for foolin' with his wife. Evan hadn't been, but no matter. Gilbey jumps up on the stand and Evan, a big man, ducks behind little George Lewis. Gilbey reaches right over George and slices Evan's throat, and the blood pours out all over poor George. Gilbey runs out of the hall, and we're trying to get our things together and get the hell out of there when he returns with a gun. Man, he's gone crazy! So we went out headfirst through the back windows. From outside we heard him roaring and swearing and all of a sudden a terrible crashing and banging. He was wrecking our instruments. He stomped my cornet—wrecked it forever. He slashed the drums, kicked in the bass, wrecked the whole goddamn band! That's when I went back to New Iberia and played no more. That was near Thanksgiving in '32, I remember," he said. Then he added, "George is a fine clarinetist."

In order to get more done, we decided to split up. So Colburn and Williams went off in search of trombonist Jim Robinson, while Bunk directed Russell, McIntyre, and me to Lewis' home. A very slender handsome man of medium stature answered our knock at 827 St. Phillip Street.

"Hello, George," Bunk said.

"Hello, Bunk. Been a long time."

"Ten years."

Bunk introduced us to George and George asked us in and introduced us to his wife, Jeanette. We took to George instantly. And this normally shy and reserved man liked us too, and said in his biography, "They asked questions and we talked a long time. There was something about them that was different, and I had a good feeling about them. There was something different about the way they talked to me and Jeanette and the way they acted. They shook hands with me, and later on David asked me did I have a horn, and I got it out and played some for them."*

George got out the worst beat-up, wired-together, rubber-band-action clarinet I've ever seen. The keys were loose, one was missing entirely, and the pad on the octave key was a ball of hardened chewing gum. But he "played some" for us all right all right! *Over the Waves* was the tune, and for the second time in less than a week my eyes were filled. I felt a bit foolish and sentimental until I noticed Russell's and McIntyre's eyes. Suddenly I remembered passing a hock shop on the way to George's. So while he started on another tune I waltzed out and bought two Boehm system clarinets and offered them to him. The one he turned down I still have. With the solid and complete horn he really wailed! It was marvelous! We had ourselves a clarinet for the session, no mistake.

George suggested his close friend Lawrence Marrero for banjo, and another friend, Walter Decou, for piano. We thanked him, said we'd call in a day or two, and set off for Decou's. On the way Bunk spotted a tall man carrying a trombone case, walking slowly along the sidewalk. "That's Jim Crow, man. I know that big rear end any place." We pulled up to his side; it was Jim Robinson. After some back-pounding greetings, I told him about the session plans, and he was "crazy to play with the old man."

* *Call Him George* by Jay Allison Stuart. Peter Davies, Ltd., London, 1961.

A couple of blocks later we came across Colburn and Williams, and the six of us drove on to Decou's. Decou was free to play any time we called him. It was while discussing with Decou the most likely day that Bunk came up with a new side of himself. He suddenly sat down at the piano and played a fine *Maple Leaf Rag* to astonish us all. None of us had the slightest suspicion he could play the instrument.

With the band arranged for came the problem of recording studio and equipment. Williams had a letter of introduction to the city's leading recording studio, so off he went. He returned howling mad to tell us, "No dice—no Negroes record in their lily-white studio!" We tried the only other professional studio and got the same damn answer. We spent the rest of the day, all of Tuesday, and part of Wednesday hunting for equipment and a room suitable—and available—for recording. Zero!

Wednesday afternoon, disgusted and soaking wet with perspiration, we slouched into Grunewald's Music Store in search of acetates. The young man behind the counter proudly announced he had a box of twelve, the *only* acetates in New Orleans! We snatched them, then told him our problems. *Mirabile dictu,* he had a home recording machine, a small Presto, he would gladly loan us. And on the third floor of Grunewald's was a piano store-room he was sure could make do as a studio. Would we be interested?

I am remorseful that I cannot recall this young man's name; it certainly should be set down here as a friend of jazz.

Thursday afternoon we cut the records. Ernest Rogers, the drummer, worked in an iron foundry and wasn't available until around three. Grunewald's closed shop at six. With only three hours, there wasn't going to be much time for any real rehearsals. We had just the dozen acetates, so the first take would be *it*—and no playbacks. After shoving the pianos around, we managed a quite comfortable space for the band and equipment. One thing was rather disturbing: The storeroom was on the top floor of the clapboard building, and in the midafternoon heat it was nothing if not a furnace. So we opened the windows to let in any breeze, and got honking horns, streetcar clankings, and the barking of dogs. And for one reason none of this seemed at the time really disturbing: The thing was to record Bunk and George and the band and to hell with the nonsense.

To get the affair started Bunk picked a tune everyone knew—*Yes, Lord, I'm Crippled and Cannot Walk.* The Presto mike, we discovered, was just large enough to feature one or two instruments and pick up most of the others. So Bunk stood front with George at his side, and the others made an arc around them. Turned out to be a happy solution. The band went over the number once, then Bunk stomped off and the legend was under way.

Some of it got on the acetates. Some of it escaped through the windows and splashed down on the street below. Colburn went out for a case of beer about three tunes later and came back to tell us he heard *Weary Blues* two blocks away, and that people were standing still in the streets, hands cupped to ears the better to hear. Most of it got into the ears of us in the "studio," and for my part the day turned into the most exciting day of music in my life. Actually, I can probably say the same for the others, including the young man who owned the equipment. He went out of his nut, and ran up and down the three flights, bringing in other Grunewald workers and friends to hear the "old men" play.

Earlier in the day I had called Orin Blackstone, the Bix specialist, asking him to come by. He said he might, but he didn't believe there'd be much use in it, as none of the old musicians were blowing much any more. He happened to walk in when the band was recording *Moose March,* and they all but blew him back to his desk at the *Times-Picayune.* He stood leaning against the wall, wagging his head incredulously. Later in the afternoon three old boozers came up from the street and held a hoedown in the hall outside, shuffling their feet, pounding their thighs, and waving their hands in the air. I say again it was the greatest day of music in my life, and more than likely in the lives of several others.

The band recorded the nine numbers now on this album in the three hours we were allowed. Once or twice Bunk's chops gave and he laid out for eight bars. But that's all. The rest of the time he blew his heart and lungs out. And so did George—and Jim—and the rhythm section. You won't hear Decou often, but he was pounding the piano all the time. The Presto simply wasn't up to recording all the music played that afternoon.

The second number was *Ain't Gonna Study War No More*. It was released as *Down by the Riverside* (under which title it has been recorded ever since) because I figured it wouldn't be politic to use the correct title when we were then up to our ears in the Second World War. *Storyville Blues* was the third number. The tune has been recorded since under several titles. *Storyville* was chosen because it's a good honest word and, as far as I knew, hadn't before been used as a song title. Bunk suggested *Moose March* when I asked for a number he'd played in the Mardi Gras parades around the turn of the century. The Moose was one of the numerous secret societies of the time. None of the others knew the tune, so Bunk played it solo for them, then they ran through it a couple of times and recorded it. Personally, I believe it to be one of the great jazz recordings. *Bunk's Blues* is just that, and the other four tunes you know.

The talking sides were made the following day on the remaining three acetates. Gene Williams asked the opening question and away Bunk went—with brouhaha accompaniment. Saturday, with the twelve acetates packed in the box, and Bunk and Williams (Gene decided to drive back to California with the three of us) as added passengers, we left Bill Russell and New Orleans.

(May 24, 1962)

68

The Legendary Buster Smith

Buster Smith
(Atlantic 1323)

I doubt whether any recording date ever met as much resistance as did this one. From its inception, long before I even conceived the idea of recording Buster, until the final note was on tape, a chain of circumstances constantly seemed to be conspiring to prevent it.

It all began many years ago with two seemingly unrelated circumstances. One was my first encounter with a 1940 Eddie Durham recording which featured an alto player named Buster Smith, who—it turned out—had been a friend and early mentor of the great Charlie Parker. Being somewhat of a discophile, I learned that Buster had not recorded since 1942, and that he lived in relative obscurity in Dallas, Texas. The other circumstance was that I was, at the time, a member of the Metropolitan Opera Orchestra. The Met on its spring tour always visits Dallas, and there the company is treated annually to a mammoth Texas-style ball at one of the big hotels. For this giant party, two bands are usually hired.

I didn't always attend these "shindigs," and one year—that was 1957—on the train leaving Dallas, I heard some of the boys in the orchestra talking about "a terrific colored band" that had played at the opera ball. One or two had remembered the name of the leader: Buster Smith.

I resolved to locate Buster on my next trip to Dallas. The next year (1958), upon my arrival in town—it was a Friday about noon—I started my search for the "legendary Buster Smith." First, I looked in the phone book, in the naïve belief that he would be listed there. After all, I had heard that he had one of the most successful bands around Dallas; and certainly he must have a phone, if only to get calls for gigs. I was quickly to be disillusioned. There were *three* Buster Smiths listed, but none of them were musicians. (I found out later that very few Negroes in the South have telephones.) The next thing I did was to call the musicians' local. I knew, of course, that there would be a separate "colored" local, but even it is not listed in the phone book. I could only reach it through its white counterpart. There was no answer at the Negro local; neither could I get any response throughout the rest of the afternoon.

In the early evening I called two well-known Dallas nightclubs, which I knew employed Negro musicians from time to time, but with no luck at either place. I was beginning to get discouraged.

That night after the opera performance the annual ball took place once again. I was entertaining very faint hopes that Buster might be hired for this grand affair as one of the bands. The Dallas Grand Opera Association was in the habit of hiring one white orchestra, a very polite society-type group, and one rougher "colored" band, playing music much closer to real jazz, so that some of the millionaires and opera longhairs could let their hair down a bit. However, even if Buster were not engaged for the job, I was sure that some of the musicians there would know where he was working. One of them *did* know—or so he thought. He said

70

Buster was at Pappy's Showland, another well-known nightclub in Dallas.

By this time it was 12:40 A.M. I promptly dashed out of the Baker Hotel to catch a cab and get over to Pappy's. When I told the driver where I was going, he said, "Oh, that's too late. Pappy's is already closed." Closed at twelve forty-five on a Friday night? Well, according to Texas laws, you not only bring your own liquor to a club, but you can not be served setups after midnight, which means that customers start leaving and, generally speaking, musical activity ceases at that time. There was no point in going to Pappy's. Again I was frustrated, but it was a curious kind of consolation to find out the next day that Buster hadn't been there anyway. He had been on a gig in Fort Worth!

On my way to my room at the Hilton, an extraordinary coincidence occurred. I bought a paper, and for some reason (I seldom do this), read some kind of a gossip column. In it I suddenly came across a little item which read: "One of the best-informed jazz enthusiasts hereabouts is Stumpy Jones at the shoeshine parlor, Columbia Hatters, on Evray Street." I thought this man must certainly know where Buster Smith could be reached.

The next morning—Saturday—I went to Columbia Hatters' emporium and asked for Stumpy Jones. He wasn't in; wasn't expected in; nobody knew where he lived; naturally he didn't have a phone. Another complete impasse.

Subsequent visits to the shoeshine parlor eventually turned up Stumpy Jones, but he hadn't seen Buster in months, and really couldn't say where he was working. Stumpy gave me one of the greatest shines I ever had, accompanied by a lengthy lecture on how Buster really wrote *One O'Clock Jump* and Basie had just appropriated it.

That afternoon I had to play a performance at the opera. There is a restaurant right outside the Fair Park Auditorium, where there was a crew of Negro waiters working. They looked pretty hip to me, and I thought I'd enlist their help. A few of them promised to ask around for Buster. So did some white jazz musicians who had come to see me at the auditorium. However, as it turned out, none of these people could discover Buster's whereabouts.

By Saturday evening I was really getting desperate, because we were scheduled to leave Dallas the next evening—and here was a day and a half gone already! I happened to be free that evening, and so decided to go to some other small clubs where I knew musicians were playing—*any* musicians. At this point, I was ready to try anything.

Finally—at about the third or fourth joint—I met one musician, a bass player named Jim Bell, who knew where Buster was that night. He was working a dance at some hall over in one of the Negro sections. Yes, Bell thought it was okay for me to go there. I took a cab, told the driver the address, and after some grumbling hesitation and rather dubious glances in my direction, he drove me to the place.

At the front door I asked whether I could come in and listen to the music. I was told that ordinarily it would be all right, but this happened to be a private dance given by the Shriners, and it would not be possible to let me in. I could hardly believe my ears. I argued with the man, telling him I was from New York and here with the Metropolitan Opera (big deal!!), and that I had "come all the way" to hear Buster Smith. Besides, it was beginning to rain. Couldn't he make an exception? No, nothing doing! He was a very officious man, determined to do the right thing.

Luckily, Jim Bell had given me a message for Buster's baritone player, a man named Grady Jones, who is secretary of the local. So I said to my adversary that I had this message to give to Jones. Could I at least "hang around" at the door until the band had a break? By this time I could already hear the band about sixty feet away at the other end of the hall. I was this close, and I *wasn't* going to give up now. He thought that that was all right. But after about ten minutes, with the worsening rain working in my favor, he softened up somewhat and decided to speak to Buster about my case.

At the next break Buster did come to the door and promptly fixed things up with my officious "doorman," who turned out to be the owner of the place. Buster told me I should sit right by the bandstand.

What I heard that night convinced me that I wanted to record Buster. I didn't know how or when; but Buster's alto, soaring effortlessly above the raucous, rocking Southwestern-style band, fascinated me. In it one could hear the pure, direct sound that Charlie Parker's ears must have absorbed in Kansas City over twenty years ago.

The second phase of "Operation Buster" took place in June 1959. I had talked to Nesuhi Ertegun about Buster, and Nesuhi agreed to let me record him at the first opportunity, if we could find a good recording studio in Dallas equipped for stereo. Inquiries resulted in our locating a studio with a good reputation, and some experience in recording visiting bands as well as local rock 'n' rollers. I was going to be in Phoenix, Arizona, in June for a lecture at the annual convention of the American Symphony Orchestra League, and I had suggested to Nesuhi that I could easily stop off in Dallas on the way back and record Buster.

On my first day in Phoenix, I contacted both the studio in Texas and Buster. This is where trouble began anew. The studio sounded fine, the engineers seemed experienced enough, and by coincidence, the head engineer was a French horn player who played jazz (a real comrade in arms), but unfortunately the studio was unavailable the week I needed it. That week—*of all times*—the organ in the studio (actually a theater during parts of the day) had to be repaired. The repair crew was all hired and set to go. With understandable reluctance, my horn player friend recommended his biggest rival, a studio in Fort Worth, the only other place that had the proper recording equipment to meet At-

lantic's very high technical standards. Another call and I had myself a studio in Fort Worth.

My attempts to contact Buster to alert him to the reality of a
recording date in a matter of days met with similar frustrations.
To contact by long distance a man who has no phone is not an
easy matter! But Buster had given me his brother Josea's phone
number. I called there and talked with a string of relatives, none
of whom had any idea where either Josea or Buster were and
when Josea might be back. I left word that I wanted to make a
session Monday next (four days hence), that Buster should
round up his band, think about repertory, and that, above all, he
should call me collect any time of day or night. That was Thursday evening.

By Saturday evening I had not heard from Buster. I called
the Josea number again. This time I was told that Buster had gotten my message, but was away on a Saturday night gig in the
northeastern corner of Texas in a town of which I had never
heard. I decided to call him directly at the dance. I waited until
about eleven o'clock, hoping to catch Buster during a break.
When the receiver lifted at the other end of the line, my ears
were assailed by an unbelievable din. It seemed as if everybody
in the place was also on the line, and through the noise I could
hear a fragmented musical background with snatches of an
unmistakable alto sound telling me that I was within earshot
of Buster. After raising our voices to yelling pitch to be able to
communicate over the noise, I thought I had made the man at
the other end understand that I wanted to speak with Buster
Smith. He had never heard of such a man. I tried to impress
upon him the fact that he was blowing an alto saxophone not
more than about fifty feet away, and that he was the leader of the
band.

"Well," he said, he'd "look for him." After what seemed like
ages, but was in reality five minutes, the voice returned with:
"There is no Robert Smith here!" I shouted to northeastern

Texas: *"Buster* Smith." "Oh, *okay!* I'll look for *him* then!" I started to say that he should just go to the bandstand and— But my intermediary had vanished into the general pandemonium. He returned another eternity later to tell me—believe it or not—that there was no "Brother" Smith there. This time I nailed him down before he got away again. I shouted at him that he should talk to the leader of the band that was playing there—I could hear him playing over the phone! Somehow he finally understood, and after considerable further waiting, I was told suddenly by a *female* voice that I should leave my number and Buster would call me back at midnight at the close of the dance.

Needless to say, I did not get a call that night. It wasn't until two the next afternoon that Buster actually telephoned. After apologies for not calling, and some unkind words about last night's place and the people that ran it, we discussed personnel and repertory.

At this point I must digress for a moment to explain that the question of repertory worried me not a little. Buster Smith today is a man who doesn't play jazz in the sense of "art music," a music to be listened to, or in the sense that a Charlie Parker played jazz. To Buster, jazz has had to mean strictly functional dance music. Solid rocking rhythms to which people can dance are far more important in Buster's everyday existence than melody or inventive improvisations per se. I knew that Buster's jazz material, in the "art" sense of the word, was limited because there is no practical use for it in the Deep South, where Negro musicians are relegated to a strictly servile function of "entertainin' the folks for dancin' "—and today dance music means primarily rock 'n' roll. In fact, Buster told me ruefully that he has been losing lots of work lately to smaller three- and four-piece rock 'n' roll groups in the Dallas area. It is understandable then that Buster's music has taken on a slight rock 'n' roll tinge, as these performances show. My repertory problem was further complicated by the fact that two of the pieces I had heard Buster play in 1958 were committed to another record company. (I don't think they have been recorded to date!)

Another problem was personnel. Some of the sidemen I had heard with Buster, while adequate for an ordinary dance, were hardly the kind of imaginative soloists one looks for on a record date. But Buster assured me that he would get the best men he knew, and, in fact, promised me a real surprise with the baritone player.

I told Buster I'd like to make the date Monday night (the next day). Could he round up his men? He thought he could, and would call me at the Hilton in Fort Worth the next day.

My hopes were rising. Early Monday morning I visited the studio, discussed microphone setups, degree of stereo "separation," etc., and told them that the date would be "either tonight or tomorrow." I'd let them know during the day. By midafternoon it was apparent that "tonight" wasn't going to work out. Buster called later and told me he couldn't get his band together on such short notice. Almost none of the men have phones and it takes time to reach each one of them.

We reset the date for eight o'clock Tuesday night. That evening I was at the studio early, eager and excited. We had all the chairs and microphones neatly set up, and looked forward confidently to a fine session which would show the world that a man like Buster Smith should not have been allowed to go unrecorded for seventeen years.

I really didn't expect anybody on time, but by eight-thirty I began to get a bit restless. I went outside in the silly hope that by waiting near the main road their arrival would be accelerated. My engineer read several Dallas and Fort Worth newspapers from cover to cover, while I stood outside watching two motorcycle cops, who used a dark side street as a hiding place, chase after speeding motorists. They made a rich haul that night, about one every ten minutes, and I was there to see it all! By ten o'clock I was really beginning to wonder. Thoughts began to cross my mind that Buster didn't really know me too well and might think I was just "puttin' him on." But, being a moderately calm individual and having basically limitless faith in humanity (that night represented by Buster Smith), I retained what in retrospect seems like an extraordinary degree of optimism and waited—and waited. Ten-thirty—no sign of the band. At eleven the motorcycle cops left off chasing Texans and reported in at the station house. Eleven-fifteen came and went. So did eleven-thirty and eleven forty-five. I was beginning to measure time not in minutes, but in quarter-hour segments!

I had called Josea's home earlier, around nine-thirty, and was told that Josea and Buster were "on their way," but would be a little late because they "couldn't locate some of the boys." Now, at midnight, I decided to call the head of the Negro local, a close friend of Buster's, whose number Buster had given me earlier, because "he lives near my house and he can always run over and fetch me." From this I assumed he was a neighbor. I called this poor man in the middle of the night. He was very friendly, but assured me that he couldn't reach Buster at this time of night, since Buster's house was "about a mile and a half away." But he said he would see him first thing in the morning. As a union official, he had sympathy for my predicament. I was paying a studio an hourly rate and after four hours still had not one inch of tape to show for it. I called Josea's number again, and by now understandably irritated, got somewhat upset at the absolute indifference and nonchalance of that charming household. Of course, I was dealing here with a peculiarly Southern characteristic! Everything is very, very easygoing down there, and if we don't do something today, why there's always tomorrow or the day after.

After due apologies—for I don't know what—to my engineer and the owner of the studio, who both said they had "never heard of anything like this," we waited another half hour, still the optimists, in case any stragglers might show up, and then closed

77

up and went home, thoroughly beaten. I decided that if I did not hear from Buster in the morning, I would fly to New York that afternoon.

Buster did call—at eight forty-five, no less! He said he couldn't get the boys together the previous night. They lived in entirely different parts of Greater Dallas, and since they had no phones, it meant that Buster had to drive to each man's house to get him. And since they never expected to hear from Buster *during* the week, working generally only on weekends, two of them had gone off fishing! Poor Buster had traveled up and down Dallas and its far-flung suburbs all afternoon and evening, pinning down his last man around eleven. I felt my wrath melting away into sympathy. He said they were all alerted and would definitely be on hand at nine "tonight," Wednesday, if I were willing to try once more.

That night Buster and his men *were* on hand, Buster and the rhythm section arriving at nine-thirty. The two-man brass section arrived fifteen minutes later. I wasn't expecting Cooper, the baritone, until ten or so, because Buster had told me that Cooper had a day job until nine and couldn't get to Fort Worth before ten. I therefore had decided to record Buster in several ballads with just rhythm. As it turned out, Buster became very shy and reluctant about this, and I could only coax the lovely *September Song* out of him.

We started late, but once the band got going, no more than two takes on any tune were necessary. Some, indeed, are represented by only one take. A few of the pieces had been in Buster's book for some time and were known to the players.

Cooper arrived around ten-thirty and lifted my spirits tremendously with his fine playing. The more I heard him play, the more anxious I became to get as much of him on tape as I possibly could. Before the session was over, I came to rely very much on his solid musicianship, indefatigable energy, and good-humored attitude. It was after one when we started on our last tune, and that accounts for the *Late Late* title. The session finished at two. Once under way, it had taken only four hours!

Although the date's outcome seemed in the balance often enough, and despite the many anxious moments I had with it, I would do it all over again. Through it all I came to know a fine gentleman and musician, and was given a chance to produce a recording in a style and a period of our American musical heritage sorely neglected today. More than that one cannot ask.

(1960)

Ellington
at
Newport

Duke Ellington
(Columbia CL 934)

Overshadowing everything else, including the introduction of a new work written expressly for this recording at Newport, Duke Ellington's performance of *Diminuendo and Crescendo in Blue* in the last set of the 1956 Festival turned into one of the most extraordinary moments in the history of this annual event.

Within an hour, reporters and critics were buzzing about it. By next morning, it was generally conceded to have been one of the most exciting performances any of them had ever heard. All were agreed that it was a triumph of the good old rocking (R&B, if you will) blues beat which has been too often missing in jazz in the last fifteen years. All were also agreed that it couldn't have happened to a nicer guy.

Typically, Duke was enjoying a perfectly successful appearance when he announced this 1937 medium-tempo blues (Duke said 1938, but it was written a year earlier), but no one was planning to break out the champagne or wave flags. Duke opened with four introductory choruses on piano; by the second, the rhythm section had already laid down a rocking beat and Duke had served notice of what was to come. Three minutes later, following the long series of ensemble choruses, Duke took over for two more rocking choruses that kicked off Paul Gonsalves playing one of the longest and most unusual tenor sax solos ever captured on record.

Gonsalves played for twenty-seven straight choruses. Of that, more later, for there are three levels at least from which this extraordinary feat must be viewed. (It should, of course, also be heard.) At about his seventh chorus, the tension, which had been building both onstage and in the audience since Duke kicked off the piece, suddenly broke. A platinum-blonde girl in a black dress began dancing in one of the boxes (the last place you'd expect that in Newport!) and a moment later somebody else started in another part of the audience. Large sections of the crowd had already been on their feet; now their cheering was doubled and redoubled as the interreacting stimulus of a rocking performance and crowd response heightened the excitement.

Throughout the rest of the performance, there were frequent bursts of wild dancing, and literally acres of people stood on their chairs, cheering and clapping. Yet this was no rock 'n' roll reaction; despite the unbridled enthusiasm, there was a controlled, clean quality to the crowd; they were listening to Duke as well as enjoying the swirling surge of activity around them. Crouched just off the edge of the stage, where I could signal back to the engineers if anything unexpected happened onstage during our recording, I had a rare view of the audience (at least seven thousand were still there, about midnight of the last night). Halfway through Paul's solo, it had become an enormous single living organism, reacting in waves like huge ripples to the music played before it.

But the management and the police, unable to sense the true atmosphere of that crowd as it felt from the stage, grew more apprehensive with every chorus. Fearful of a serious injury in the milling crowd, which by now had pressed forward down the aisles (the open area between the boxes and the elevated stage was already jammed with leaping fans), producer George Wein and one of the officers tried to signal Duke to stop. Duke, sensing that to stop now might really cause a riot, chose instead to soothe the crowd down with a couple of quiet numbers.

Out of sight of the crowd was an unsung hero who is quite possibly the person most responsible for this explosive performance. No one will ever know for sure, but perhaps the Ellington band might never have generated that terrific beat if it weren't for Jo Jones, who had played drums that night with Teddy Wilson. Jo happened to be in a little runway below the left front of the stage, at the base of the steps leading up from the musicians' tent behind the bandstand. From this vantage point, hidden from the crowd by a high canvas, but visible from the shoulders up to the musicians, Jo egged on the band with nothing more than appreciation and a rolled-up copy of the *Christian Science Monitor*. As Duke (whose voice you can hear from time to time) drove the band in the early stages of *Diminuendo and Crescendo*, first the reed section and then the trombones and finally the rest of the band picked up on Jo, who was shouting encouragement and swatting the edge of the stage with the newspaper, about eighteen inches from my squatting haunch. (As this target has grown more inviting with the years, I was careful to stay an arm and a half's length clear of Jo at all times.) The saxes began hollering back at Jo, then the rest of the band joined in, and by the time Gonsalves had sprung the dancers loose, it seemed that bassist Jimmy Woode and drummer Sam Woodyard were playing to Jo as much as to anyone else. Even the superplacid Johnny Hodges, who will probably not raise a half-masted eyelid come millennium-time, smiled and beat time back at Jo.

Gonsalves dug in harder and harder, and when he finally gave way to Duke, the release was electric. But only for an instant, for Duke himself was swinging, and when the band pitched in with the low-register clarinets plumbing *misterioso* depths, the tension built anew. (Don't miss the rhythm section's excruciatingly delayed return after the first chorus with the clarinets. What would normally be a four-bar break turns into seven!) With Duke and Jo still whipping up the band from opposite sides of the stage, the last choruses climbed to a climax topped by Cat Anderson, Duke's high-note specialist, who booted everybody home after the fifty-ninth chorus. Flat here and there? Nobody complained then, and don't bother us now, boy!

As we were saying about eight hundred words ago, Paul Gonsalves rates some examination on his own. His staunchest fans would never rate Paul among the giants of the saxophone, but after his feat at Newport one wonders who else could have sustained twenty-seven choruses without honking or squealing or trying to take the play away from what really counted—the beat. I can think of two or three others who might have done it—but I just as easily can imagine them running into complications of their own making. But that matters little, because the point is that Paul did it.

The key, obviously, lies in knowing how to tread the narrow path between Spartan simplicity and embroidery to a degree just short of destroying the hypnotic effect that Gonsalves achieves by adhering to the rhythm section's conception. This is not the place for the soloist to take over: He cannot grab the spotlight; he must remain one with the driving beat and yet not fall into dullness. A "display" saxophonist would probably have burned himself out within ten choruses, thus reducing the permanent value of this performance as it happened to develop (although the crowd might have enjoyed it just as much at the time).

Thus the Paul Gonsalves solo is not really a solo at all, but a leading voice supported by many parts, and never letting down the conception of those parts: the beat laid down by the drums, bass, and occasionally Duke's piano, and equally important the reacting support of the crowd, the girl who danced, the enthusiasm of the rest of the band (which did not play at all behind Paul, but which kept the beat with him and drove him on with shouts of encouragement, which Paul must have sensed were something more than just routine showmanship) and Jo Jones' wadded *Monitor*.

And as we were saying a thousand words ago, until *D. and C.* came along, Duke figured to have been remembered at Newport for his new work, written for this appearance. When George Wein approached me with the idea of Columbia recording at the 1956 Festival, he said he had asked Duke to write a composition for Newport; a few days later Duke played in New York, and agreed to finish the piece (which he and Billy Strayhorn had already started) and to record at Newport. He came through handsomely, as the three movements of this *Suite* attest, especially when one considers that the band had had only two short rehearsals while on the road prior to the Newport performance. The *Blues to Be There* themes are among the most memorable bits of Ellingtonia to come along in years. By the way, note how audience and orchestra (including Duke, usually quite vocal in his cries of encouragement from the piano) are busy concentrating on the new music during this performance.

Opening the other side of this album, ahead of Gonsalves Rides Again, is the Johnny Hodges showpiece, *Jeep's Blues*. This, too, could be the top item in any other Ellington collection. But *Diminuendo and Crescendo* was really the climax of Ellington at Newport '56 and the proof is right here, uncut and already mellow.

The introductory remarks at the start of this recording are by Father Norman J. O'Connor, Catholic chaplain of Boston University and one of New England's staunchest jazz enthusiasts.

From time to time, a flood of soloists appears in this album, and it seems advisable to list them in the order of their appearance. In the first movement of *Festival Junction* (which is also the title of the movement itself) are Jimmy Hamilton (clarinet);

Ellington (piano); Willie Cook (trumpet); Gonsalves (tenor sax); Britt Woodman (trombone); Harry Carney (baritone sax); Quentin Jackson (trombone); Russell Procope (alto sax); Cat Anderson (trumpet).

Procope (this time on clarinet) and Ray Nance (trumpet) are the soloists in the second movement, while Hamilton and Gonsalves are heard again in the third, along with trumpeter Clark Terry. In *Diminuendo and Crescendo in Blue,* a few bars of Nance's plunger-muted trumpet and Carney's baritone sax are heard in the last two choruses of the first long ensemble, and Hodges is heard for a few measures against the brass in the fiftieth chorus. Remaining credits are covered in the preceding text.

There is still more Ellington at Newport in a Columbia album which includes Buck Clayton's All-Stars (CL 933), as well as a complete personnel listing of the Ellington band. Other Columbia Newport albums are CL 931, which features Louis Armstrong and Eddie Condon, and CL 932, by the Dave Brubeck Quartet and the Jay & Kai Quintet.

(1956)

DAVID HIMMELSTEIN

Setting
the
Pace

Booker Ervin
(Prestige 7455)

We had not slept for four days and four nights and, as water and sky merge on the vasty deep, so for us the diurnal world had become a single, unbroken gray space. Sleeplessness, ancient drug of prophets, coursed our bodies; a waking dream of antimatter that mirrored our souls and paralleled our journey to the beginning of night. To Munich, Germany, where two Jewish boys traveled on business where they had no business—once had, nevermore. A beginning and an end.

How? (Let all metaphysical speculation await the full exposition of our existential position, if you can.) How: I, to lead a tour of jazzmen throughout the Continent, Don Schlitten, to make this record (What stuff our dreams are made of!), and Jaki, Reggie, and Alan, to make both, flew off toward a sun that afterward hid (in shame?) for a fortnight. To London, where we couldn't land, then to Orly (Paris), where we did (and got free lunch, several drinks, and boosted a bottle of wine); back to London, where we stumbled into a waiting room to be saved by Air-India's ground service from being transported bag and baggage to Beirut ("Maharahja Service" also means English girls in blue uniforms—quick thinking and sandwiches—bright and beautiful as the jets that lift us high to Cloud Cuckooland). To Dusseldorf, where Don and I caught a bus under a sign that mocked us with its I. G. FARBEN welcome, winking in bloody neon; to a train that hurtled us across the whole graveyard of Europe, east past Idiotstadt, through Beersville and a night that flashed like ack-ack on the swollen shrunken pusses of the rustic fellow passengers who pressed around and the stream of Red Army strutters, men without feelings like demons, flanking everyone—an obscene, slow-motion embrace of funeral wreath and tommy gun; a Dance of Death to the rhythms of a third-class carriage that reeked faintly of soap and stale cheese. Finally, to an exhausted dawn of fogs and Berlin.

Like traveling players in a comedy of the Absurd, our arrival, by mistake, at the Friedrichstrasse station (East, not West, Berlin) pitched us headlong center-stage; an entire garrison of soldiers poured into the corridor of our coach, yelling ("Hauptman, Hauptman"), with small arms at the ready (submachine guns, baby!), to arrest us (Yipes, we're on the wrong side of the Wall!) and trundle us onto Kafka's version of the Toonerville Trolley, which delivered us into the outstretched tentacles of the so-called "friendly Berliners." So much for Cold War parodies.

The Russians, who got their savvy about the Huns in the nose from the stench of their burning motherland, devised the Wall to set brother against brother, thereby keeping the rest of the neighborhood safe. This plan, an Oriental stratagem for the containment of wild animals, has worked so well that this once prancing, spangled city—divided—has been transformed into a circle of Hell whose ashen inhabitants snuffle after the blood of their kin. Welcome to Canniballand.

A day and night among the Harpies. Chaos, a fortune of small stupidities, broken promises, and the shadow of the

Swastika on every face. By this time our collective paranoia shouts: Don't eat their meat. It is befouled by an unclean touch and their linen has been whitened by the moon. So it's pork chops and greens (Southern-style!) cooked by Mae Mezzrow, Mezz' ex-wife, at Dug's Night Club (dig?), where Leo Wright, his dark face lighting new hopes in our shriven hearts, played brilliantly, his alto inspired, in part, by our desolation. At last, the Music! Dr. Jazz! Life Preserver, Hear O hear! A fountain of fresh water sprung from the briney. And Booker, too, was there, witness and savior.

The hallucination continues. In Munich now our trio (Booker, royalty in exile, freshly fled from Spain with some mysterious burden—solid, silent, spectral—looking like a Latin effigy of Christ wrenched from its gory cross, has joined our little force, mutual protection against the icy arrogance blasting from amidst this alien corn) is greeted at the airport by our guide—a midget! A petty Virgil, a Münchenkin, a man-boy to lead us. Or, as Pres once put it, half a motherfucker.

Hysterical reunion: Jaki, Reggie, Alan, Don, and I (the five who began the quest rejoin in Hades) in Munich to play a concert (eight to eleven) and record two albums from midnight until the plane takes us back to Berlin (shudder) in the morning. Sonny Rollins, a gray eminence, arrives collar up brim down, with wife and a hundred suitcases at our headquarters—Hotel Plätzl, the Alvin of a different day. But where is Dexter, and when?

Munich is our midget trying to make a call from a row of pay phones fixed at a normal height but still above his tiny reach. One after another he tries as futility and desperation dance wildly in his arms. Communication exists but is not possible; we are lost in a universe of useless machines. Should a man's reach exceed his grasp? His and ours, truth and omen. For us, a special death, the majestic shade of George Tucker (O Navigator!) haunts the empty concert hall. And the microphones of Heaven stand abandoned by their Engineer.

An incredible concert. The Sonny Rollins Trio with the mighty Dawson, schlagzug, and Niels–Henning–Orsted–Pederson–Oscar–Pettiford (the wunderkind) on bass opposite Art Blakey's art nouveau orchestra with Jaki (wow!), Reggie, Nathan Davis (new star tenor), and Freddie Hubbard ("Man, all I want to do is swing the world, man"). But where is Dexter, and when?

Packing up as the madly enthusiastic fanheads exit this Hall of Kultur, Schlitten's tired eyes spell "Where's Dexter?" and we sit in folding chairs, folding and nodding like addicts, limbs swollen with the oil of fatigue, scratching the invisible itch, forlorn. Here's Dexter! Stop-motion. Yellow goggles, tan, tam and tenor, cigaretted six and a half feet of trench coat high, elbows and knees, palm upturned, swings into view. Ladies beware, Dexter's here! Let joy be undefined.

'Round midnight at the Plätzl. Reggie missing in action, searching Munich for a proper instrument to record with. More heavy dues, arrangements for the session botched by our hosts, their ninety-seventh consecutive goof and a new world's record. In our room, a few precious horizontal moments stolen—the bed, like a lotus, soft and strange. Dexter retires to his bebop ablutions and reemerges, a garden after a summer rain, pours himself a small drink, and, flourishing it with a rhythmic shuffle, laughs lightly.

The entire party regroups in the lobby and two taxis caravan us to the outskirts of town. The groove is gay and good, the drive refreshing, and Jaki's comic chatter provides a murmurous leitmotif. We arrive in the Hunnish suburbia, at the address of Willy Schmidt's studio—the building a darkened blockhouse, looking arsenal and deserted among the neat houses. We fan out, black shapes against the purple night, surrounding the place like a commando team. But Willy has gone home, perhaps cursing the Americans who didn't show.

The false energy of our dream begins to slip away in a communal sigh. On the way back, Schlitten learns to use a German pay phone. (The midget! Roused from slumber, he sits on the immense flotilla of his hotel bed in the dark, wiping the cobwebs away with his miniature hand—ring of gold and diamond—perhaps cursing the Americans who rant at him in the middle of the night.) But finding Willy Schmidt in Munich is like finding Bill Smith in Brooklyn. You need time.

2 A.M. at Plätzl, the euphoria of dejection. Booker, waiting five days to make his record and battered by the boots of a thousand hassles to make it, suddenly bellows out his wrath at the inhospitable gods. Dexter disappears. Jaki, still chattering away in a telephone booth, manages to locate Reggie. Out of nowhere, meet Mr. Benny Bailey, trumpeter, expatriate and personal friend of Willy S. Don calls and cajoles. We win, it's on! Dexter reappears, in a different mood, the only man in the world who can walk in a sitting position. The darkness grows darker.

A return to suburbia, with expectations dampered. Jaki's chatter has almost ceased and Dexter mulls the pause between long thoughts. The Autobahn strokes by and I laugh bleakly out at it. It doesn't laugh back.

3 A.M.: Willy Schmidt's studio, complete with kitchen, bar, and bath, the perfect spot for our honeymoon. Frau Schmidt has just whipped up a batch of Teutonic sandwiches and we devour them, prejudices notwithstanding, washing them down with great clouts of cognac (Dexter: "It's international!").

Booker gets right down to business and the quartet slams into *Cookin' at the Jamboree (The Trance,* Prestige 7462), while Dexter, listening, puts his horn together—new Selmer, new sound—then turns and walks through the control room, past Schlitten's mustache, into another room. A few moments later scales and exercises emanate from within. A knock on the front door reveals a party of Czech students (coed) on a jazz tour of Western Europe who heard that "Sonny Rollins was having jam session here." Smiling evilly, like Charon, I lead them into the studio.

90

For the next two hours, Booker records with the rhythm section: Jaki, a Tiresias chattering our downfall between takes, his green cap like a leaf perched on a giant apple; Reggie, intense and earnest; Alan, tired but game. And all the while Dexter woodsheds in the back room, getting it together. Then, vaulting into the spotlight, he comes on. Dexter lifts his golden wing as Booker does and—*Dexter's Deck*.

Booker leads off, going "outside" at once, no problem with Jaki at the tiller. He preaches an emotional and intellectual analysis of his own style, echoing Dexter's phrases (his major influence) with his own transmutations. Language evolves. Listen again, you have to dig it to dig it. Now Dexter's turn—a nine-and-a-half-minute autobiography. Dexter's my name, bebop's my game. Right down the middle *(Mona Lisa? And the Angels Sing?)* an anthological style, the art of quotation and permutation. Jaki tries to go "out," but Dex will have none of it, except as a joke. Intimations of Pete Brown and a nod to Booker in the upper, upper register. And, of course, swing, swing, swing, swing!

A cowboy from Texas, rio grande mustaches and the souls of countless Federales notched upon his weapon, and a paladin from the Golden West stand locked in mortal confrontation like Colossi astride the banks of some moving thing—a river, a human street, time—beating the savannahs with fists of sound, their melodies charming the serpent and the lamb into soft liaison. O Earth, how terrible is thy rage and joy! O Peaceable Kingdom! O America! A vision and a visitation.

Setting the Pace. Dexter erupts like a volcano, flowing molten from great depths; Booker follows, a dragon breathing flames until they come together. Dexter's off mike, but who can expect even a Willy Schmidt to keep his head in the face of such insanity (the music is all here, and that's what counts!). Fours crackle like the Fourth of July, lines twining into an umbilicus of music, then fuse and become the root, the essence—life! life! Or the motive and cue to passion.

Amid this great booming, buzzing creation, I nod and fall away (Frau Schmidt thinks I'm dead!), a Jew, on the lone, resting with the finality of a wandering Greek shipwrecked on a foreign shore. The control room is a fluorescent coffin and I sleep, my mind darkening like deep water, and dreamlessly doze in a chair as my troubled heart, turning toward home, sings.

(September 1966)

TOM PIAZZA

Barry Harris Plays Barry Harris

Barry Harris
(Xanadu 154)

Almost noon. The snow falls endlessly and aimlessly; it has for hours. The sidewalk of 42nd Street is choked with slush; the slush is gray and gray trucks grind it into a soup which collects in pools that hug the curbs at each corner. My destination faces Sixth Avenue and has three letters—RCA.

Silent elevator up to seven. When I get to Studio B, no one is in the dimly lit control room. The air is heavy with the imperceptible hum of machines that have been left running. It is a room full of calibrations; rows and rows of sliding numbered bits and switches in a green defunctive gloom. Stillness.

The door outside clucks shut. George Duvivier walks into the studio, wheeling his bass. I watch him through the control room window; the live microphone in the studio registers the scuff and ruffle of his coat coming off, the case unzipping from his instrument.

The door outside opens again and a wash of nervous energy and talk carries Don Schlitten and his wife,

93

Nina, into the control room. Don—thin, intense—takes off his coat, smoothes his mustache, looks at the control board, and starts pacing. He is happy that only a couple of people have been invited; there will be less chance of any interruptions or scenes. The fans, musicians, and writers who usually turn up at his sessions have been making it hard for him to concentrate. Nina says, "You wouldn't believe how many people talk to Don while he's working! How can people who love music talk while it's happening?"

On the other side of the control room glass a young man, wearing a wool hat and hunting jacket, appears, looking around at the studio. He is followed by a girl about the same age, college age, and then about four more come into the picture with the air of students on a field trip. Then another wave of people, and now there is a small crowd in the studio, walking around, craning their necks at the high ceiling and looking at each other. Schlitten stares at them. Barry Harris walks in behind them, smiling like a cross between a gangster and a scoutmaster, buried in a trench coat, accompanied by Leroy Williams.

Schlitten finds out that the strangers are students from a class that Harris conducts. The question of where the students are going to sit is still forming itself in Schlitten's brain with the proportions of an ancestral curse when engineer Paul Goodman, who has arrived unnoticed, points out a series of risers, set up with folding chairs, far to the right in the studio. They are out of the sight lines of the control room and in perfect position to watch the trio record. The studio is used occasionally for slide shows, and the chairs and risers had been left there. Intimations of a benevolent Creator replace the ancestral curse. The students gravitate toward the risers.

Microphones are being arranged, Schlitten is getting his signals straight with Goodman, Barry Harris is lighting a cigarette. Harris' first Xanadu album contained only compositions by Tadd Dameron (X113); his second was made up largely of songs composed by, or identified with, Bud Powell (X130). Schlitten thought it was time for an album consisting solely of tunes composed by Harris himself.

Out in the studio, Harris is showing Duvivier the voicings for a ballad that the pianist has written, based on the chord structure of *Embraceable You*. The students, who have settled in, are making practically no noise—the atmosphere is that of a class. Doctor Harris guides Doctor Duvivier through an examination of the skeleton, noting the appropriate joints and structural peculiarities. Doctor Duvivier seems to agree that it is a fine subject.

Schlitten has turned down the lights in the studio, and the mood has deepened with them, to that level at which music is no longer just a demonstration of principles, as it is in a class, but an experience, wherein one moment is connected to the next by laws belonging to the uncalibrated provinces of taste, impulse, and wit. This is the level at which music disappears as an object of analytical thought, removing us from the conventional perception of time and involving us, to the degree to which we surrender ourselves, in a world in which the very articulation of the landscape is its meaning.

The institutional beige of the studio has deepened, with the dimmed lights, to a burnt orange. Curtains run, in narrow vertical pleats, the entire thirty-five feet from ceiling to floor. Small lamps, set into the ceiling, spill light down the curtains to where we sit. Harris and Duvivier are running through another of the pianist's new originals, this one based on *I Got Rhythm*. The piano and bass lines curl around each other like vines.

It is one o'clock and they are ready to begin recording. Don Schlitten comes out of the control room and gives a short speech to the students assembled on the risers, the kind of speech a favorite teacher would make before an important test: "If you have to cough or sneeze or fall off the risers, wait until the take is over..."

Schlitten is back in the control room; Leroy is set up, and Schlitten's disembodied voice comes over the speakers: "Gentlemen . . . *The Rhythm,* take one." Harris counts off a bouncing medium tempo and the trio begins.

There has been a nip of tension introduced by the rolling tape. If performing tends to make most musicians more self-conscious, performing for posterity further increases the more or less conscious sense of weight resting on each note. Ordinarily, in a studio, there is not even the feedback of an audience's reaction; a musician has the sense of playing for someone other than himself, but he can't see their face or sense their spirit. Today, however, there are the students, with whom Harris has an especially warm relationship.

They complete two takes, stopping after the second because of an electrical disturbance to make an adjustment in the placement of the drum microphones.

To no one in particular, Schlitten says, "It's man versus machine. The more machines, the more fuckups."

The control board sits, studded with small lights, in the underwater darkness of the control room. Green lights, red lights, beige gauges with yellow blips next to them, orange buttons lit from underneath. There must be times in the lives of engineers when trying to figure out the board's eccentricities is like playing chess with a computer. There is something akin to malignancy in its muteness, sitting there all dressed up and waiting for someone to make the right move.

Finally the microphones are ready for another take. This one is faster, but there was some mental static injected along with the electronic kind, and Harris isn't happy with it. They decide to wait before trying *The Rhythm* again. Instead, they run through the *Embraceable You* hybrid, which Harris calls *Back Yard.*

After the run-through, Schlitten asks if they are ready for a take. Harris replies, "Yeah, here we go," and counts off. He and Duvivier go through the ins and outs of the introduction, which is a series of alternately bright and clouded lines played in unison by bass and piano, reminiscent of some of the recordings Duvivier made with Bud Powell in the early 1950s. After the in-

96

tro, and a moment out of tempo, they play the melody, a warm, sunny thing, then Harris begins a long solo. Everyone, now, is carried along, around corners, through dry and lush country. George plays after Barry, then Barry plays the melody again. They come to rest on a soft forest floor of dark chords and the spirit floats upward, through sweet notes in the treble like sunlight on branchtips, down to a final tonic in the bass, which comes like sleep. A moment passes, and the mood passes like a shadow. Everyone applauds.

Harris listens to the playback in the control room, after which they decide to do another take of *The Rhythm*. Duvivier plays an introduction and the piano and bass have the theme for sixteen bars; Williams joins them on the bridge, which Harris plays in chords this time. Harris' solo is alive from the first notes. Quick references to other melodies float up, shine through the surface, then metamorphose into something else. The connections make themselves with the greatest of ease and two choruses tell it all. A bass solo, fours with Leroy, the theme and out. They will use this take and call it *Chances Go Around*.

Now they talk over and play through another of Harris' new originals, called *Father Flanagan* in honor of Harris' lifelong friend, pianist Tommy Flanagan. Harris' esteem for Flanagan is huge, particularly regarding Flanagan's harmonic sense. Harris once said, in conversation, "Tommy Flanagan knows something special, like a secret, about chording; I don't know where he got it, but he's known it since he was in his teens." Harris has put an unaccompanied opening section, played in chords, before the body of the tune. After a quick rehearsal of the group section, they turn on the tapes, Schlitten says, "Take one," and Harris begins the piece, alone.

A horn player, playing a solo, can be compared to a downhill skier, tracing the curve of an unbroken line to its ending, determining its shape, as he goes along, on the basis of a million small signals from muscles and eyes and ears. If he is good, he draws on resources owned

by few, resources that give one grace, allowing one to make instanta-
neous choices that lend smoothness to the ride. Better, he may be able to
call on rarer, less definable resources that give him something like dar-
ing, liberating him to make choices that open the mouth of failure so
much wider, making success that much more beautiful.

A solo pianist, on the other hand, is a soliloquist with ten voices;
the largest part of his art is the ability to mix colors so to create a
climate, an atmosphere, a mood. He can make one chord, voiced
tissue-thin, span a short, speechless moment, or smoke up a section
with billowing sounds and run a sharp line of thought right through
the middle of the clouds. So it is less a matter of the musician measur-
ing his thoughts against the fixed passage of time, showing his re-
sourcefulness in the way he contrasts his own movement with that of
the backdrop, than of the musician creating an independent cosmos of
his own, with its own sunlight, its own troubled moon, if he should
hear it.

A thick spell has settled. As he finishes the intro, Harris plays
a break, in single notes, leading into the body of the tune. In the
middle of the break, Harris' concentration is interrupted; he
went very far into the music on the introduction and, perhaps,
coming out of it, became a little too conscious of how excellent
it was. He breaks the trio off at the second bar and stops the
take. Schlitten, anxious for the momentum to be maintained,
says, almost immediately, "All right, this will be number two."

To Harris, Duvivier says, "How will you ever play that one
again?"

Harris laughs and says, "I probably won't."

Schlitten's voice comes over the speakers: "Take two, still
rolling." The microphones are all around, perched and hovering.

Harris starts the intro again, but stops after one phrase.

Schlitten calls out, "Take three."

To make a statement directly, without evaluating it beforehand,
making it because it is right on a level deeper than theory—a gift out-
right; to play out of your heart and have it all be true is an improvis-

ing musician's deepest desire. It is not something one can wish for; it is a blessing to which one comes close by playing as musically as one can at all times. Most of the time, music is a search, a playing off of one sound against another, a fascination with mathematics, a love of form. There are times, though—you can't predict them—when you are freed (maybe once a year, maybe twice in a career) from the constraints of technique and doubt and are carried as if on a river, and what comes is as euphoric, still, and detached from mediation as the music in a dream.

Most of the time, music does not come so perfectly; moreover, once a phrase is played, it cannot be erased and rephrased. (But don't worry, sonny; Mr. Technology will scare the ghosts away.) Each new equivocation or boldness or brilliancy adds another factor to the performance. The shape of the thing is created from inside, moment by moment, the way a person creates himself and becomes a little different, better or worse, with every choice he makes. Improvising musicians rarely like the records of their own that their fans treasure; they are too aware of the missed chances. It is their obsession to improve, always, and they are constantly striving for something just beyond reach. To the listener, though, these losses and gains, to the extent to which he sees them, are the medals and wounds of a struggle to attain, and the fact that there are losses means less than that the attempt was made.

Now Barry plays alone, the theme of the introduction again, more reflective now, then sweeps long runs very lightly like a breeze in the middle of the night bringing a sweet, troubled dream to an end. When it is over, everything is quiet for what seems to be a long time. After five seconds, Don Schlitten says, "Perfect," over the speakers.

Luminescence, which Harris recorded for an album produced by Schlitten for Prestige over ten years ago, is based on *How High the Moon.* They discuss the tune briefly, decide on a solo routine, and start a take right away. After the introduction, a series of jabbing accents on the upbeat, Harris misses his entrance and sings a couple of bars instead, breaking everybody up, before stopping the take. They start another immediately and, at the same place, Williams forgets to come in. Duvivier says, "My turn next." He does come in on the third take, though, and they play well, although not as well as they would like. Afterward, they decide to do another right away. Take four is excellent.

After the playback, Harris announces, "We're going to do *Cherokee*," and asks for title suggestions for his new line on those chord changes. He suggests, "Pocahontas ... some Indian name ..." Someone volunteers Minnehaha. Harris says, "Yeah, Minnehaha. Ha ha ha."

Harris sings the line, a pair of eight-bar figures to be answered by drum fills, for Williams. It is fast and intricate, and Harris laughs at the expression on Williams' face as he finishes singing. He sings it again, faster, and Duvivier says, "Got that?" Everybody laughs.

They begin the run-through and, in the middle of Harris' solo, which seems to get more brilliant with each measure, Schlitten says, over the speakers, "Don't waste it." They are ready to record.

An eight-bar drum break leads into the head, played at a ridiculous tempo; thirty-two bars and then the bridge, played ad-lib—Harris is burning notes like rocket fuel—to the end of the head, then the break—Harris blows out a long four-bar line which arches like a skier taking off from a jump with perfect form; the line doesn't stop at the end of the break, it slides right down into tempo, Duvivier playing a pedal tone for a couple of bars just to charge the batteries ...

Bebop is the farthest flag on the frontier of music that demands instant harmonic resourcefulness, rhythmic inventiveness, and technical mastery. Cherokee *is the archetypal bebop test; the bridge forces the musician to play in four different keys in sixteen bars, the test being whether you can be as inventive in the keys of A natural and B natural as in the more often-used B flat.*

And you must be cool while tracing this speeding line of single notes, making use of substitute chords and other harmonic alternatives which must be under your fingers at a moment's notice, deployed not flatly and mechanically but with an interesting texture of rhythmic placements and displacements. No show of strain—man, everyone knows it's hard; the trick is to make it seem easy. And quoting—quoting, especially, shows the connections working, shows humor in the middle of a test, shows that your mind is working as fast as your fingers.

Harris, cool but Romantic, playing lines as if a saxophone were playing them, stringing parallel phrases like lines of crystals or pearls, switching from D diminished with a half step under each note to a B-flat scale laid over the Cm7 to F7, switching them with the ease of a Savoy lindy hopper, laying them down and running them into each other like a railroad car switching tracks at five hundred miles an hour. The center of your heart when you're on the bridge of Cherokee *is defiance, in the broadest sense: to defy fate by not tripping where the going is most slippery, to stick your tongue out at fate by making a joke as you leap over the canyon. Not that you think of these things as you leap; oh, no . . .*

It ends in a whitewater of chords on the offbeat, with cymbals frothing. It has been the afternoon's climax; Duvivier asks them to play the take back, just "To see how it lays."

During the break, Baroness Nica de Koenigswarter, friend to many musicians, comes in. Barry decides to make the title of the next tune some kind of cryptogram of her name. At first he says *I Can,* then, teasing, *A Cin.* They finally call it *Inca.* It is a lovely bossa nova over the changes of Tadd Dameron's *Lady Bird,* the melody played in Dameron-like chords. The observers, who had numbered about twenty-five, have dwindled to fifteen. It is around five o'clock. Finished with *Inca,* which is completed in just one take, they go on to the last tune, a new blues. The third take of what they finally call *Even Tempered* has the spirit of a closing sermon.

It is five-thirty and it will be dark out. George Duvivier packs up his bass. The students who remain talk in twos and threes. After some good-byes, I take the elevator down with a friend from the class.

We stand on the corner of Sixth Avenue. The snow comes out of the dark sky, between the steel and glass buildings, falling without hurry, timeless and austere as a roll call, on and on. The taxis rush by, the buses and cars, all sounding horns, different cars, the same sound, everyone hurrying now to get home; it is six o'clock, the hour of forgiveness, when everyone returns to the warm place, like shadows. As we stand on the corner, the snow falling on our shoes, Barry goes by, heading for the garage to get the car and drive back to New Jersey. My friend crosses the street; we wave and then I turn and walk toward Broadway.

(1978)

PART THREE

Straight
Ahead

DAN MORGENSTERN

Dan Morgenstern is probably the most universally liked and respected jazz critic alive. He was editor of **Down Beat** from 1967 to 1973 and has been the director of the Institute of Jazz Studies at Rutgers since 1976. His warmth and love for jazz music and its musicians comes through in these two sets of notes; the Coleman Hawkins notes won a Grammy Award in 1974.

Memorial Album

Pee Wee Russell
(Prestige 7672)

In the early evening of March 29, 1960, I walked into Beefsteak Charlie's, a midtown Manhattan bar frequented by jazz musicians. With some surprise, I spotted a familiar figure at the bar—familiar, but not at Beefsteak's.

Pee Wee Russell, who'd turned fifty-four two days before, didn't hang out there—or in any other bar, for that matter. He'd done his share of that sort of thing—more than his share—but after his miraculous recovery from a near-fatal illness some years before, he had stopped.

But here he was, by himself, having a quiet drink. I didn't yet know Pee Wee well in those days, though I'd been enthralled by him for years, and Pee Wee was shy with people he wasn't familiar with. But I sidled up to him and ventured a greeting.

"How do you feel, chum," he acknowledged in that unforgettable sotto voce way of his. "Have a drink." Pee Wee was in a mellow mood, and it soon became apparent why. "We just made a record," he told me, "and it was a good one—I think."

That was almost as surprising as finding him there. Pee Wee was not as self-effacing as some people think, but he was his own severest critic, prone to shaking his head and waving a hand "no" when his solos were applauded, and only very rarely satisfied with his recorded efforts.

But about this session, he was not at all apologetic. In particular, he was pleased with the rhythm section. "It was modern," he pointed out. "And the piano player is one of the best I've ever played with." Pee Wee was particular about piano players. He was, in fact, particular about everything concerning music, but years of enforced association with contemporaries he'd outgrown decades ago had made him adaptable. He had learned to endure, and hold his head above the water.

No such problems this time out, though. No liabilities in this band. And no Dixieland chestnuts on the program, either. Not even a traditional front line. It had been more than a year since his last date as a leader, and in this kind of setting, Pee Wee was ready to do some serious playing.

As for most of the great jazzmen we call, for lack of a better term, mainstreamers, the fifties and early sixties were problematic for Pee Wee. As often as not, he had to play in settings far from perfect. Buck Clayton, that sensitive and elegant stylist of classic swing trumpet, was making a living playing at Eddie Condon's, where the staples on the musical menu were *That's A Plenty* and *Muskrat Ramble*, with an occasional ballad medley for respite. Oh, there was some good music made there, to be sure,

106

and I wish the club were still around, but Buck deserved a less restricting framework. He had it here.

Pee Wee had given up the Condon routine years before, and led some good bands of his own, but the tribulations of leadership soon became more than he was willing to cope with, and so, the gigs were infrequent and often less than congenial. Things were to get better in a couple of years, but at the time this record was made, it provided a welcome relief.

Now that Pee Wee's gone, it has become a precious gift. Every note he put on wax is something to be treasured, and fortunately, he managed to get quite a few things down for keeps. This album, however, is special; there are no dull spots to wade through. It's all of a piece.

It has been almost seven months, at this writing, since the bad news. If you love jazz and the people who make it, and have been with the music for a while, you get used to bad news—some expected, some not—and learn to live on as the ranks thin, accepting the inevitable.

Yet it is difficult to be resigned about Pee Wee's death. Every being is unique and irreplaceable, but he was more so. And he still had so much music in him to give; at sixty-two, he was not a shadow of former greatness, but rather the substance of new discoveries; as good as he'd ever been—perhaps even better. And music aside, Pee Wee was a lovable man. A few hours in his company could light you up for days to come. He was no saint, but he was holy.

Some unfortunates couldn't dig Pee Wee's music. Among them are some noted sages of jazz, one of whom only recently complained that Pee Wee spoiled a record which in fact was salvaged from mediocrity by his presence.

To me, he was a permanent revelation. In my early listening days (those days when you first discover the things that make the music part of you), I found a record of *Hello Lola* and *One Hour* by the Mound City Blue Blowers. I picked it up because I'd read that it contained some great Coleman Hawkins solos, and the ballad side made me fall for Hawk for good. But there was something else on that side that made me play it over and over—a solo by a clarinetist named Pee Wee Russell.

He turned the scene around when he started to play on that. It had been recorded in 1929, the year I was born, and I was sixteen when I heard it. But it sounded "modern," strange at first, then as clear and inevitable as something by Louis or Prez. I still love that solo, and it still sounds as fresh to me as it did those many years ago. It was my real introduction to Pee Wee's world, a world complete in itself and full of rare delights. He was a jazz musician to the core, and he never played an untrue note. Some wrong ones, maybe, though he could make wrong sound right, but never a false one.

He was often called odd, and there were people who considered his way of playing something to patronize. Belittling Pee Wee, however, only revealed the smallness of the belittler. It hurt him, nonetheless, as when a younger clarinetist, whom he sometimes sat in with (and without meaning to, played rings around) said, not softly enough to escape Pee Wee's acute ear, as his guest had left the stand (addressing his pianist), "Well, now we can play some real music."

Pee Wee didn't let on, but he never came back, and he never played with that cat again. What hurt him more than the insult was that he had liked the man, and considered him his friend.

Among the many peculiar theories about Pee Wee was the one that he was some sort of natural musician who played his instrument in hit-or-miss fashion, a kind of happy accident. In fact, he was a thoroughly skilled professional, who'd done his share of section work in more or less jazz flavored dance bands, doubling alto and tenor saxophones. He played the way he did because he wanted to, not because he was without legitimate skills. He was good enough at that sort of thing to have become a studio hack, but he was an artist by choice and temperament, and he cherished his freedom.

Pee Wee was one of the survivors of a generation of white jazzmen (though he was inordinately proud of his Indian ancestry) who discovered, without help or handbooks, the beauty of the black man's music and became part of it. All of these men were (or are) true originals. Some garnered more fame or notoriety than Pee Wee, but in some ways he was the most remarkable of them all. From the start, his music was unique, yet it could fit almost any surrounding. In later years, he never looked back. He was totally uninterested in recreation, only in spontaneous creativity. While others played the old songs, Pee Wee taught himself new ones, and thus he found new listeners. His work of the last decade, I think, will stand with the finest music from that time—and of the time. When this record was made, Pee Wee, as always, was caught in the act of reinventing himself.

We have here one of the most compatible and relaxed rhythm sections imaginable. Any horn player with a liking for swing could not help but be inspired by such backing, and Pee Wee Russell and Buck Clayton are swingers.

Osie Johnson, whose playing sometimes could be a bit choppy, is flowing throughout; Wendell Marshall plays the right notes in the right places with the right time, and Tommy Flanagan is a jewel.

Buck Clayton is an ideal partner for Pee Wee. Both are melodists, but of pleasantly contrasting styles. Buck is symmetrical and lucid, Pee Wee asymmetric and oblique. And they both listen as well as play.

There are two great blues on this LP, both originals by Pee Wee (who could write marvelous pieces). *Midnight Blue* is a happy blues, climaxed by some fine four-bar exchanges between the horns. *Englewood* is a mean blues, opening and closing with splendidly funky clarinet. Each hornman takes a pair of brilliant

109

choruses, and in the last ensemble, Buck's vocalized trumpet essays *West End Blues*. This track alone is worth the admission price.

The other pieces are all standards, none of them shopworn. *The Very Thought of You* is the only ballad, and Pee Wee's soulful solo is beautifully complemented by Buck, muted and tender. This song was recorded by Billie Holiday, with a clarinet spot for Lester Young, my second-favorite clarinetist. Pee Wee and Prez had a lot in common—in respect to feeling—and Pee Wee's solo here ends on a Lesterish note. Dig his coda, too, and Tommy Flanagan's half-chorus.

What Can I Say, etc., starts with some remarkable ensemble playing. All three soloists have spots, and Pee Wee opens his in his special trumpet bag.

Lulu has nice tempo, and Pee Wee displays his lower register, leaping into high for part two of his solo. Buck saves some great glisses for his climax. The closing ensemble demonstrates the virtues of intelligent interplay—no arranger could improve it.

On *Troubles,* Flanagan sounds remarkably like a modern Jess Stacy. Buck reaches for some high ones, while Pee Wee goes into his second chorus with a growl that is like a signature.

Anything for You, a tune Pee Wee liked and recorded several times (once on tenor), has a remarkable clarinet solo, almost entirely based on the opening phrase. Buck is particularly strong and joyful in the collective finale.

Well, those are some things I especially enjoy about this record. It captures some happy moments in the life of a great jazzman. He liked it, and so will you.

(September 1969)

The Hawk Flies

Coleman Hawkins
(Milestone M-47015)

Even among the chosen few, the extraordinary men and women who make up the peerage of jazz, Coleman Hawkins stands out.

To begin, there is his sound, a thing of beauty in and of itself. Hawkins filled the horn brimful with his great breath. Sound was his palette, and his brush was the instrument that, for jazz purposes, he invented—the tenor saxophone.

In this post-Coltrane age, the tenor sax is so prominent a feature of the landscape that it's hard to imagine it wasn't always there. Lester Young once said, accurately, "I think Coleman Hawkins was the President first, right?"—here meaning *president* in the sense of founding father. Which wasn't the sense in which Billie Holiday had laid "Prez" on Lester—at a point in time when the President of the United States was a great man, number one in all the land.

Tenor time in jazz begins in 1924, when Coleman Hawkins joined Fletcher Henderson's band. In a decade there, he first mastered, then established the instrument. While trumpet still was king, it was due to Hawk that tenor became president. Thus jazz became a republic in the Swing Era. King Louis was peerless by definition, but his powerful message unlocked the magic in other noble souls. If we hear young Coleman Hawkins both before and after Armstrong joined Henderson, the point is clearly made.

The saxophone family of instruments had been invented by Adolphe Sax to mirror the range and variety of the strings; he wanted his instruments to sing, to have the warmth of wood and the power of brass, and thus created a hybrid of wind mouthpiece and brass body, unlocked by a new system of keys. He did this in the 1840s, but with the exception of Bizet, Debussy, and later Ravel, no major "serious" composer knew what to do with the new arsenal of sound. Until it was discovered and mastered by jazzmen in the early 1920s, the saxophone remained a brass band and vaudeville instrument—a novelty.

Coleman Hawkins' first instruments in St. Joseph, Missouri, were piano and cello. (Of all the saxophones, the tenor most resembles the cello in range and color.) As a boy, he heard and saw the Six Brown Brothers in vaudeville. They used the whole range of saxes, from sopranino to contrabass, and with all their clowning really knew how to play. Young Coleman began to explore the saxophone.

Exactly when this occurred is not entirely clear. Hawkins, like so many other performers, prevaricated about his age. It was widely accepted that he was born on November 21, 1904; a date he unsuccessfully tried to adjust to 1907. Still, underneath incessant joking and good-natured teasing about age with his friends (Ben Webster: "I was in knee pants when my mother first took me to hear you." Hawkins: "That wasn't me; that was my father. I wasn't born then!"), there ran a current of doubt, and when Charles Graham, doing biographical research, obtained a copy of Hawkins' birth certificate, it read 1901!*

By the time "the Father of Tenor Saxophone" left for Europe in March 1934, he had already created the two prototypical tenor styles in jazz: the fast, driving, explosive riff style and the slow,

---

* Author's note: This document turned out to be the birth certificate of a sibling (female) who'd died in infancy; Coleman was in fact born in 1904 (though his cabaret card stated 1912). Later in the piece, I refer to Roy Eldridge as ten years Hawk's junior—he was in fact seven years younger.

flowing, rhapsodic ballad form. He made the mold, he was the model: Already, Ben Webster, Herschel Evans, Chu Berry, Budd Johnson, and many more had sprung, fully armed, from his high forehead.

To Europe, where the greatness of jazz had been felt mainly through records, Hawkins brought it in the flesh. Sidney Bechet had spent time there back in the twenties, and Louis Armstrong himself had flashed like a comet through England, Scandinavia, the Low Countries, France, Italy, and Switzerland earlier in the thirties. But Hawk came and remained; the first fixed star of magnitude.

When his erstwhile Henderson colleague, Benny Carter, that master of the alto sax, clarinet, trumpet, and arranger's pen, crossed the Atlantic a bit later and also decided to stay, the two often hooked up. Together and individually, they put their stamp on European jazz for decades.

The process was reciprocal. Hawkins' love for certain of the better things in life—good food, good drink, good clothes, pretty women, fast cars—was apparent before he left his homeland, but Europe sharpened and deepened his tastes. His sense of his own dignity and worth also expanded in the warmth of European appreciation and adoration. From here on in, Hawk was a cosmopolitan.

Meanwhile, there were not just contenders to his crown back home, but a whole new tenor style, introduced by Lester Young. Only a few of Hawk's great European recordings had made their way into the hands of American musicians during his absence. The climate seemed right for battle and the tenor brigade was ready for "Bean" (as musicians then called him, *bean* being a synonym for head, i.e., brainpower) when he came home in late July of 1939, just before the outbreak of World War II. Chu Berry, Ben Webster, Don Byas, and Lester himself were gathered to greet Hawk at a Harlem after-hours spot called Puss Johnson's (there were many such music spots; the reputation of Minton's is all out of proportion). The master arrived without horn (but with a striking lady), listened, and refused to be drawn into battle. A few days later he returned with horn and reestablished his sovereignty.

Hawk's victory became official with the release, late in '39, of the biggest record of his career: *Body and Soul.* Consisting of just two choruses—framed by a brief piano introduction and short tenor cadenza—it stands as one of the most perfectly balanced jazz records ever made. After more than three decades, it remains a model of flawlessly constructed and superbly executed jazz improvisation, and is still the test piece for aspiring tenorists.

Although young tenor men in increasing numbers were taken with Lester's cooler sound and unorthodox phrasing, the Hawkins approach remained firmly entrenched (as the newfound popularity of Ben Webster with Duke Ellington and Don Byas with Count Basie proved in the early forties). There also arose a school of tenors equally influenced by both: Illinois Jacquet, Buddy Tate, Gene Ammons, and Dexter Gordon are examples.

Furthermore, that leader of the new style soon to be labeled *bebop,* Charlie Parker, symbolized the possibility of a Hawkins–Young fusion. Though fashionable jazz criticism has emphasized only Young's influence on Parker, there can be no doubt that Hawkins, especially in terms of harmony, approach to ballads, and use of double time, also profoundly touched Bird's conception.

The influence was a two-way street. Hawkins was the first established jazz figure of major stature to not only accept but *embrace* the new music, which he rightly saw as a logical development. Consider this: Hawk was the *only* name leader to hire Thelonious Monk, the strange piano player from Minton's house band, for a downtown gig (on 52nd Street) and to use him on a record date (the earliest music heard on this remarkable collection, and Monk's studio debut). And this: For a February 1944 date with a larger band, Hawkins hired Dizzy Gillespie, Max Roach, Leo Parker, and other young modernists to back him. And this: At the end of '44, Hawk took to California a pioneer bop group that included Howard McGhee and Denzil Best. As early as 1947, Hawk used Miles Davis on a record date; a few years later, he had him in his band. The 1947 date on this album clearly reflects Hawk's commitment to the new sound, and his ability to fit himself into it. (Note also the inclusion of a Monk tune, perfectly interpreted.)

Hawk didn't just adapt to bop; profoundly touched by Parker, he entered a whole new phase of musical development at an age when most players have settled permanently within a given framework.

The new Hawk was most clearly visible in the blues. Prior to the mid-forties, Hawkins rarely played blues, and never with much of what we now call *funk*. But Bird brought a new blue stream into jazz, and Hawk was nourished by it (hear him here on *Sih-sah* and *Juicy Fruit*). And Bird's song in Hawk's ear didn't end with the blues. You can feel it throughout the '57 session, and in the magnificent *Ruby, My Dear* which stems from a Monk–Hawkins reunion album that costarred John Coltrane. (The rest of that date, by the way, can be heard on *Monk/Trane*—Milestone 47011.)

For many years they had affectionately called him "The Old Man." But he still looked, felt, and played young and it was the Old Man's pride that he could keep up. No resting on laurels for him; virtually everything new was a challenge. But for a while, when Lester's way of playing tenor dominated the scene, and bop had little time to look back, Hawkins fell somewhat out of favor. When producer Orrin Keepnews gave him carte blanche to pick his own men for the '57 date reintroduced herewith, the result was the first loose, modern jazz date for Hawk in some time. It compares most interestingly with the session of ten years before, and not only for the work of Hawk himself and repeaters J. J. Johnson and Hank Jones. (It is also interesting that Hawk did not choose a bop rhythm section for himself.)

Throughout the fifties, with Norman Granz's Jazz at the Philharmonic and also on his own, he frequently teamed with old friend Roy Eldridge, ten years younger but a fraternal spirit. From 1957 on, the Metropole in New York's Times Square area became their home base. Most jazz writers (except visitors from Europe) shunned the place, but musicians did drop in to hear Roy and Hawk: among them, Miles Davis, Sonny Rollins, and John Coltrane.

At the soulful establishment across the street, the Copper Rail, the players and their friends congregated to eat and drink. Even when they were three-deep at the bar, you could hear Hawk's laughter, or his voice emphasizing a point, from anywhere in the house. Though he was not a large man, his voice had a presence remarkably similar to his saxophone sound. Hawk was strong in those days. The new tenor voices, significantly that of Sonny Rollins, seemed closer in conception and sound to him than to Lester, and his star was once again in ascendance. He and Roy made periodic tours abroad. Recordings were again fairly frequent. His personal life was happy. His health seemed robust.

"You have to eat when you drink," he used to say, and he was still following his own rule. A girl I knew thought nothing of cooking him eight eggs for breakfast, and he could go to work on a Chinese dinner for two or a double order of spareribs in the wee hours of the morning with the gusto of a hungry lumberjack. In the course of a working day, he'd consume a quantity of scotch even Eddie Condon would have deemed respectable, but he could also leave the booze alone when it got to him. When Lester Young died in 1959, not quite fifty, the Old Man told me how he used to try to make Prez eat when they were traveling together for Jazz at the Philharmonic. "When I got something for myself, I'd get for him, too. But I'd always find most of it left under his bus or plane seat when we got off."

Hawk liked Lester very much, but the only tenor player I ever heard him call "genius" was Chu Berry. Other musicians he bestowed this title on were Louis, Bird, Art Tatum, Dizzy Gillespie, and Monk—the latter a personal favorite.

At home, Hawk rarely listened to jazz. His sizable collection was dominated by complete opera sets (Verdi, Wagner, and Puccini) and also included a lot of Brahms and Debussy. Bach and Beethoven were there as well, and some moderns, but Hawk liked music with a big sound and romantic sweep best of all. With his luxurious hi-fi setup, he could fill his comfortable Central Park West apartment with sound, and the commanding view of the park went well with the music. Sometimes he'd play the piano, which he did surprisingly well—always music of his own.

In the final years, which his friends would rather forget but can't, Tommy Flanagan would sometimes drop by and make Hawk play the piano and try to copy down some of the tunes. Hawk was always a gifted composer—even with Henderson—but never had the patience to write the stuff down. By then, the expensive hi-fi equipment had fallen into disuse, the blinds were often drawn to shut out the view, and the sound most frequently heard was that of the TV—on around the clock to keep the insomniac company. As often as not, there'd be food defrosting in the kitchen—chicken, chops, ribs, or steak, but "By the time it's ready for me to fix," he once told me, "I've lost my appetite from this whiskey." He knew exactly what he was doing to himself, but some demon had hold of him.

It had nothing to do with the socio-psychological clichés of art and race so often applied to "explain" jazz artists, but it did have much to do with the fact that he was living alone now, and that his aloneness was of his own making. His last great love gone because in his jealousy he could not accept that a woman could love a man much older than herself, he now chose to accelerate the aging process he had previously hated and successfully fought off. He let his grizzled beard and hair flow freely, and let his once immaculately fitting suits hang from his shrunken frame.

Only work could shake him out of his depression, but now it seldom came. He'd never been one for managers and agents; if people wanted his services, they could call *him*. But only a few employers—mainly the loyal Norman Granz, sometimes George Wein, a club owner here or there—would still come through. My friends and I got him some gigs. It was a vicious circle: Because he didn't work much, he was rusty when he did play (he had always disdained practicing and lifelong habits don't change), and because he was rusty (and shaky), he wasn't asked back. Even quite near the end, a few nights of work, leading to resumed eating, could straighten him out, and he'd find his form. But there was no steady work to make him stay on course.

Perhaps it would have been too late; he hated doctors and hospitals and refused all suggestions of medical attention. And since his voice, incongruously, remained as strong as ever and his ego just as fierce, it was difficult to counteract him. He welcomed company but never invited anyone. His daughters would come by to visit and straighten up the house when they were in town. Frequent visitors included Monk and the Baroness Nica de Koenigswarter, but the closest people near the end were Barry Harris and drummer Eddie Locke.

Monk was at Hawk's bedside when it had finally become necessary to take him to a hospital. Monk even made the Old Man laugh—but it was for the last time.

Coleman Hawkins was a legend in his own time: revered by younger musicians, who were amazed and delighted at his ability to remain receptive to their discoveries; loved by his contemporaries, who were equally astonished by his capacity for constant self-renewal. He was one of those who wrote the book of jazz.

The art of Coleman Hawkins transcends the boundaries of style and time. Fortunately, it is well documented. The great sound and mind that is one of the landmarks of jazz lives on, as in these grooves, awaiting your command to issue forth once more.

Even among the chosen few of jazz, Coleman Hawkins stands out. Hear him well.

(1973)

IRA GITLER

Ira Gitler has been an unflaggingly entertaining and witty presence on the jazz scene for well over forty years. The house annotator for Prestige in the 1950s, and extremely prolific for other labels as well, **Gitler** has written more liner notes than almost anyone else. He is currently a columnist for **Jazz Times** and the author of **Swing to Bop**, an acclaimed oral history of the beginnings of modern jazz.

Body and Soul

Al Cohn and Zoot Sims
(Muse 5356)

In listening to a test pressing of this album, someone was moved to say, as the twin tenor tendrils of Al Cohn and Zoot Sims intertwined around the melodic trellis of *Emily,* "Now, there's a friendship." She was as right as Leonard Feather back in 1960 when he called them "the Damon and Pythias of the tenors."

Al and Zoot have had a perfect blendship since January 1948, when they first met in a parking lot in Salt Lake City at the time Al joined Woody Herman's Second Herd. The musical-social association that began then grew during their travels with Woody and further solidified in the immediate post-Herman period in New York, when they had the opportunity to play together in various small groups and at many informal sessions.

Off the stand they drank together, played softball together, visited each other's apartments, and generally strengthened the bond between them. In 1957 they finally formalized their musical affinity by forming a working quintet which spotlighted the two tenor saxophones and occasionally featured their assorted other horns. Although for the next two years they recorded and worked within the new format on an intermittent basis, the group really came into its own in 1959, when Sims and Cohn began working regularly at the old Half Note. Between the several engagements each year at the club on Manhattan's Lower West Side, there were visits to the jazz spots of other cities. Al continued to write arrangements for a multitude of aggregations (including the Cohn–Sims quintet) and both men recorded on their own as well as team-style.

1960 marked the last time they recorded in a two-tenor with rhythm format. The inordinate length of time between recordings for the team makes this one's value go beyond its intrinsic musical worth, which is very high, indeed. The fact that Al and Zoot have not worked together as often in the 1970s as they did in the 1960s is yet another reason that this studio gathering had such a special aura.

The lists of Al's and Zoot's friends do not stop at one. The same characteristics of warmth, humor, and just plain old-fashioned humanity that made their own friendship a reality have drawn many admirers into each man's orbit. The atmosphere in the studio on the afternoon this session was taped was one of quietly joyous celebration. The feeling was verbalized in certain ways, but mostly it was unspoken. The good vibes that were ricocheting around the room were as implicit as the good notes they reflected. With former Herman mates like Terry Gibbs and

Lou Levy visiting from the West Coast, and ex-bandmate and colleague Frankie Socolow in attendance, this session had all the positive aspects of an alumni reunion.

Both Zoot and Al can communicate a wide range of emotions through their playing. (Forget about hate.) Each has had his knocks just by virtue of living on this planet for forty-five years, but each has the kind of spirit which is able to deflect the flings and marrows of egregious Gorgons. This optimism in the face of reality comes out in the music and is one of the appealing, attractive, uplifting elements in the righteous rhapsody we call jazz, generally speaking and specifically as it applies to Cohn–Sims. There is nothing so potent in the pro-life arsenal as a sense of humor. Al and Zoot are not wanting in this department.

Cohn, the Brooklyn native transplanted to the Poconos, is renowned as a raconteur of droll and ribald stories. The lost art of telling a joke has not gone astray because of his efforts. And he's not bad with a pun-ishing ad-lib, either. He was an S. J. Perelman head while still in his teens and into the Marx Bros. and W. C. Fields then, too. Al loves to do *The New York Times* crossword puzzle, is an avid fisherman, and sleeps in a Saran Wrap nightshirt on a bed of pine needles.

Native Californian Sims, the Westerner who found happiness in New York, exhibits humor of a drier bent. Once, at a record date when someone swallowed only one half an upper and was about to discard the rest, Zoot admonished: "Think of all the kids in Europe who are sleeping." He's just as likely to spring a singing song title on you, like *Ray Sims with the Moon; Zoot Sims to Me I've Heard That Song Before;* or his ever-popular *Sol Schlinger Awhile.* He enjoys reshaping driftwood into bird and animal forms; makes some mean chili and guacamole; has been known to Ping-Pong it up; and sleeps nude in the top of a double bunk bed without a ladder.

The excellent rhythm section which backs the twin cantors

of caloric clout here is made up of three diverse personalities who blend beautifully, enabling Sims and Cohn to forget about anything but projecting their thoughts and feelings in an inspired manner over a welling billow of harmonic-rhythmic plenitude.

Jaki Byard, the sometimes unpredictably unorthodox and ofttimes brilliantly versatile, historically encyclopedic pianist, worked with Al and Zoot at Lennie's on the Turnpike in Boston, the old Half Note, and is capable of being intelligently avant-garde, seriously raggish, unstridently stridish, or any other way you want to play it. Most of the time he enjoys swinging in any of its many guises, like straight ahead with the saxophone seraphs. Presently, Mr. Byard is a Professor of Music at the New England Conservatory in Boston.

One of the deans of the contrabass in American music is George Duvivier, a veteran of the New York recording, radio, and television studios, where his path has crossed with Zoot and Al on innumerable occasions. For tone, time, propulsion, and all-around musical knowledge and experience, Monsieur Duvivier has few peers. Lately, he has been alternating with one of those peers, Milt Hinton, in the Bobby Rosengarden orchestra on *The Dick Cavett Show*.

Co-leader of the Thad Jones–Mel Lewis big band, drummer Lewis is a subtle accompanist who achieves a driving beat without forging huge metal sculptures in the process. He is able to swing a large organization or a small unit and if you were present for the Gretsch afternoon at Wollman Amphitheater during the 1973 Newport–New York Jazz Festival, you heard him play an unaccompanied drum piece that was as notable for its lack of bombast as for its invention. A "musical" drummer, Mel is, in his own way, carrying on the tradition of the late Tiny Kahn.

The repertory of a working Cohn–Sims group is, of course, well stocked with originals by Al, but it also contains material from other writers from the jazz ranks, like trombonist-arranger

Billy Byers, whose *Doodle Oodle* is based on the changes of *There'll Be Some Changes Made*. When there are some changes to be made, Al and Zoot negotiate them rather adroitly as in this up-tempo, romp-stomp of an opener. Al's keening choruses—with a finishing quote from the old Paramount News theme, *The Eyes and Ears of the World*—precede Byard's, and Zoot's—with overtones of Ben Webster in his throaty sound—follow Jaki. Duvivier does some walking on his own before the tenors, in the same order, engage in a round-robin with Lewis.

Emily, mentioned at the outset, is by the Academy Award-winning Johnny Mandel and was first heard in *The Americanization of Emily*. Mandel, a former trombonist-bass trumpeter-jazz arranger, is an old buddy of Zoot and Al, who have long enjoyed interpreting his music.

The tenors take turns with the lead as they state the melody in lovingly tender terms, Zoot beginning the chorus and Al finishing. Each backs the other with superb empathy before setting out on successive wondrous solo flights in the same order.

Next is the *Samba Medley*. We are long past the fad period of the bossa nova, but the good that it rendered unto American music has survived. Zoot did Djalma Ferreira's *Recado Bossa Nova* in 1962 at the height of the craze. The lilting, minor-key melody lends itself well to the kind of torrid rhythmic impulses that regularly throb through the Sims tenor.

Byard delineates *The Girl from Ipanema* without quite ever revealing her original contours but tells us a lot about the inner woman. Then Cohn expands on *One Note Samba* (like *Girl*, a creation of Antonio Carlos Jobim) in a dissertation demonstrating that whether it is one note or many, it's what you do with them that counts.

Al's *Mama Flosie* is dedicated to his wife, Flo, a fine singer known professionally as Flo Handy. It's a funky holler of a rolling, bluesy forty-bar pattern played in fast waltz time. Cohn and Sims each have two strong solo choruses, gathering mo-

124

mentum as they go. After two insouciantly swinging choruses by Byard, Al and Zoot return to trade thoughts.

Body and Soul is the tenorman's domain. Coleman Hawkins planted the flag there in 1939 and it has been the bearer for this standard ever since. For the neophyte, *B&S* has been both stumbling block and proving ground; for the seasoned pro, a vehicle allowing the deepest kind of soul-plumbing. Al pulls out a plum here, a plum-sized diamond. This is a heavy performance of Johnny Green's masterpiece, adding to its already weighty heritage. If there be such a thing as continued cosmic consciousness, Hawk must be smiling behind this one.

When the Cohn–Sims quintet began, Zoot doubled alto; Al doubled baritone; and on certain numbers both whipped out their clarinets. Eventually, the essence of the group was boiled down to the two tenors. In 1972, however, Zoot again turned to a second horn. This time it is the soprano (he calls it "Sidney" for Bechet) and it has become a love affair, arousing anything but jealousy in his wife, Louise, and culminating in the kind of performance exemplified by Rod McKuen's heart-touching *Jean* from *The Prime of Miss Jean Brodie*. Tune, tone, sound, and substance are wedded in a wistfully affecting way as only Zoot can do it.

Gary McFarland wrote the plaintive *Blue Hodge* for Johnny Hodges, who recorded it in 1961. Zoot steps right out with full-toned ease. After Jaki's solo, it is Al's deep-throated moans which carry forth the blues. Duvivier's nimble fingers pluck the tenors back into the final chorus.

That's the music, an immaculate execution of a body and soul-pleasing array of songs. I use *immaculate* in the sense of a perfection that is achieved as a by-product of professionalism that can be reveled in and marveled at because it never loses anything at those really important levels. Al says it well when he talks about Zoot's current work. "He's playing better than ever," comments Cohn. "He's never lost that spontaneity and he's become more polished. Some players get polished and, with it, more mechanical. Not Zoot. I enjoy his playing more than ever."

Zoot feels that Al is "one of the greatest musicians and men I've ever met. It's always a pleasure to play with him. He's great now, but if he played all the time, concentrated on it, he'd even be more sensational."

Sims was referring to Cohn's busy writing schedule, which takes precedence over his playing hours. Recently, he has arranged part of the score of *Raisin,* the musical version of *Raisin in the Sun.*

The indications are, too, that the team of Sims and Cohn is once again going to be more of a factor on the live jazz scene. The release of this record should further increase the renewed demand for their combined services.

Audiences are apt to react the way Cannonball Adderley did one night at the old Half Note. Since he had just come from his own job, he arrived at closing time in the midst of the last number of the morning. Placing his ample frame in the club's entrance with his back squarely, or roundly, against the door, he cried: "Alvin Gilbert Cohn! John Haley Sims! Don't stop now!!"

(1976)

NAT HENTOFF

Although he writes little about jazz today, **Nat Hentoff** was one of the best and most engaged jazz writers of the 1950s and 1960s. Of all jazz critics, Hentoff seemed to have a large sensitivity and empathy for musicians; he was an intimate of some musicians who couldn't stand any critics at all, most notably Charles Mingus. He has authored and edited many books on jazz, including the seminal oral history **Hear Me Talkin' to Ya**, with Nat Shapiro.

The Clown

Charles Mingus
(Atlantic 1260)

William Butler Yeats' Crazy Jane, who felt beneath the "sanity" of conformity, said once that "Love is all unsatisfied that cannot take the whole body and soul; Take the sour if you take me, I can scoff and lour and scold for an hour."

And in *A Coat*, Yeats added: "There's more enterprise in walking naked."

When you take Mingus as a man and as a man who makes music, it helps to take—or at least try to understand—the whole of him if you want to comprehend fully what he and his music are about.

Mingus tries harder than anyone I know to walk naked. He is unsparing of phoniness and pomposity, and is hardest of all on himself when he feels he has conned himself in any respect.

In his dealings with people, he is unpredictable because people are. If you make any attempt at honest communication with him, Mingus returns the word with love. He is an open human being. If he feels his love has been betrayed or exploited or misunderstood, his initial instinct is to strike from his hurt, sometimes physically, sometimes verbally, very often in his music.

Mingus is one of the very few ingenuous people I have known, and I remain surprised at how he remains ingenuous after all he has experienced and seen in the cities of this country and in the *Tonight at Noon* that is part of the world of jazz. He doesn't give up. He continues to trust; to give; to flagellate himself emotionally to be "better" and more understanding of others; to have the courage and the strength to look for help when he feels he needs it.

Mingus feels the slightest draft, sometimes even when no draft is there. He sometimes reacts to an actual or invisible draft with instantaneous, unreasoning emotional directness. And sometimes, he does all he can to avoid a situation he knows will detonate his hurts and rages (for there is not only much love in him but, as in all of us, much of "the sour" as well). I've seen him leave the room when a drunken Southerner began to make all-too-explicit racial allusions. Mingus didn't want to embarrass his hosts, and he was in the midst of another of his frequent resolutions not to explode, whatever the provocation. The drunk followed him, backed him into a corner, and finally, with a shattering quickness, Mingus knocked him out. He was shiveringly upset, angry at *himself* more than at the man. "I wouldn't have hit him at all," he said, "but I was afraid he was going to hit me."

Once Mingus has reacted with an emotional explosion to hurt or pressure, he's able to profit and grow by what he has learned of himself and of others in the situation. He is honest with himself, so far as any one can be, and so he changes and continues to change; and at each stage of his development, he gives all of himself that he can find. Like all vital jazzmen, his music is his autobiography.

Mingus is verbally articulate as well, and it's illuminating to follow the one immovable, uncompromising line of continuity that connects his development through the years—the line of personal and musical integrity and relentless self-searching. He may have a reputation for being an avant-garde composer, but he knows where he's come from. In 1951, at twenty-nine, he wrote in a letter to Ralph Gleason, printed in *Down Beat:* "There is something to be learned from every score of the great composers, old and modern; each page bears evidence to the musical tightrope walker that he has looked only at his own tiny rope, not realizing that men have not only walked ropes years before him, but tiny threads—perhaps the water. And can we not all learn one more step while restudying what might possibly aid us in walking the earth tomorrow?"

In 1953, he told me in Boston in an interview for *Down Beat:* "We've now fallen into standardization. Great artists like Bird, Prez, Dizzy, Max Roach, Blanton, and Charlie Christian have worked and suffered to develop their own style. Then the copyists come, singing their praises while stealing their phrases. And worse yet, these copyists have more success than the creative artists from whom they have stolen. Personally, to unmask those who copy, I have no other solution than to write and play my own music in accord with the real emotions of the moment when I am writing and playing."

And in 1956, in *An Open Letter to Miles Davis* in *Down Beat,* Mingus wrote: "Just because I'm playing jazz, I don't forget about *me.* I play or write *me,* the way I feel, through jazz, or whatever. Music is, or was, a language of the emotions. If someone has been escaping reality, I don't expect him to dig my music...My music is alive and it's about the living and the dead, about good and evil. It's angry, yet it's real because it *knows* it's angry."

In the summer of 1957, Mingus was one of six composers commissioned to write a jazz work by Brandeis University for a concert to be part of that university's Fourth Festival of the Creative Arts. Another jazzman, pianist Dick Katz, reviewed the concert for *Jazz Today,* and his review of *Revelations,* the Mingus composition, transcends the piece in part and tells quite a lot about Mingus' body of work as well: "It is a powerful piece which began with an almost Wagnerian brooding-like intensity, expressed by way of an insinuating pedal point. It also revealed some beautiful dissonances and ingenious orchestration. I was quite taken by the striking patterns of sound and the way it reached its climax with a kind of centrifugal force. It was a very determined piece of music; and as one of the participating musicians said to me later, 'When it was over, you really *knew* something had happened!' This, I think, is high praise. Mingus is indeed a strong personality and is quite able to express it in his music."

As for his four originals in this album, Mingus begins by pointing out: "I selected these four over two others that were more intricate because some of the guys had been saying that I didn't swing. So I made some that did. This album also has the first blues I've made on record."

"*Haitian Fight Song,* to begin, could just as well be called *Afro-American Fight Song.* It has a folk spirit, the kind of folk music I've always heard, anyway. It has some of the old church feeling, too. I was raised a Methodist but there was a Holiness Church on the corner, and some of the feeling of their music, which was wilder, got into our music. There's a moaning feeling, too, in those church modes. Try a song like Dizzy's *Woodyn You,* for example, and make some changes; fit a church minor mode into the chord structure, and you'll hear what I mean. I'd say this song has a contemporary folk feeling. My solo in it is a deeply concentrated one. I can't play it right unless I'm thinking about prejudice and hate and persecution, and how unfair it is. There's sadness and cries in it, but also determination. And it usually ends with my feeling: 'I told them! I hope somebody heard me.' "

"Blue Cee," Mingus continued, "is a standard blues. It's in two keys—C and B♭—but that's not noticeable and it ends up in C basically. I heard some Basie in it and also some churchlike feeling."

Reincarnation of a Lovebird, Mingus starts to explain by saying: "I wouldn't say I set out to write a piece on Bird. I knew it was a mournful thing when I was writing it. Suddenly, I realized it was Bird. Then, on developing it, we tried to play little things that would bring back that era."

"I like the line a lot," Mingus added. "I think it can be played in different ways. I think it cries. It's mainly about my misunderstanding Bird. I never thought that *he* might not have thought he was as great as everybody said he was."

There had been a desolate, terrifying night at Birdland shortly before Bird died during which the band had included Bird, Bud Powell, and Mingus. At one point in the night, Mingus announced over the microphone that he was disassociating himself from the confusion (and that's a euphemism) on the stand.

"Bird came back later that night," Mingus can't forget, "and kissed me on the cheek. 'I know you love me,' Bird said. And I did. It was Bird who had called me out of the post office in December 1951, when I had almost decided to stay there. And Bird encouraged me about my writing. He never mentioned whether he thought my bass playing was good or bad, but he always thought I was a good writer. In California in the mid-forties, he heard a poem-with-music I'd written, *The Chill of Death.* He heard it in the studio; they never released it. He said that was the sort of thing I should keep on doing, and that I shouldn't be discouraged."

"In one way, this work isn't like him. It's built on long lines and most of his pieces were short lines. But it's my feeling about Bird. I felt like crying when I wrote it. If everybody could play it the way I felt it. The altoist did, finally."

The Clown originated this way: "I felt happy one day. I was playing a little tune on the piano that sounded happy. Then I hit a dissonance that sounded sad, and realized the song had to have two parts. The story, as I told it first to Jean Shepherd, is about a clown, who tried to please people like most jazz musicians do, but whom nobody liked until he was dead. My version of the story ended with his blowing his brains out with the people laughing and finally being pleased because they thought it was part of the act. I liked the way Jean changed the ending; leaves it more up to the listener."

"We rehearsed once at my house, and then did it in the studio. His narration changed every time. He improvised within the story. As for the musicians, Jimmy is the leader in this piece, behind the narration. We play around what he does. When we do the work in a place where we have no narration, Jimmy is the clown."

Jean Shepherd, incidentally, is a New York radio bard whose free-association stands on WOR have enlisted behind him a growing legion of "night people" who profess vehement nonconformism with "day people" but manage to be quite conformist within their rebelliousness. He also writes for *The Village Voice*, and has presided at various New York jazz concerts and Sunday afternoon jam sessions.

Pianist Wade Legge, born in Huntington, West Virginia, and raised in Buffalo, is twenty-three and has worked and recorded with Dizzy Gillespie and a number of New York-based combos. Jimmy Knepper, twenty-nine, was born and brought up in Los Angeles. He's worked for Charlie Barnet, Charlie Spivak, Dorothy Lamour, Stan Kenton, Woody Herman, Vido Musso, Claude Thornhill, Charlie Parker in Philadelphia for several weeks in 1951, and others. During the preparations for the afore-mentioned Brandeis concert, Jimmy cut each part on all the works, some of them unusually exacting, with accuracy, sensitivity, and strength.

Dannie Richmond, twenty-three, was born in New York, raised in Greensboro, North Carolina, returned to study at the Music Center Conservatory in the Bronx, and then went on the road with rhythm and blues units like Paul Williams and the Clovers and Joe Anderson. Until last year, he played tenor exclusively, but when he decided to leave rock 'n' roll, he switched instruments. "I left rock 'n' roll because it was a matter of walking the tables and lying on the floor, and I couldn't do what I wanted to do." Back in Greensboro, he discovered he had a natural ability for keeping time, and became a drummer. Mingus is his first "name" jazz gig.

Curtis Porter, born in Philadelphia, September 21, 1929, grew up in Detroit. His rhythm and blues experience has been extensive, including gigs with Ivory Joe Hunter, Ruth Brown, Paul Williams, and much of the time with the Griffin Brothers. He left the field at the end of 1956, and the Mingus band is the first regular jazz assignment he's had. "I think," says Porter, "that more jazz groups should tell stories like Mingus does instead of just playing notes and techniques."

Another thing Crazy Jane said was that "Fair and foul are near of kin, and fair needs foul." And she also said, "Nothing can be sole or whole that has not been rent."

I have no idea whether Crazy Jane would have dug *The Clown* and these other three, but I expect Mingus might enjoy meeting Crazy Jane, who, of course, is no crazier than were William Blake or Leadbelly or, for that matter, Mingus.

(1957)

133

Milt Jackson
(Atlantic 1269)

Milt Jackson a while back took part in a friend's record date. There were contractual reasons why Milt's name couldn't be used, but the leader quickly solved the problem of what pseudonym to put in the notes by simply calling Milt "Brother Soul."

The question of Bags' "soul" came up again in a conversation with Dizzy Gillespie. "Why, didn't you know?" asked Dizzy. "Milt is Sanctified. That's why he plays so soulful. His whole family is Sanctified."

When a man is Sanctified, that's another way of saying that his early—and in some cases, continuing—religious experience was absorbed in one of the Churches of God in Christ. In these churches, the services are based largely on music, and it is music of a releasing freeness, music in which the congregation collectively and individually gives from within the innermost reservoirs of the spirit and receives in turn the strength of having been opened to the honesty and joy of each other. The most deeply swinging, exultant gospel singing comes from the Churches of God in Christ and from those similarly uninhibited church units that are members of the Holiness Churches.

It is not generally realized that a number of modern jazzmen first felt the passionate possibilities of self-expression in improvised music while still small children at Sanctified churches.

"Soul" is clearly the most essential quality of a jazzman, and

Milt has as much of that open emotional strength as anyone in his jazz generation, and more than most. There are other corollary qualities that are also needed. One is an almost automatic dedication to playing. A jazzman whose desire to play is limited only or mainly by the expectation of a paycheck is apt to be more a craftsman than a creator. The *players* are those who find whatever informal sessions exist wherever they themselves may be, or who, if necessary, create their own sessions.

Bags loves to play. There was an evening at Music Inn at Lenox one summer when several musicians, who hadn't had enough of playing at a concert, headed into a nearby town looking for ad-lib room. They found a place, but as could be expected, there were no vibes. Bags, undaunted, wailed at the piano. "He may not have had a whole lot of technique," reported one of the other musicians later, "but what he played was pure soul and I wouldn't have traded that for any number of runs. That's another thing. Everything he played was right to the point. It was as wholly, unwastefully swinging as anything I've heard."

There is also a certain stick-to-itiveness, as ancient newspapermen used to say, about Bags. Woody Herman recalls a night in Cuba when Bags was in the band. "He was using a set of vibes we'd gotten for nothing, and you might call it a collapsible model. In the middle of his solo on one number, the legs of the set started to spread out in opposite directions. Bags followed that set down, playing all the way. When he finished, he was almost on his hands and knees." The instrument, after all, still was soundable and Bags hadn't finished his solo, so he saw no reason to stop until he had.

Woody, who is far from an impressionable leader, having worked with hundreds of musicians under the most revealing of conditions, still shakes his head about Bags. "He's a fantastic musician. And one of the things about him that impressed me was his great knowledge of tunes. He was and is a young man, but he remembers songs I've long forgotten. He remembers all about a song, the bridge, the right changes. That depth of repertoire is a long-lost quality with most young players, but not with Milt."

Yet another aspect of Bags, and I don't know whether this has ever been printed before, is that he has perfect pitch. "When I first met him," said Dizzy, "he was about the first musician I'd known who had perfect pitch." Perfect pitch alone doesn't make a musician any more than possession of the most demonically complete I.B.M. machine necessarily makes a statistician. But when a jazzman has the other qualities, perfect pitch is a fructifying bonus.

An essay on Bags, the more the subject comes into relief, could continue to an unconscionable length. A few more points, however. Bags is somewhat like Gerry Mulligan or Monk or Coleman Hawkins in that he possesses and can project what might be termed an inherent theatricality. It's not self-conscious posing, but rather an instantly arresting power of personality (and music as expressing that personality) that he projects without thinking about it. André Hodeir, in *Jazz-Hot*, writes that when Milt begins to play, "it's not necessary that an electrician envelop him in a reddish light." There is "the Jackson climate," which is born in himself and is imposed, Hodeir adds, on even the least informed listener. Later in his essay, Hodeir continues his point: "Certain jazzmen, and not the least, succeed in creating a climate in the course of an exposition (of a tune) but if they have to connect an improvised chorus, they're not able to sustain that climate. With Bags, there's nothing to worry about. The Jackson climate once established, the chorus develops as if it were in its natural milieu. Bags impregnates himself with the musical atmosphere that he has brought into being and he draws the substance of that atmosphere for his improvisation." In other words, Bags is that rare artist who is always himself, and whose force of individuality, particularly in a blowing session, can do much to determine the gestalt of the situation.

There's more to be said—Bags' lyricism, his command of the

blues (or is it the other way around?), his rhythmic sensibility—and for a long, detailed analytical survey of Bags, I would strongly recommend the two-part essay, "Bags' Microgroove," by André Hodeir in the March and April, 1956, issues of the French magazine *Jazz-Hot*.

Bags is a shy man, and is not apt to become very communicative verbally until he has known someone for a while. I recall a description by British critic Tony Hall in the *Record Mirror* in the course of a favorable review he was writing of Bags' previous Atlantic LP, *Ballads & Blues* (Atlantic 1242): "When I met Milt in Paris last November, wandering sad-faced around the Club St. Germain-des-Prés, singing obligatos to what the resident group was playing, I asked him how he felt about that particular date. He blinked behind his specs, shrugged and said: 'Man, it's business.' No more, no less."

I'm sure Bags had more to say, good or bad or both, but it takes time for him to decide whether any musical occasion can be at all clarified by verbal discussion. So, since this was a casual meeting and a casual question, he decided with characteristic functional brevity to leave the subject verbally opaque.

In talking about this set, Bags had a good deal more to say. Like his colleagues in the Modern Jazz Quartet, Bags is critical of his work and especially of sessions associated with his name. Yet he feels able to say that he's "very happy about this one. I've been a very firm believer in good support; I chose the men for the date; and I feel it all worked out—the arrangements, the playing, and everything." Quincy Jones was the arranger and wrote *Boogity Boogity* and *Blues at Twilight*. The other originals are by Bags, except for Julian Adderley's thoroughly appropriate *Sermonette*.

The first track, Milt recalls, "was to have a title that would fit the whole idea of the album. What is 'soul' in jazz? It's what comes from within; it's what happens when the inner part of you comes out. It's the part of playing you can't get out of the books and studies. In my case, I believe that what I heard and felt in the music of my church—I went until I was full-grown—was the most powerful influence on my musical career. Everyone wants to know where I got that funky style. Well, it came from church. The music I heard there was open, relaxed, impromptu—soul music."

Heartstrings underlines the soft, flowingly romantic side of Bags' spirit. He is one of the master ballad players in jazz, because it is a form of expression he can identify with. Being a direct spirit, he does not feel it is square or unhip to give way to this kind of lyricism when he feels it. "I also started to write the words to it," he recalls, "but I never finished them out, not yet anyway. It has something to do with 'You're playing around with my heartstrings.'"

The Spirit-Feel was only marked "up-tempo" as a title at the time of the conversation with Milt. I had recently interviewed Mahalia Jackson, and she used a recurring term, *spirit-feel,* that stayed in mind. Milt thought it might fit this track and the overall intention of the album. *Ignunt Oil* is an idiomatic term for whiskey.

A couple of other questions remained. In print and in conversation, Milt has long been referred to familiarly as Bags, but I'd never heard any explanation of how he had acquired the sobriquet. One explanation was that when joined Dizzy's band, the uniform had hung baggily around his spare frame. But Bags' recollection goes back to Detroit after he'd been released from the Army. "I did quite a lot of celebrating with a lot of late hours, and so I had little bags that had gathered under my eyes. The musicians called me 'Bags' and it stuck."

I was also curious as to what disadvantages—as a corollary to all the obvious advantages—there were in having perfect pitch. "It's mostly," Bags answered, "in listening to records. If the turntable is a little too slow and I know how it's supposed to be, it becomes irritating." It's fortunate, turntable whims aside, for many record companies and musicians that Bags isn't a critic.

And the final query was Bags' reaction to occasional comments by jazz musicians and critics that being in the MJQ holds him down. "No, not actually," he answered without hesitation. "It may not sound or look like it when you're listening out front because it's all so well planned, but I still get to play more or less what I want to play. I'm relaxed. I've always been able to adjust myself to a situation. When I first joined the MJQ, there were times when I looked at the planning as a handicap, but now I've come to look on it as an asset. In terms of business, and musically, too. Discipline can be a good thing, and having been under discipline can be a help when you do let loose."

John Lewis adds, "Milt is not only a consistently fine solo improviser, but he is an excellent group player, too. And he keeps on developing. In all areas."

The musicians on the date, it need only be further said, all belong. They're all free, soul brothers.

(1957)

Warne Marsh

Warne Marsh
(Atlantic 1291)

The road to self-discovery, let alone recognition by others, is difficult for any creative artist—in jazz as in classical composition, as in painting, as in politics, etc. Circe is around every corner, and all the mirrors are bewitched. There is no guarantee that the longer and harder the odyssey is, the more fruitful and satisfying will be the ultimate insight. In sad fact, most people never do find themselves and communicate mainly what they hope other people want to hear.

In the case of Warne Marsh, the apprenticeship has been long and often exceedingly bleak, but finally, all the stumbling years are beginning to seem worth the journey to Warne, because he has found who he is in jazz and what he wants to do. This album is one product of this second stage of his career, and his forthcoming association with Lennie Tristano in a group will be another.

Warne was born in Los Angeles, October 26, 1927. His mother, a first-rate violinist, played in one of the string quartets that directors or relatively wealthy actors hired in the days of silent films to provide background music for the acting. Warne's own first instrument was the piano, which he studied from six to ten. In grade school, he picked up the accordion until he got to that size of the species which he could, in fact, no longer pick up. At about twelve, he spent a short time with the alto, but took the advice of his junior high school teacher (who also taught him privately) and switched to tenor. During high school, Warne studied tenor for a year and a half with studio musician Mickey Gillette and had half a dozen "jazz" lessons with Corky Corcoran. "The only thing I remember is that he ridiculed Lester Young because of what he regarded as Lester's small sound and the way he held his horn."

The tenor who most impressed Warne then was Tex Beneke, since most of the kid bands of that time were playing Glenn Miller arrangements and listening to the original. But Coleman Hawkins and Ben Webster soon moved into Warne's hagiology; and while in the service, he became opened to Charlie Parker around 1947. When he came to New York and started studying with Tristano, he also began to really hear Lester Young.

Before the Army, Warne worked in a band that played at the Hollywood Canteen and also worked Ken Murray's Blackouts for

140

some six months. The Teenagers, largely an outgrowth of that band, went on to do Hoagy Carmichael's NBC show for some six months with Warne still included. He was about halfway through his second term at the University of Southern California as a music major when he was drafted. For nine months, he played in a special service band at Camp Lee, Virginia, and for the final nine months was part of the A.G.F. band at Fort Monmouth, which situation allowed him to come to New York often.

Warne had met trumpeter Don Ferrara at Camp Lee; Don was corresponding with Lennie Tristano; and Warne was impressed at what he learned of Lennie. For four months, while still in the service, Warne studied with Lennie. "That changed the direction of everything," he recalls. "Until then I'd figured on getting to know three or four instruments well, sitting back in L.A., and doing studio work. But then I was discharged and did go back to L.A., and nothing seemed to be happening. Hal McKusick got me on Buddy Rich's band the following summer of 1949 and I stayed with it long enough to get to New York. I went back to Lennie, studied four complete years with him, and intermittently for the three years after that.

"What did I learn from Lennie?" Warne continues. "Integrity. There's no bull with him as to what the music is *supposed* to be. You simply study what is recognized as having been great so far in jazz. A student who has any listening experience first gets an education in Louis, Prez, and Bird—before any theory. From there, Lennie applies the basic ingredients—harmony, ear training, rhythm, the understanding of what goes into improvising without actually telling the student what to play. Lennie did make that mistake in the early years, but now he leaves the conception itself to the individual player. In short, he teaches the essentials. As for exercises, for example, he used to make them up directly from the jazz material; now he has the students make up their own exercises under his supervision so that they learn to cover the whole horn.

"As I said, the big thing I got from Lennie was the feeling that if music was worth that much to him, it could mean that much to me to play only what I wanted to play."

After using up the 52–20 checks from the government, Warne worked for a time with the sextet Lennie had with Lee Konitz and Billy Bauer. It was that year, 1949, in which the sextet made the Capitol sides (*Marionette, Sax of a Kind, Wow, Crosscurrent, Intuition,* among them) that were to influence many musicians here and abroad and that first made Warne Marsh's name at all known in the field.

The sextet played several of the jazz clubs, but in time the group dissolved, with Konitz going to Kenton, Bauer and Arnold Fishkind into studio work, and Tristano devoting his full time to teaching. In retrospect, Warne feels, as do many observers, that the 1949 Tristano records were important in helping to presage the renaissance imminent in jazz of multilinear improvisation and were also influential in terms of the long lines of the soloists and the light, cool tonality of Konitz and Marsh.

Warne feels that although Tristano knew then the significance and potential of what the sextet was trying to do, the other members had to grow as individuals, had to absorb what they had learned, and had to leave the group and develop on their own to accomplish both ends. "I, for example," he notes, "had put so much emphasis on learning and developing new ideas, but hadn't given myself a chance to absorb them, and the only way to do that is just getting out and playing."

For the next few years, Warne worked days half the time, mostly in various forms of clerical work. He'd leave a job when Lennie had the urge to return to the road for a couple of weeks, and then had to come back to find another. He was also teaching at the school as one of Tristano's assistants, but was not jamming as yet. "I still hadn't recognized the importance of it; I still had the idea that study would produce everything and that I didn't need experience."

In August 1955, Lee Konitz and Marsh worked at Jazz City in Los Angeles for a couple of weeks, and Lee also got Marsh on the Hollywood Bowl jazz concert that year. When Konitz returned east, Marsh stayed in L.A., mostly taking it easy for several months and thinking about where he might be going in music. In July 1956, a group was formed with drummer Jeff Morton, pianist Ronnie Ball (another Tristano alumnus, as was Morton), bassist Ben Tucker, tenor Ted Brown (also a Tristano student), and Warne. The group stayed together until February 1957, making a couple of albums during that period. Warne gigged around the coast, and especially remembers a couple of stimulating weeks at the Blackhawk with Art Pepper. One night he received a call from a girl he knew in New York. She was in a nightclub where Horace Silver's quintet was playing, had him listen to the music, and he was on his way back. "Things were just dull out there. And it was when I got back this time that things really began happening for me. I began to understand myself, what I was doing and why."

Since returning, Marsh has been back in association with Tristano, who set up this record date; and he has worked with Lee Konitz (at the Cork 'n' Bib, several Mondays at Birdland, and several weeks at the Half Note). Warne and Tristano are currently planning a quartet to which Marsh looks forward "with real anticipation. Things are just beginning to break finally."

After all the years of looking and learning, Marsh has come to a number of conclusions. "Seven or eight years ago, we were determined to be original to the point of not allowing any influences in our work, not even the good ones. Now a man like Bird is coming to mean a lot more to me as an influence. For example, the crucial matter of actually improvising with a group. There are standards that cannot be bypassed or overlooked, and so far as I'm concerned, Bird set those standards. Bird, especially during his 1945–50 period, was able to improvise a good deal of the time, and that's not happening today. The emphasis on improvising is dissolving. While the groups as a whole are absorbing the ideas and the level of playing Bird has established, while they're improving *collectively,* very few people are continuing to grow as improvisers.

"There are players today," Marsh went on, "that I respect more for their musical ability than for what they do with it. Several have been very stimulating to me. But they don't do as much as they're capable of. Despite the distortions and distractions of playing in nightclubs, Bird was able to get to the point where he played all music. I mean, he got outside of himself by going through himself and eliminating everything in his personal character that might tend to distort his music. It became purely musical expression.

"He didn't expand what he started with but he showed the goal—not to have the music distorted by any elements of your personality that might tend to take away from it as music. That's the difference between an artistic approach and the approach of a personality. The artistic approach doesn't mean you yield self-expression, but it does mean that emphasis is placed on talent rather than personality. Certainly, emotion or feeling is still at the base of the playing. Putting it another way, it's a matter of how one's ability, one's talent, is used—either with complete integrity and artistically or primarily as a means of maintaining a 'personality,' by which music is used to express personality rather than as an expression in itself. By doing it artistically, however, it's the essence of your personality that is transmuted into music; the 'I' is no longer italicized."

On three of the five numbers, there is no piano. "The reason was the freedom the absence of a piano allows harmonically, with regard to improvising a chord structure as well as a melodic line. A lot of piano players will use the same positions of a chord over and over. Without them, you can voice a chord your own way. And, there's also rhythmic freedom."

As for Marsh's colleagues, Ronnie Ball, English born, has

been in America since 1952, and has worked with, among others, Lee Konitz, Chuck Wayne, and J. J. Johnson and Kai Winding. Paul Motian, born in Philadelphia, March 25, 1931, didn't become a professional until after leaving the Navy in 1954. He has worked with Oscar Pettiford, Tony Scott, Don Elliott, and Zoot Sims, among others. His major influence is Kenny Clarke, and he also admires Max Roach, Philly Joe Jones, Art Blakey, and scores more.

Paul Chambers and Philly Joe Jones of the Miles Davis band are familiar to even peripheral jazz partisans. "Philly Joe was very stimulating," says Warne, "particularly after the drummers on the West Coast. They keep time well and they're good musicians, but the spirit is different." As for Paul: "I can't say enough about his playing. I'd like this album to be considered both of ours. He has that essential element; his music is just music. There's no horseplay in it. It's all music."

(1957)

DAVID HIMMELSTEIN

One of the most imaginative and talented *writers* to deal with jazz during the 1960s, **Himmelstein** has written very little about jazz lately. His notes for Prestige are classics of the genre.

Out Front

Jaki Byard
(Prestige 7397)

Adozen or so years ago, John A. (Jaki) Byard was a local Boston legend. Born in Worchester, Massachusetts, in 1922, Jaki, whose mother played piano and his father (a candy maker) played baritone horn in the local marching band, began taking piano lessons from Miss Grace Johnson Brown when he was eight years old. All he remembers learning in those tyro days are the C scale and numbers like *Humoresque, The Scarf Dance,* and *Waltz in C♯ Minor.* Tiring quickly of salon music, Jaki was fairly relieved when, two years later, the Depression relieved him of this burden when, as he puts it, "My father wound up as a janitor. The Machine Age came in jumpin' and aced him out of his thing. There were no more candy makers. It aced me out of my piano lessons, too."

Between the ages of ten and sixteen, Jaki's talents

developed, so to speak, naturally. Without the benefit of formal training, he was left to pick out tunes on the home piano and sounding on his mother (unsuccessfully) for a saxophone, the instrument which really inspired him. (This childhood ambition was not to be realized for some twenty years.) In the evenings, he went to the local dances, especially the ones at Dan Dundee's Deck (admission: four bits), where the great bands of the thirties played one-nighters.

"I saw Fats Waller there. All the bands—Basie; Fletcher Henderson with Hawk; Isham Jones; Joe Venuti; Lunceford, who had hit with his little thing and it was romping; Chick Webb with Ella. I used to sit right down in front of the stage, diggin' the cats half-asleep. Diggin' them in their youth, in their prime." It was, of course, a better instruction than any academy could offer, and youthful enthusiasms leave an indelible impression. "Out of all the bands, the only one I used to dig was Fatha's band. Fatha Hines. That was the only band that intrigued me."

During this eventful period, Jaki played his first gig when he volunteered to play piano with a local white band led by Doc Kentross. "The first night I fell down and cut my hand. I played the gig with six stitches and as the evening went on my hand blew up like a football." But I kept saying 'You gotta make the gig, you gotta make the gig.'" His interest in composition stems from this period also since, in order to make the band, he had to take the music to Waller's *I'm Gonna Sit Right Down and Write Myself a Letter* home and learn it on piano.

Jaki's father, always a help musically, gave him pointers, both practical and general. "My old man hipped me to Teddy Wilson. He used to drag me into the house to listen to those Goodman things and he said that that style was going to be a big thing. He also forecasted that tubas would come back into the bands and they did. He had a trumpet and I started playing it. He showed me a few things. The man then was Eldridge, and Walter Fuller who was with Hines. Those were the licks we played."

Jaki joined his second local band (colored this time) called Freddy Bates and His Nighthawks, holding down the second trumpet chair. It was a band with four horns and he stayed about a year. Lenny Waterman, a guitarist, gave him some good advice and hipped him to Bix (who had recently died) and Django Reinhardt. It was with this band that Jaki did his first arrangement: a scoring of Hawk's famous *Body and Soul* solo for the four horns. "I wrote it in quarter notes—everybody knew how it went anyway." The drummer in the Bates band left to form his own group and asked Jaki to join—on piano. "He (the drummer) asked me to play piano for him because he didn't dig this other kid that was playing like Fats Waller. He dug me because I used to play like Fats, but I was digging Hines and Cole."

Ready to start a serious career in music, Jaki, by 1941, had saved enough to begin taking piano instruction in Boston when Uncle Sam sent his GREETINGS. The next five years were spent in khaki, but they were not unmusical. After a halfhearted attempt to join the band at Camp Devon as a trumpeter ("They had too many trumpet players. But that's where I first heard about Dizzy Gillespie—he was playing like Eldridge then, but he was beginning to get his own thing..."), he was shipped down South.

Forsaking music, he threw himself into a life of hedonism ("I became a hustler"), but fortunately he was barracked with Kenny Clarke and pianist Ernie Washington. "I had given up the piano, so I learned the trombone—to stay out of the field... Ernie Washington was one of my influences, you know. Between the two of us—he was playing glockenspiel and I was playing trombone—we had a time. We got together on piano and had sessions and had a ball together." (The trombone came in handy, as did the bass, violin, guitar, and all the saxophones, which Jaki later learned before he went into composition seriously, but we're getting ahead of ourselves.)

Jaki headed for Boston after the duration; with the war over, there was a small entertainment boom. He played around Boston with Danny Porter and with the bands of Dean Earle and Hillary Rose, the Boston pianists to whom Jaki had listened at the dances back in Worchester. He then spent two years as a member of the Ray Perry trio, and it was that jazz great who encouraged him to take up the saxophone (Perry, who was noted as a jazz violinist, was a formidable alto player as well), pointing to Ray Nance, Sonny Dunham, and Benny Carter as examples of musicians successful at "doubling."

Gigging around locally, Jaki played with everyone; during a period with the Sal-Sala group—a white rehearsal band—he organized the Saxtrum Club (a portmanteau name from the words *saxophone* and *trumpet*) at whose headquarters the members of bands playing shows in town could go after hours to jam.

In 1947 Jaki went on the road with Earl Bostic and, being one of the first "modernists" to be hired into that organization, he collected his share of woes. "We never did get along ... He didn't exactly dig my influence. I was always talking about Bird ... and Bird didn't have any tone for him. My man was Bud Powell ... and Erroll Garner ... and them cats played behind the beat ... And he liked to go forward. That's when I learned about going back and going forward ..."

From Bostic, Jaki went to Canada, losing his small savings on a band that folded and becoming a member, for a while, of the Islamic faith, an experience which deepened his attitude toward study ("I had a beard then, too"). Hearing Oscar Peterson and Art Tatum around this time caused him so much frustration that he abandoned the piano and turned to his first love, the saxophone. ("I bought a tenor for a hot forty bucks ... My stick used to be Ben and Hawk ... Ben, mostly. That was my stick on ballads ... that beautiful sound ... One of my favorite sax players was Chu Berry. I often wonder what would be the condition of jazz if cats like Chu, Herschel Evans, Fats, Bix were living today. I used to adore Willie Smith. With Lunceford he played some fantastic things. Now I'm saying that in the same breath as Eric Dolphy. One of his main influences was Willie Smith..."")

Back in Boston, Jaki organized his own rehearsal band, attempting to build "the hippest bebop band around." Inspired by Boyd Raeburn and Eddie Sauter, with personnel that included Joe Gordon, Sam Rivers, and Lenny Johnson, it went down the drain, and Jaki went on the road with a Negro review—Larry Steele's *Smart Set*, for which he wrote some of the music ("That was a sad thing") and worked in the band, along with Thad Jones, Gigi Gryce, and Jimmy Crawford.

Returning to Boston, Jaki began what he ironically describes as "the Nat Pierce era" and he found a berth at the Melody Lounge in Lynn, Massachusetts. His group included saxophonist Charlie Mariano, with whom he formed an abiding relationship, and cornetist-violinist Dick Wetmore ("Fabulous. He was influenced by Bix, but he loved everybody...and heard everybody."). The pressures of the business increased and Jaki gigged around as the Byard legend began to take root. Working at the Stables and the Jazz Workshop in Boston, he became the center of the flurry of activity that erupted with the emergence of the Herb Pomeroy band. Organized as a Tuesday–Thursday group at the Workshop, Jaki joined the band on tenor. "That's when I got my saxophone thing really going further...playing in the sax section. Serge Chaloff was part of it. Bad, man! That band was the most fiery one of all. Now, that's when they should have recorded it. Later, the spirit went out of it because it began to get too academically involved."

Breaking away from Pomeroy, he began "to form my own dynasty." A group of young musicians fell under the Byard sway, including Don Ellis and Al Francis and, especially, the late Dick Twardzik. For several years he led his own trio at Wally's and Savoy-on-the-Hill also in Boston, breaking ground for his present work.

Jaki started coming to New York for the Monday night sessions at Birdland in 1958. That summer he spent at the Cape, playing the compositions of Rube Bloom a half hour a week for forty dollars, and then Maynard Ferguson called him. He stayed with that band awhile, disgruntled that his talents as a composer-arranger were being ignored. He frequently visited the Showplace in Greenwich Village and heard Mingus and Eric Dolphy. ("Eric was one of my favorite musicians. If you hear some of the last things he recorded, in Europe, on alto, you will hear the direction the alto is going in reality . . ."). Quitting the Ferguson band, he joined Mingus.

"Mingus had to get a piano player that could play 'old-fashioned' for his Town Hall concert. There ain't too many cats that can go that way, play stride . . . I used to dig rent parties. There was a cat named Walter Henderson who used to play at rent parties around Hartford, Connecticut, and I used to go down there to visit my grandmother who lived there. I'd go all around to these parties with my parents. I used to sit right by the piano . . . this Henderson would get that thing going in F♯, it was a lot of fun." Notably, although his work with the volcanic bassist was seldom heralded, the great success of the 1964 Monterey Festival was in large measure personal, since Jaki had arranged the raved-about music.

Now, after his tenure with Mingus and a few dramatic record dates in a rhythm section with Alan Dawson behind tenorist Booker Ervin, *The Freedom Book* (Prestige 7295) and *The Space Book* (Prestige 7386), he has formed his own group (including drummer Dawson), which should serve to bring him into the vanguard of both public and musical attention. Jaki, of course, goes his own way with his own views on the matters, both musical and extramusical, at hand!

"I attribute some of my piano thing from listening to Garner, what I get from his impressionistic approach. Of course, first of all, Hines. Then Powell, Haig, and Tristano—who I think is one of the most underrated cats. Some of the things he used to do—he was there!

"One thing that bores me on piano is hearing the same thing over and over again. So I try to build myself as a *piano stylist,* but I don't want that to become like a gimmick thing . . . I don't want to say, like, 'This is an imitation of Art Tatum,' which it isn't because no one can do it and even if they can hooray for them . . . I don't think this gives you a badge. But if you can relate to an audience, you can try to get the *feeling* of those people you dig. This is the only way I can get myself across because I can't get up there and play single lines all night. If I do, I can't go away feeling satisfied . . . I can't play one way all night and I wouldn't want to. If you stay in one groove, you can't reach the people . . . And hardly any of us can be ourselves pianistically; not with the people who've been before us, you understand what I mean? I try and go into each phase of the piano with respect and, this is something I don't like to hear, I don't play 'tongue-in-cheek.' People say this about me and it's not true. Someone might ask me to play a certain way and I play it. I don't like the blasphemy thing that some cats put on. They play a certain thing and then—'Hey-heh-heh'—they laugh, you know. I think that's wrong. If they're going to do it, they should do it all the way . . ."

A Note on the Music

Out Front is dedicated to the late Herbie Nichols, an extraordinary jazz pianist and composer whose work remains sadly unappreciated.

Two Different Worlds is the title number from a nonmusical film.

Searchlight is the blues. "Can you picture the searchlights sweeping low and slowly across the water? They never do hit the object." (Laugh.) "The mood is slow. Peaceful and a little happy. Yeah, happy." Booker Ervin—"The surprise element. I don't think the people here are ready for him, actually. He doesn't sound like he's practicing, does he?" Richard Williams—"Would you call that 'traditional'? This sort of gives him a different sound, a different feeling, instead of all those notes. Meaningless. He has a tendency to play a lot of notes, but this is beautiful. Beautiful."

European Episode is a dance suite in six parts which Jaki (himself a dancer) hopes to choreograph and present in concert with twelve dancers and a seventeen-piece orchestra. The rapid opening section is subtitled *Journey to Brussels,* and celebrates his arrival in the Lowlands. The second has a ragtime feeling and is called *One-Step,* the name of an early popular dance ("Like, 1921 style"). Part three is called *Gallery* and relates an experience Jaki had in a small European art gallery that had a beautiful piano in one room. The different chords describe different paintings. Part three merges into the fourth, an excursion in modality, named *Gerald* after Jaki's extraordinary young son. Musically, Jaki dedicates it to "the lovers of the Miles Davis Quintet." *Express* is an airplane trip ("...sit back, *javarooooom,* one stop and you're there!") and the final section, *To Milan—Lions,* etc., is the enigmatic conclusion whose title summons up all kinds of Italian fantasies. ("By the way, all the passages of 'stride' playing here are dedicated to you-know-who.")

Lush Life is Billy Strayhorn's boyhood ballad. (It was penned in 1938.) ("We should call this track a demo. Straight ahead. But that's where I think a ballad should be—easy, pianistic, and beautiful. Billy Strayhorn's sure a beautiful cat, isn't he?")

When Sunny Gets Blue was recorded some six years ago and is a good example of the Byard approach to the alto. ("I started really playing alto at Wally's with the trio. I had a tenor, but I had an urge to play alto. Hear that part? Bird played that cliché on *Billie's Bounce.* This is dedicated to all the Bird lovers.")

A Final Word from Jaki

"I'm against all those that talk hate. I don't hate them, I pity them. I pity their poor souls. I'm against what they're talking about. If

153

they spent more time trying to spread more happiness, express good music, good thoughts, and clean language, they would accomplish more as a family, as Americans. They have too much to say and are saying nothing. Many of them are failures, musically and as people... Don't try to mess with my music, just leave me alone... Don't try to tell me I should play avant-garde all night. They come up to me and say 'blackie' this and 'whitey' that. I don't want to hear that, either. That has nothing to do with true music and true living. That's corner talk, poolroom talk... They are rejected knights in nightclubs..."

(1965)

Lucky Strikes

Lucky Thompson
(Prestige 7365)

Most musicians would make lousy critics. Not that they have bad taste necessarily, but their particular stylistic proclivities often stand in the way of their critical judgment. There are immortal jazzmen who watch *The Lawrence Welk Show* each week because they like the band, and the classic case is Louis Armstrong, who favors Guy Lombardo and Teresa Brewer. An exception to this rule (and a couple of others) is Eli (Lucky) Thompson, whose taste and judgment are as impeccable as his musicianship.

"Music," he said recently, listening to records in my living room, "is the most interesting thing in the world." Sonny Rollins made him smile at first, then laugh out loud. "There's such great humor in the man's playing. I love to listen." On Chu Berry: "What a player! He's the only one who could play four bars alone and be swinging that hard by the time the rest of the band came in." On Coleman Hawkins: "Yeah, yeah. The master." Lester Young: "What a sound. Listen. Play that again [*Clap Hands, Here Comes Charlie* with Basie]. What a sound! There's a whole world in that solo. Would you please play that again?"

Lucky Thompson, one of the great tenor saxophonists of his generation—this *obiter dictum,* by the way, is not original; it comes from both the dean of conservative jazz opinion, as well as from a pioneer modernist critic—is a curiosity even in the curious environs of what is arbitrarily called the jazz world. His career, his life, and his music are a unique footnote to undercurrent themes in the American Drama. A jazz novelist would have a field day; and Lucky (is that really a misnomer?), says simply, "Music is my only vice." He is not a man much given to hyperbole.

The Career

A number of qualities emerge from the star-crossed journey of this superb saxophonist. Despair, loneliness, and frustration have dogged many jazzmen (indeed, the same might be said of any sensitive person in our society), but few have reacted with the resilience, inner strength, and determination that have marked the Thompson career since he left Detroit, twenty years ago, as a fledgling musician.

His peregrinations, admirably outlined in Dan Morgenstern's notes to Lucky's first Prestige album, *Lucky Thompson Plays Jerome Kern and No More* (Prestige/Moodsville 39), have brought him into conflict with people he calls "the vultures"—a breed of human offal that preys on a musician's weaknesses and insecurities, draining him of his resources and constantly offering corruption as an attractive method of "reaching the top"; happy only when the artist wears their heavy chains, does their bidding, eats their craw. Lucky, somehow always in an uphill battle either to keep a big band together or to prop up faltering compatriots or simply to play his music, has earned a reputation for telling "the vultures" what they can do with their "ideas." And in such certain terms that they have tried to drive him out of the business. When pressures became too great, he went into retreat—a sojourn on a farm in the country, where he built his own furniture and learned he could survive on his inner life and the mere necessities without missing the glitter or the glamour—and to Europe, where, even during thin times, he was accorded a measure of genuine respect on a large scale that is seldom found on this side of the Atlantic. God bless the child that's got his own.

The Man

Lucky Thompson has never given up the struggle. Optimistic in the wake of private disasters, he is a man with one face, a set of values, and two extraordinary sons: Bo-Bi, eight, and Kimmie, four. Bo-Bi is an astute judge of people (especially his father) and Kimmie a tiny tornado. Little boys are by nature exasperating, and the Thompson boys are no exceptions. What is exceptional is their understanding of the demands on their father, their patience and indulgence. It is difficult enough for one to become a "good father" on a part-time basis, but Lucky is at it, time and a half. Perhaps it is because they are so "much in the son" that the boys have already developed strength beyond their years. For, as the city of Florence is a museum without walls, so their life is a classroom without desks; they learn constantly—morally, philosophically, and practically—from an excellent teacher. They are already young men of character and Henry James could ask no more.

At a record date, like the one that produced this album, Lucky's fanatic devotion to music becomes immediately apparent. No sooner is one take finished, when Lucky is hauling out music for the next, running it down, checking the other parts. "Yeah, yeah," he says, nodding in approval while listening to a playback, looking like both the matador and the bull. "Music is the master. If you don't give it everything, it will whip you." His technical facility, perhaps the most accomplished of his generation, is constantly searching for challenges, constantly trying to fulfill itself. This, in turn, makes powerful and unusual demands on his sidemen. And, consequently, the musicians with whom he surrounds himself, like those assembled for this session, must have at their command an awesome amount of ability.

The Music

There is the history of the saxophone in Lucky Thompson's music. But for that very reason, do not expect the past here. Great as his playing has been—in 1947 on *Just One More Chance* (a jazz masterpiece), with his own groups in the late forties, with Stan Kenton, with Oscar Pettiford on the famous trio sessions, with the Dave Pochonet Quartet in Paris, or with Miles and J.J. on *Walkin'*—this is a different Lucky Thompson. The elements of his style—out of Hawkins through Byas and Webster—are still there, but now one hears more Prez and more Bird. Can a man remind of so much and still be authentically himself? The answer is yes, and one has only to play a few bars to rest assured that the sum is distinct from its parts.

The sound is new—leaner yet still soulful and sensuous on tenor—for this promises to be the beginning of a "new" era in the Thompson saga. As the fifties saw a rediscovery of the still-fresh giants of swing, perhaps the sixties will bring the prime movers of the revolution once known as bebop, but now fully absorbed in the jazz mainstream, back into the forefront. Surely, this is one of the ends toward which Don Schlitten, who produced this excellent date, works. Lucky Thompson may well be one of the first to reemerge and an important part of the "new" Lucky is the soprano saxophone. The soprano is an instrument that lay dormant in jazz for a lot of years, the exclusive property of the inimitable Sidney Bechet, until Steve Lacy found a modern dress for it and Coltrane popularized it as an avant-garde property. Lucky, needless to say, plays it like no one else—in fact, the four soprano tracks on this album are, to me, the high points of the record.

Once, rehearsing for a nightclub engagement, Lucky played the introduction to *Yesterdays* as a duet with bassist Richard Davis. Davis, who Lucky alternately calls "The Tank" and "The Monster" because of his tremendous drive and finger-busting technique, played his part with a bow, making celloish figures. Both improvised freely, out of tempo, one bowing, the other blowing soprano. They came together finally, miraculously finding the same, thrilling note. After a moment, Lucky turned away and looked down at his straight horn. "Yeah, yeah," he said, looking up suddenly. "That's what this thing is all about"—pointing to the soprano—"you know? Yes, really, the cello is the sound that I hear when I play this. This fellow here"—pointing at Richard—". . . well, what can you say?"

Hank Jones has been a friend of Lucky's since boyhood. "Brother Jones," says the leader, "is a terrible man. You can't fool him and if you make a mistake, he's right there to make it sound like you meant it." Jones, the possessor of the most beautiful "touch" extant, adds his unique sense of "rightness" to the proceedings, comping and soloing on a formidable level. Connie Kay, the resident drummer in the Modern Jazz Quartet, rounds out the all-star rhythm team.

The music, all written and arranged by Lucky (except Ellington's *In a Sentimental Mood* and the lovely Bronislaw Kaper motion picture theme *Invitation*), is melodic and intimately personal. Although there are a variety of tempos, there is no screaming, and an avoidance of cliché, gimmickry, and pretention. Lucky is a melodic improvisor; and jazz is rooted in song: its *vox humana* aspect, often overlooked and today oversimplified, is the magical ability of an instrumentalist to bend his horn to shape the artist's needs, to make it an extension of his own, personal voice. It is a magic at which Lucky is a Merlin. In listening to this record, all you need to think about are the names of the tunes. Each has a particular message. All you need to hear is track number one: Duke's *In a Sentimental Mood.* If you're not a Lucky Thompson fan after that, I pity you. It's just a man and a good melody. But a *jazzman,* a great one. *Lucky Strikes.* And he's wicked, man. Yeah, yeah.

(1964)

MARTIN WILLIAMS

Considered for years to be the dean of American jazz critics, **Williams** brought a seriousness, intellectual sophistication, and broad cultural context to his jazz writing that few others could equal. His book **The Jazz Tradition** is one of the landmark works on the music. For years the director of the Smithsonian Institution's jazz program, **Williams** died in 1991.

Count Basie in Kansas City

Count Basie
(RCA Victor LPV-514)

In mid-December of 1932, in the depths of the Depression, a group of musicians entered the RCA Victor recording studios in Camden, New Jersey, for a marathon recording session. They were the members of the Bennie Moten orchestra, one of the leading bands of the Midwest—of the country, for that matter—an organization which had been recording for Victor since 1926 and for another company three years before that. The men were demoralized, literally hungry, and the long session was almost the last act of this particular manifestation of the Moten band. As clarinet and alto soloist Eddie Barefield has put it, "We didn't have any money

... we had to get to Camden to record, and along comes this little guy Archie with a raggedy old bus, and he took us there. He got us a rabbit and four loaves of bread, and we cooked rabbit stew right on a pool table. That kept us from starving, and then we went on to make the records. Eddie Durham was doing most of Bennie's writing then; I made *Toby* that time. We just turned around and made it back to Kansas City. We hung around there for a while, not doing much of anything..."

Certainly, there is nothing either in the music or in the frequently joyous way it's played on this LP to indicate that the band was in such straits at the time. Or glance at the soon-to-be-illustrious personnel. There is "Hot Lips" Page as the group's trumpet soloist; there are Dan Minor and Eddie Durham as trombone soloists, with Durham also contributing guitar solos and arrangements; there is Barefield; there is Ben Webster on tenor saxophone; there is William, later "Count," Basie on piano; and there is Walter Page, whose firm, steady, but exhilarating four-beats on bass had as much to do with the character of this music, probably, as anything else. And there is a style of music which is fresh and rather unlike Moten's previous music and which, in just a few years, would dominate big band jazz.

But in late 1932, apparently few people wanted to hear it. They wanted to hear earlier Moten instrumentals like *Moten Stomp* (which sounds quite dated now), and they wanted to hear *South* (which Moten had first recorded in 1924, and which in its 1928 version could be heard in urban jukeboxes well into the early forties). But they didn't want to hear this music which sounds so frequently vital and undated, even now in the mid-sixties.

We have kept that 1932 session intact and in the order of the original recording, omitting only two selections outright—one almost entirely taken over by the Sterling Russell vocal trio, the other to a vocal by Josephine Garrison. The first piece, Barefield's *Toby*, introduces the major soloists, Durham, Page, Webster (notice how the riff that accompanies him becomes the next chorus, transferred to a brass lead), Basie, Barefield, and (in my opinion) Minor on the brief open trombone solo and Durham on the plunger solo. These surging, inventive, shouting brass and reed figures here may remind one more of the later Lunceford style than the later Basie style. The performance probably holds a special meaning for those who were lucky enough to hear the band when, as Barefield puts it, "Lips Page would play maybe fifty choruses and we would make up a different riff behind each chorus."

Moten's Swing succinctly reveals what this band achieved. Here, by late 1932, was a large jazz orchestra which could *swing* cleanly and precisely according to the manner of Louis Armstrong—a group which had grasped his innovative ideas of jazz rhythm and had realized and developed them in an ensemble style. Further, the piece features original melodies on a rather sophisticated chord structure borrowed from a standard popular song. Notice also how much Fats Waller there is in Basie's solo— the stride masters James P. Johnson and Luckey Roberts were Basie influences in his early days, and Waller gave Basie instruction. Notice also how personally melodious Lips Page is. And notice that the figures usually played today as *Moten's Swing* are only the final riffs in this performance.

Blue Room opens in a somewhat older style, but there are the chimes Basie provides behind Lips. Then, hear the way the spurting riff figures begin to appear under Barefield's wry solo. Finally comes the thrilling brass and reed riffing, which not only takes us into the later world of Count Basie, but which in itself is one of the most beautifully played passages in all recorded jazz.

New Orleans was Jimmy Rushing's vocal for this session, but it also has a wonderful, eruptive moment on the verse of the piece by Ben Webster, who sounds a lot less like Coleman Hawkins here than he is supposed to have sounded at this early point in his career.

162

The Only Girl I Ever Loved contains a rather square style vocal by the Sterling Russell Trio, but the side is notable as a sample of the group performing at slower tempo. There are also brief, effective flashes of Durham's guitar; there is Ben Webster; and there is an ending which, in effect, reinterprets the piece as if it were *Moten's Swing.*

Milenberg Joys, like *Prince of Wails,* reinterprets a piece from the earlier jazz repertoire in the new style. Basie is lightly humorous in his deliberately old-timey introduction, and do not miss the saxophone figures, nor the way the rhythm walks behind them, nor the chase between Barefield and Webster toward the end.

Lafayette is one of Durham's contributions to the new repertoire, not quite so lean and spare in the writing as his later arrangements for Basie, however.

I am sure that *Prince of Wails* would be an exceptional performance if only for the forceful and handsome, not to say joyous, striding of Basie's piano—we tend to forget how beautifully he could play this style and what glee there was in it. But also do not miss the way Walter Page comes in behind Webster, the figures behind Lips, and the way that the ending in effect rewrites *Prince of Wails* as if it were *Toby.*

Walter Page was the solid foundation on which this band was built rhythmically. And Walter Page's Blue Devils, his Midwest group of a few years earlier, was the source of its style and of many of its best sidemen, beginning with Basie and Jimmy Rushing, then Lips Page, and ending with Walter Page himself. It is fascinating and instructive to see how the Moten band evolved as these men gradually joined it. Indeed, the earlier Moten records which sound best today are apt to be those on which the ex-Page men appear and contribute.

The Jones Law Blues comes from Basie's first recording session with the Moten band, and it features a brief Basie solo. But the style is older and shows one of the Moten band's earliest debts, for it might almost be one of Jelly Roll Morton's late RCA Victor records. *Small Black* is more typical of the late-twenties Moten—"peppy" rather than really swinging, with solo moments from Ed Lewis, Bus Moten, Durham, Woody Walder, and (I think) Harlan Leonard on alto clarinet. For this version, we have expanded Basie's interesting solo space by first using the chorus from an earlier take and then including the solo originally heard in this take. The first shows Basie's other major influence after Waller, Earl Hines. There is more Waller in the second solo, but there is Hines, too, and the remarkable thing is how well Basie had brought the two styles together as one so that they don't sound like a patchwork.

The New Vine Street Blues is a remake of a piece first recorded in 1924—an unusual twenty-four-bar, long-meter structure. It is an altogether remarkable, sustained performance, much less overarranged and much more emotionally cohesive than most of the Moten records from this period. This, by the way, is a previously unreleased "take," chosen because the solos seem a bit stronger. I assume that the effectively Bechet-like clarinet solo, which has so much to do with developing the mood of this performance, is Woody Walder, who had been with the Moten band on its earliest records, and that the baritone solo, which manages some slap-tonguing without raucousness and without breaking the mood, is Jack Washington. I also take it that the plunger introduction is Ed Lewis, although this playing is rather different from the Nichols–Beiderbecke style he uses on his other solos here.

This is also a new "take" of *Won't You Be My Baby?*—included for Rushing's marvelous singing—he comes on as if he wrote the piece himself, which, as a matter of fact, he did! Rushing was largely a ballad singer in those days, but here he has the plaintive wail of a blues celebrity of the twenties—that wail plus his own ubiquitous good humor. The performance also shows an effort at a steady four-beat rhythm.

Oh! Eddie is arranged, or overarranged, in the old style, but it has Basie (it also has Bus Moten's accordion jiving around with the brass), and the last chorus teasingly sketches out ideas that later turned up in *Moten's Swing*.

That Too, Do is a blues, but a blues with a bridge in the instrumental choruses(!), and Rushing's only recorded blues vocal with Moten. The title is rather like "that fuss" or "that mess," a kind of mock disparagement of the piece. Notice that each of Rushing's choruses had a life of its own on a later blues with Basie. Also notice that provocative call-and-response between "preacher" Ed Lewis' trumpet and the band's "congregation." (Incidentally, if the bass figure that introduces *That Too, Do* gets under your skin, listen to King Oliver's *Snag It* or to the Modern Jazz Quartet's first recording of *Django*.)

When I'm Alone is more typical of the balladeer Rushing of this period, and the piece shows the tempo at which the four-beat swing of the later band was worked out. Also, watch the hints of things to come in those crisp brass figures at the end.

Somebody Stole My Gal almost had to be included if only for Basie's scat singing. The "jungle" jive that introduces it is perhaps all-of-a-piece with the *vo-de-oh-do* baritone, trumpet, and tenor solos, but Basie's piano contribution to the introduction is a moment of lighthearted joy, and in those brass figures at the end we are, once more, warming up for *Moten's Swing* and jazz to come.

(1966)

Ornette Coleman
(Atlantic 1317)

I believe that what Ornette Coleman is playing will affect the whole character of jazz music profoundly and pervasively, but I am not unique or original in believing that what he is doing is new and authentic. For two examples, Percy Heath, bassist with the Modern Jazz Quartet, has been praising him for over two years, often to deaf ears. "When I first heard Ornette and Don Cherry, I asked, 'What are they doing?', but almost immediately it hit me. It was like hearing Charlie Parker the first time: it's exciting and different, and then you realize it's a really new approach and it makes a really valid music." And John Lewis, pianist and musical director of the Quartet, said last winter after hearing him, "Ornette Coleman is doing the only really new thing in jazz since the innovations in the mid-forties of Dizzy Gillespie, Charlie Parker, and those of Thelonious Monk."

What Ornette Coleman plays can be very beautiful and it can have that rare quality of reaching out and touching each member of an audience individually. His melodies are unusual, but they have none of the harshness of self-conscious "experimental" borrowings. When we hear him, he creates for our ears, hearts, and minds a new sensibility.

It is probably impossible for Ornette Coleman to discuss music without sooner or later using the word *love* and he has said, with the innate modesty with which he seems to say everything, "Music is for our feelings. I think jazz should try to express more kinds of feeling than it has up to now." He knows well, then, the source and reason for his music. He also knows that he does not "own" it himself, nor "invent" it, but is responsible to something given to him. As is so necessary with an innovator in the beginning, he is not afraid to play whatever his Muse tells him to play: "I don't know how it's going to sound before I play it any more than anybody else does, so how can we talk about it *before* I play it."

What he has done is, like all valid innovations, basically simple, authentic, and inevitable—but we see that only once someone of a sublime stubbornness like Coleman's does it. The basis of it is this: If you put a conventional chord under my note, you limit the number of choices I have for my next note; if you do not, my melody may move freely in a far greater choice of directions. As he says of his improvising, "For me, if I am just going to use the changes themselves, I might as well write out what I am going to play." This does not mean that his music is "aharmonic" as is the music of a "country" blues singer, a Sonny Terry or a Big Bill Broonzy; nor that he invites disorder. He can work through and beyond the furthest intervals of the chords, and he has said, "From realizing that I can make mistakes, I have come to realize there is an order to what I do"—which, among other things, is as good a definition of maturity as I have ever heard.

As several developments in jazz in the last few years have shown, no one really needs to state all those chords that nearly everyone uses, and as some events have shown, if someone does state them or if a soloist implies them, he may end up with a harassed running up and down scales at those "advanced" intervals like a rat in a harmonic maze. Someone had to break through the walls that those harmonies have built and restore melody—but, again, we realize this only after an Ornette Coleman has begun to do it.

Since the world of jazz has been thickly populated with false prophets for the past ten years, Coleman may need his credentials and it seems to me that among them are these: Like the important innovators in jazz, he maintains an innate balance among rhythm and harmony and melodic line. In jazz, these three are really an identity, and any change in one of them without intrinsic reshuffling in the others invariably risks failure. Further, he works in terms of developing the specific, implicit resources of jazz, not by wholesale importations from concert music. Like most of the great ones, Coleman has a deep and personal feeling for the blues which is unmistakable. *Peace* seems to me a lovely example of that, and of how his playing adds to the emotional range of jazz. These things, and the fact that he breaks through the usual thirty-two-, sixteen-, and twelve-bar forms both in his compositions and in his improvising, all spring from an inner musical necessity, not from an outer academic contrivance. I think that compositionally *Congeniality* is an excellent introduction to many of these things, to the authenticity of his work and the way he is extending the whole idea of instrumental composition in jazz. Finally, to say (as some have) that the solos on such a piece do not have a relationship to his melodies is quite wrong. As a matter of fact, most jazz solos are not related to their theme-melodies, but to the chords with which the themes are harmonized. Coleman and Cherry may relate to the emotion, the pitch, the rhythm, the melody of a theme, without relating to "chords" or bar divisions. To a listener, such relationships can have even more meaning than the usual harmonic ones.

Ornette Coleman started to play alto in 1944, when he was fourteen, in Fort Worth, Texas. He remains largely self-taught on his instrument, but inspired by a cousin, James Jordan, who was a music teacher in Austin, he studied books on harmony and theory quite early and thoroughly. One of his earliest influences was Red Connor, who had played with Charlie Parker and who, according to Coleman, played then the way Sonny Rollins and John Coltrane do now. Coleman has also heard and admired altoist Buster Smith, who now works in Dallas, and Smith was, as Parker said, "the guy I really dug."

Early jobs included carnival and rhythm and blues bands from which he was usually discharged for playing something the leader didn't like. Once in New Orleans, a crowd smashed his instrument, apparently because *they* didn't like his playing. 1952 found him stranded in Los Angeles, where musicians at sessions would tell him he didn't know harmony and was out of tune. After a return to Fort Worth, he went back to Los Angeles in 1954; that was the crucial year for him, when he really broke through to the freedom that has characterized his work since. Still disapproved of, he supported himself and his wife, Jayne, and soon a son, with day jobs while he stuck to his convictions about music.

In 1956, he met trumpeter Donald Cherry, who grasped what Coleman was doing, and began musically to breathe as he breathes. Cherry, who is six years younger than Coleman, moved from Oklahoma City to Los Angeles at four, and has gigged with professionals since 1951.

Bassist Charlie Haden is more than an asset to this recital; he too has grasped the essentials of Ornette's music and contributes to it. In his work here, I think one can see most clearly at least one of the things that Coleman's music has already achieved in group improvising. By abandoning conventional bass positions and the usual ideas of harmonic bass lines, he has found for himself and his instrument the pitch in which a piece and the improvisors are playing (Ornette sometimes wrote out a bass range for him), his bass forms a percussive-melodic part that participates much more directly in the music, rather than functioning as a contributing "accompaniment." Hear him especially on *Lonely Woman*. Finally, drummer Billy Higgins, who was brought into the group by Don Cherry, can shift tempos and play freely around the rhythm and time while maintaining the basic movement of, and swing of, a jazz beat.

The titles to these instrumental compositions are neither the usual ironies or throw-away, but are intended to mean what they say. *Congeniality,* for example, was originally named for a wandering preacher but, Coleman says, "I'm not a preacher, I'm a musician, so I named it for what I think a *musician* feels toward an audience."

The tapes for this LP were edited during the third summer session of the School of Jazz at Music Inn in Lenox, Massachusetts, where Ornette and Donald Cherry were students. Ornette asked Gunther Schuller, who is a composer and French horn player in both jazz and classical idioms, practicing jazz critic, and instructor at the school, for help in the editing. Schuller's remarks on Ornette will follow but because of what he says I will preface them by the note that his (Schuller's) own works have been praised for "one of the most immaculate senses of form in contemporary composition." He says, "Perhaps the most outstanding element in Ornette's musical conception is an utter and complete freedom. His musical inspiration operates in a world uncluttered by conventional bar lines, conventional chord changes, and conventional ways of blowing or fingering a saxophone. Such practical 'limitations' did not even have to be overcome in his music; they somehow never existed for him. Despite this—or more accurately, *because* of this—his playing has a deep inner logic. Not an obvious surface logic, it is based on subtleties of reaction, subtleties of timing and color that are, I think, quite new to jazz—at least they have never appeared in so pure and direct a form. Ornette's musical language is the product of a mature man who *must* speak through his horn. Every note seems to be born out of a need to communicate. I don't think Ornette could ever *play at* playing as so many jazzmen do. The music sits too deeply in him for that, and all these qualities are the more startling because they are not only imbued with a profound love and knowledge of jazz tradition, but are the first new realization of all that is implicit in the music of Charlie Parker."

(1959)

170

LEONARD FEATHER

Probably the most widely published jazz writer ever, **Feather** wrote many books, including **The Encyclopedia of Jazz**, and was probably the all-time liner note champ, in terms of sheer amount if nothing else. Always a clean stylist, **Feather** was for years the jazz critic for **The Los Angeles Times**.

Harlan Leonard and His Rockets

Harlan Leonard
(RCA Victor LPV-531)

The chief of the cashiers' section in the Los Angeles Internal Revenue Office for the past four years has been a heavyset, orderly man whose appearance denies his sixty-one years. His present responsible position in the department is the culmination of a carefully planned climb that began when he joined it in January 1949. Not too many of his associates are conscious that this man, whose nickname is Mike but who was born Harlan Quentin Leonard, had another and somewhat more glamorous career that preceded his present relatively prosaic life.

The band known as Harlan Leonard and His Rockets enjoyed very little public recognition. During the years of its outstanding contribution, from 1936–40, it was virtually ignored by the relatively few historians who were then chronicling the events of jazz. (Dave Dexter, then with *Down Beat*, was a notable exception. From Kansas City himself, he led the small but faithful Leonard cheering section.) The band was among the most underrated of its day; moreover, its personnel, at one time or another, included several musicians who went on to international prominence, and at least a couple who deserved to but never did.

Harlan Leonard was born in Kansas City on July 2, 1905. He played saxophone in the high school band, studying with several prominent Kansas City musicians, including a well-known band-leader of the day, Paul Tremaine.

He made his professional debut at the age of eighteen with Bennie Moten's band. "The first records we made were so long ago," he recalls, "the recording was preelectric. I stayed with the Moten band until 1931. Then they changed the personnel around and some of the men, including me, went out with a band directed by Thamon Hayes. There was another reshuffling in 1934 and I took over as leader. The following year we went to Chicago and played in a big show at the Cotton Club there."

Leonard organized a second band in 1936. The personnel changed slightly from time to time, but basically this was the same unit heard in the present performances. Leonard recalls that Charlie Parker worked with him briefly around January of 1939, playing third alto to the leader's first. "He was a wonderful fellow, but we just couldn't count on him to show up, so he didn't stay with us long."

For those of us who were fortunate enough to be on the scene at the time, the culminating point in the career of this band appeared to arrive on February 4, 1940, when the Rockets were booked for a six-week engagement at the Golden Gate Ballroom in Harlem. For the first week, an astonishing initiative was undertaken by the management. The Golden Gate was going all out to compete with the Savoy, which lay two blocks farther south on Lenox Avenue; accordingly, in a burst of generosity the like of which was never observed before or later in the history of Harlem jazz, four big bands and a trio were booked in simultaneously, all occupying different bandstands and taking turns throughout the evening. The big bands were those of Leonard, Les Hite, Claude Hopkins, and Coleman Hawkins. The trio, led by organist Milt Herth, occupied a bandstand at the far end of the room. Tiny Bradshaw acted as master of ceremonies.

Little was known about Harlan Leonard at the time. Les Hite, though California-based, was somewhat more familiar, having made a number of records with Louis Armstrong. What happened during that phenomenal week, as might be expected, was an atmosphere of competition that stimulated each band to its optimum level. The excitement in the ballroom reached a pitch that has never been duplicated. The Golden Gate was a vast, somewhat chilly arena, large enough to accommodate thousands of dancers as well as the hundreds who stood around one bandstand after another as the sets followed each other in rapid succession.

The two outstanding soloists of the Harlan Leonard band were Hank Bridges and Fred Beckett. Bridges and the other tenor man in the band, Jimmy Keith, were admirers of their counterparts in the Count Basie band, Lester Young and Herschel Evans, though it is the Evans side of Bridges' personality that is apparent on most of his solo work here. Beckett, who died in January 1946 in St. Louis, showed evidence of a greater control of the trombone than perhaps any other contemporary except Jack Teagarden. He has often been cited by J. J. Johnson as the real precursor of modern jazz trombone.

In addition to Beckett, Bridges and several other soloists, the band was impressive on the strength of its clean, brisk section work. Harlan Leonard led the reeds, rarely soloing; Edward Johnson was a strong and dependable lead trumpet. Leonard was also fortunate in having such arrangers as James Ross, Richard Smith, Eddie Durham, Buster Smith, and Rozell Claxton.

During the band's New York visit, Leonard made an important addition to his roster of arrangers. "One day," he recalls, "I ran into Tadd Dameron at the Woodside Hotel. He was broke, and looking for work. I took him along with me to Kansas City and for a while he played piano in the band as well as writing a lot of our arrangements." Dameron, represented as a writer on the last two of the four Leonard sessions, earned a worldwide reputation a few years later as one of the first arrangers associated with the bebop revolution.

Recognition for a big band during the Swing Era often depended on the fortuitous success of a single ballad record. Ironically, Andy Kirk's orchestra, contemporaneous with the Leonard band in Kansas City, made the jump from obscurity to jukebox ubiquity, not with a tune that represented its essential jazz qualities, but with a simpering vocal version of *Until the Real Thing Comes Along.* Similarly, Tommy Dorsey subdued his virtuosity as a jazz trombonist after *I'll Never Smile Again* had established him with crooner-conscious audiences.

It could have happened to Harlan Leonard just that way, for his was the first band to record *I Don't Want to Set the World on Fire.* Unfortunately, he treated it as a jump tune; later it became a great hit as a ballad. He could have been lucky, too, with *Southern Fried,* which did so well for Charlie Barnet and others; but his own version made only a small dent and was not even issued under that title (it was originally known as *Hairy Joe Jump*).

And so, luck having never crossed over to their side of the street, the Rockets were never fired into an orbit of economic security and critical acclaim. After drifting for another year or two, Leonard moved in October of 1942 to Los Angeles, where he replaced Freddie Slack's band at Zucca's in Hermosa Beach. A few months later he brought his family out and put his two children in school there. (His son, now thirty-nine, is an Air Force major and a jet pilot.)

The band played a year at the old Club Alabam. Gradually,

the draft made its inevitable inroads on the personnel. "We played our last date," Leonard says, "at Shepp's Playhouse in Los Angeles early in 1945. Our pianist then was Nellie Lutcher. After we broke up, I decided the time had come to get out of the music business entirely. I didn't even want to own a saxophone, because then I might have been tempted to accept a job again. I was out of everything for a year, then floated around in unimportant jobs, at Lockheed, at the post office, until I finally found my niche in '49."

The personnel and solo credits for the sixteen performances in this album were painstakingly checked for a discography compiled in 1963 by a loyal fan of the Leonard band—Johnny Simmen of the New Jazz Club in Zurich, Switzerland. Through personal and written contacts with former members of the band, he established every detail beyond any reasonable doubt. Harlan Leonard confirms this: "Mr. Simmen's information is quite accurate and represents a tremendous amount of research. I think he knows more about my band than I do myself."

Rock and Ride, a Tadd Dameron arrangement, features a chase trumpet chorus comprising alternating eight-bar passages by William H. (Smitty) Smith and James Ross, in that order. Bridges plays sixteen bars on tenor, followed by sixteen bars featuring Keith. Jesse Price has a couple of drum breaks near the end.

Dameron Stomp has never previously been issued. The soloists are Ross, Bridges, trombonist Walter Monroe, and then Smitty. *Skee,* arranged by James Ross, features Bridges, Beckett, and Smitty.

The languorously pretty *A-La-Bridges* is, in this writer's opinion, the band's most memorable performance, credit being due in equal measure to the solos of Bridges and Beckett and the arrangement by Dameron.

Ross, Monroe, Keith, and bassist Winston Williams are heard from in *Too Much,* which also shows off the reed section to advantage. *Take 'Um,* another item never before released, is a rollicking showcase for Bridges. *Ride My Blues Away,* arranged by Buster Smith, features Bridges and vocalist Ernie Williams, a superlative blues singer who certainly must be classed along with Jimmy Rushing among the preeminent artists of the day in this idiom.

Eddie Durham's arrangement of *I Don't Want to Set the World on Fire* is included mainly as a matter of historical interest. The tempo is too fast for singer Myra Taylor, and the solos (Ross, Bridges, Beckett, Ross again, Keith) are too brief to accomplish much.

Solo credits on the second side are as follows. *Rockin' with the Rockets:* Effergee Ware, Beckett (muted), Smitty (in second chorus); Keith (release, second chorus); Bridges, Ross, and pianist William S. Smith in the third chorus. *Southern Fried:* Smitty, Keith, pianist Smith, Ross, Bridges. *Parade of the Stompers* (a Rozell Claxton arrangement): Smith (piano); Ross, Bridges. *Mistreated:* Bridges, Ross, and Smitty backing Williams' vocal. *Keep Rockin'* (a Dameron arrangement): the two William Smiths, Ross, Bridges, Monroe, Keith, and Smitty riding it out. *"400" Swing* (Dameron): Bridges, Keith; a chorus of Ross-and-Smitty four-bar chases; Beckett. *Please Don't Squabble:* Beckett, Ross, Bridges, and Smitty under the Williams vocal. *My Gal Sal* (arr. Richard J. Smith): Bridges, Beckett, pianist Smith, Ross, Keith. (Arrangements, unless otherwise stated, are by Ross.)

Listeners not previously familiar with the work of the Rockets will certainly concur with Simmen's summation that "individually, and collectively, this band had something to say, and said it well." For Harlan Leonard himself, listening to these performances as we picked out the best available for reissue was an experience that brought waves of nostalgia for an almost-forgotten era. For young jazz historians, these sides will fill a gap that has existed far too long in the microgroove annals of big band jazz.

(1967)

WHITNEY BALLIETT

Certainly one of the finest prose stylists to write about jazz, **Balliett** has been the jazz writer for **The New Yorker** for going on five decades. His books include **The Sound of Surprise, Such Sweet Thunder**, and many others. A master of the unusual metaphor, **Balliett** has consistently written the finest extended profiles of jazz musicians that I know of.

Boss of the Blues

Joe Turner
(Atlantic 1234)

Jazz would be an empty house without the blues. For the poetry, temper, restlessness, and depth of the blues have been inescapably annealed to jazz. A jazz musician who cannot drive his blues down so they shake you a little is suspect. And people who do not like blues are, like Cassius, lean dogs. The blues, born out of the troublous mind of an oppressed people, have become a kind of universal flag of sound. They are, of course, also a state of soul. Thus, Leadbelly once said: "When you lay down at night, turn from one side of the bed all night to the other and can't sleep, what's the matter? Blues got you. Or when you get up in the mornin' and sit on the side of the bed—may have a mother or father, sister or brother, boyfriend or girlfriend, or husband or wife around—you don't want no talk out of 'um. They ain't done you nothin' and you ain't done them nothin'—but what's the matter? Blues got you. Well, you get up and shove your feet down under the table and look down in your place—may have chicken and rice, take my advice, you walk away and shake your head, you say, 'Lord, have mercy. I can't eat and I can't sleep, what's the matter?' Why, the blues still got you . . ."

The blues are generally regarded as an expression of sadness, misery, or melancholy. But the truth is, the blues—depending wholly on how they are performed—are an accurate register of all emotion. They can be sad, miserable, low-down sad. They can be angry-sad. They can be haunting. They can be lilting, salubrious, joyous, bubbling. They can be wildly exuberant. They can be funny, sardonic, and even nasty. They can be ironic. They can be dirty. The blues have no other intention than being a direct emotional thrust. Created as a balm and safety valve, they still serve the same purpose. Like any art form, they can gather up the listener and, if he is willing, anoint him.

In its simplest form, the blues is a twelve-bar construction based on three chords (in the key of B♭, the commonest blues key, these chords would be B♭, E♭, and F) the last two of which incorporate partially flatted notes, or "blue notes," the blue third and the blue seventh. The simple rondolike arrangement of these chords within the frame of one chorus—B♭, E♭, B♭, F, B♭—builds to a kind of climax with the F chord and then slides away to a neat resolution in the final return to B♭. In short, the blues chorus is a classic form that has simplicity, variation, and an endless allowance—because of its ingenious construction—for improvisational flexibility. No matter how much window dressing may be added, however—subchords, a myriad of notes, intricate rhythms

—it is always the blue notes, queer and twilit, around which the poignancy of the blues revolves.

No one knows much about the origins of the blues; they developed, along with such other Negro vocal music, as spirituals, work songs, and so forth, sometime in the last century throughout much of the South. Ezra Cornell, the founder of the university, wrote his wife in the early 1810s that he had "the blues." Of course the term as he used it may have had nothing to do with music; it may simply have been derived from the color itself. At any rate, there must have been blues not long after the Civil War. There are blues in the repertoires of the two country brass bands Fred Ramsey recorded a few years ago in the backlands of Alabama, and there is some reason to believe that these musicians use the same materials their grandfathers did. In the 1920s, people began to realize that the blues were a coherent musical form. The big record companies sent units around the country to record the great rural folksingers, such as Blind Lemon Jefferson, Speckled Red, and Big Bill Broonzy. Abbe Niles, in 1926, wrote a still penetrating analysis of the blues in a foreword to a collection of W. C. Handy blues. George Gershwin imagined the blues, and wrote *Rhapsody in Blue*. By the end of the decade, the first era of the blues was well under way. Peculiarly enough, it was dominated by women. There were the five Smiths—Bessie, Mamie, Laura, Clara, and Trixie (none of them related)—Ma Rainey, and Chippie Hill. In the thirties, as instrumental jazz grew in strength and variety, the blues, which had largely been a vocal music, gradually became an instrumental property. Yet, a second generation of male blues singers appeared: Joe Turner, Jimmy Rushing, T-Bone Walker, Teddy Bunn, Hot Lips Page, and Jack Teagarden.

Vocal blues are generally less varied in expression and mood than instrumental blues. Blues lyrics tend toward the melancholy, and the human voice is, after all, a limited instrument.

Blues lyrics are often set in the form of a couplet, with the first line repeated twice. They are in iambic pentameter, and there is a kind of Pope-like caesura in each line. Blues lyrics are among the most touching folk poetry ever conceived:

> If you see me comin',
> > hist your window high
> Oh, if you see me comin',
> > hist your window high
> And if you see me goin',
> > hang your head and cry.

One of the most durable of the great blues shouters is Joe Turner. A bulging tower of a man who weighs over two hundred and fifty pounds and stands six feet two, Turner was born in Kansas City in 1911. He was singing professionally at the King-fish Club by the time he was fourteen, and Mary Lou Williams remembers him, as a bartender, shouting the blues with Pete Johnson at the Sunset Club. Turner first achieved some sort of prominence in 1938, when he was brought to New York for a Carnegie Hall concert, produced by John Hammond, that was in large part responsible for the boogie woogie craze that lasted into the early forties. After this, he worked for a time with his own group in New York, and recorded both under his own name and with Joe Sullivan, Art Tatum, and Pete Johnson. Turner dropped into obscurity after the war, reappeared a few years ago, and made his first hit record—a simple blues—on Atlantic.

The blues are played and sung in a very special way by the majority of Kansas City musicians and singers. They are explosive, but fragile; they are intense, but unruffled. They have a kind of beefy sophistication. Turner uses little vibrato, almost no gravel-voicing, and simple but effective dynamics. He has a big baritone voice that has an almost flat, slatey quality to it. It is never musky or lorn. It is hard and certain and gives the im-

180

pression that the listener must contribute exactly as much as Turner himself. Turner's blues are not passive. Like many blues singers, he tends to slur his words, so that certain passages dissolve into mere balls of sound. He uses a good many long notes, and has a fine sense of delayed rhythm. Above all, Turner's singing has power and definiteness. Indeed, it is as if he were *driving* his voice into your mind.

This album, which demonstrates some of the clearest and most forcible singing Turner has put on record, was made in a couple of sessions in New York. The simple, suitable arrangements were done by Ernie Wilkins. The musicians need little explanation. Pete Johnson, the master blues pianist, worked with Turner for years in Kansas City, and has cowritten three of the tunes here. Frank Wess, Freddie Green, and Walter Page are, of course, also associated with Kansas City. Here are some of the best moments in the album: the irresistible noodling quality—listen to Brown's lazy-daddy trombone behind Turner—of *Morning Glories,* a charming tune that was, according to Turner, in vogue in Kansas City; Turner's sudden humor in the two choruses that are tacked onto the end of *St. Louis Blues;* Wilkins' ingratiating background figures, and Lawrence Brown's two choruses on *Wee Baby Blues;* the great tension that is achieved in the final choruses of *How Long Blues;* Turner's half-spoken, half-moaned apostrophe—"Mmmmmyeh"—at the end of his first chorus on *Girl;* all of Pete Johnson's solos, and in particular his easy-rocking opening chorus on *Cherry Red,* which is everything the blues were meant to be.

(1956)

Gerry Mulligan Quartet
(Pacific Jazz PJ-1207)

A little less than ten years ago, a schism—caused by the unexpected and inescapably brilliant melodic lines and dervy rhythms of Dizzy Gillespie, Charlie Parker, Lester Young, and Bud Powell—split jazz in two. The older musicians, the hot, simple men, suddenly went into obscurity and were replaced by a host of young imitators who poured cooly from every wood to follow unquestionably the new Pied Pipers. Louis Armstrong became old hat. Benny Goodman was put to pasture. Art Tatum became as obsolescent as the great auk. Then, about four or five years ago, another group of young jazzmen, revolutionary reactionaries all, began springing up. Some of their names were Oscar Peterson, Gerry Mulligan, Louis Bellson, Ruby Braff, Urbie Green, Bobby Brookmeyer, Frank Wess, Joe Morello, and Howard Roberts. In their earliest interviews, they spoke of how they too had been influenced by Parker, Gillespie, and Powell, but they also mentioned Nat Cole, Tatum, Jo Jones, Davy Tough, Armstrong, Buddy Rich, and Ben Webster.

It soon became clear that one of the most imposing and persuasive of these musicians, all of whom unfashionably combined an awareness of the new Cadillac-length lines with the bearish old warmth of Herschel Evans, was Gerry Mulligan, an original melodist, a creative, arresting arranger, and the first baritone saxophonist of sufficient breadth to challenge the immemorial tenure of Harry Carney. For it had been Mulligan, with the arranger Gil Evans, who had been at the bottom of the handful of rebellious, questing Capitol recordings issued under Miles Davis' name in 1949. These warm, moving efforts were notable for their unique small band instrumentation—trumpet, trombone, alto saxophone, baritone saxophone, French horn, tuba, piano, and drums—as well as the integrated, loosely swaying ensembles that were as important as the solos. ("It was a kind of smaller version of Claude Thornhill's band," Mulligan said recently. "If there had been a good clarinet around at the time, we probably would have used him too.") Three years after the Davis session, Mulligan started a second upheaval by organizing, in Los Angeles, a pianoless quartet composed of his baritone saxophone, a trumpet, bass, and drums. Almost instantly the piano became as popular in modern jazz as the bowler in Texas, and innumerable quartets, which attempted the same deceptively simple mobile counterpoint and soft, melodious movements, sprouted with every conceivable combination of instruments. Mulligan became famous, moved out of debt, got married, and eventually took an apartment on Central Park West. And the schism began to heal.

Mulligan himself does not look much like your ordinary revolutionist. At twenty-eight, he is tall, thin, and stooped, has a monkish cap of red hair, a pale face that goes balloon-red when he is playing, and a broad, relaxed mouth. In fact, if it were not for his nervous, voluble, direct, and sometimes snappish way of speaking, and hands that continually shape air, Mulligan would resemble Uriah Heep. His dress, however, can be a quite accurate reflection of his inner fires. Recently, in Boston, he sauntered unselfconsciously down gray old Boylston Street in a flapping flag-colored checked coat that seemed to sputter in the sun of that city of tired tweeds and brown hats. Mulligan is highly articulate, and this articulateness is composed of sharp judgments and a pleasant, almost aggressive honesty. As he said recently and variously: "A lot of people say that I'm arrogant, and I suppose I am. But I haven't got the time to make these people feel differently." "At any given time I'm liable to play differently than at any other given time. I have no control over this. I react to any group I'm with." "I don't think I'm playing well now. You can't put your horn down every six months and expect to." "I live a crazy life. In fact nothing in my life is normal except me." "These experiments within modern jazz for new extended forms are fine, but no form at all is not a new form. And who wants to memorize all those progressions, anyway?"

Mulligan was born a Catholic in Queens, New York, the fourth and youngest son of an industrial engineer. Before he was a year old, his family had moved to Marion, Ohio, and when his schooling was over, at the age of seventeen, in Philadelphia, he had lived, in addition, in New Jersey, Chicago, Kalamazoo, Detroit, and Reading. His first instrument was a ukelele. He also took piano lessons, learned the ocarina family, then the clarinet, although he had asked his father for a trumpet. In 1944, Mulligan left school, where he had led several bands, and went to work as an arranger for Tommy Tucker, turning out in the three months that he stayed a trunkful of material, some of which is still in use. He spent the next six months or so as an arranger and sometime tenor saxophonist with Elliot Lawrence, joined George Paxton, and eventually, for a year, Gene Krupa. During the next few years, he worked as a freelance writer and sideman around New York, made his first recordings, with Brew Moore and George Wallington (he had just taken up the baritone saxophone seriously), had various rehearsal bands, which occasionally practiced in Central Park because no one had money for a studio, and, shortly after the Miles Davis date, hitchhiked, over a period of months, with waystops at Reading and Albuquerque, to Los Angeles, where he stayed more or less permanently until his recent move east. On the West Coast, he wrote for Kenton and worked marathon twelve-hour gigs on Saturdays and Sundays at the Lighthouse, Hermosa Beach. In 1951 he landed a Tuesday night job at the Haig, in Los Angeles, where he did some experimenting with a trio composed of guitar, his instrument, and drums. Then, almost inadvertently, after he had met Chet Baker, he hit upon the instrumentation of the quartet and was recorded by Richard Bock of Pacific Jazz, the cream of which can be heard in the twelve reissues, recorded between 1952 and 1953, that make up this record.

Mulligan is a fresh and convincing melodist. (Writing a pure and ingratiating melody is like putting together a sentence that, by virtue of its perfectly chosen and arranged parts, has grace, rhythm, and meaning. A rare talent in any sort of composed music, it is woefully rare among modern jazz musicians, a great many of whom began in 1940 or so the interesting practice of writing their own material. Out of these hundreds of tunes, one remembers, perhaps, such things as *Move, Four Brothers, Swing Street, Subdivided in F, Lullaby of Birdland, Now's the Time,* and *Trickleydidlier.*) Listen on this record to *Jeru, Nights at the Turntable,* and *Swinghouse,* and elsewhere to *Walkin' Shoes.* In his writing for both small and big bands (Mulligan is, of course, one of the finest big band arrangers in the business today), he is no innovator in the sense that Teddy Charles or Lennie Tristano presently are with their adventures into extended forms, free improvisations, and left-field harmonies. On the contrary, the quartet sides, with their warmth and narrow brushes with a kind of dixieland impulse, often sound strangely old-fashioned. In the way of the modernists, though, Mulligan believes in controlling firmly through rehearsals and his writing the voices he had at hand, adding, for instance, counter lines and organ chords—with human voices, his own instruments, or with several instruments— to the spiritless void that can appear behind the soloist who has nothing but a rhythm section for support and impetus. He also feels that humor (*I'm Beginning to See the Light* here), rather than the owlish musings of so much modern small band jazz, has a definite place in jazz, which he grants a happy music. Mulligan's talents as a baritone saxophonist are equally capacious, but at the same time more erratic than his writing. His solos are apt to repeat earlier choice phrases, his tone sometimes goes thin, his constructions sound strained. His style is a wide one, and ranges from the delicate sonorities present on most of these sides to a damn-the-torpedoes booting that, when it first was manifested to the public at large during the 1954 Newport Festival, surprised those who had docketed him as a miniaturist. Above all, when Mulligan is in form, he is quite capable of producing one of those rare improvisational statements that move the listener as no other instrumental music can. Witness, for example, his solos on *Little Girl Blue* on the recent Gerry Mulligan Pacific Jazz album PJ-1201.

Mulligan, who can be high-strung and moody, is now feverishly at work with still another group, which, although it will not cause any tremors like those that followed the Davis and quartet sides, will continue to lessen the needless gap between the "modernists" and the "traditionalists." A sextet with trombone, tenor saxophone, trumpet, bass, and drums, and the leader's occasional piano and more frequent baritone saxophone, it builds quite complex structures that feature fluidly written contrapuntal ensembles, meaningful cradles for generous amounts of solo work, and an omnipresent swing. And sometime soon Mulligan hopes that he can rehearse still another group that will combine older musicians with younger ones. If he succeeds, he will have a music as fascinating as a structure designed by the Roebling brothers and Le Corbusier.

(1955)

GEORGE FRAZIER

The gray eminence of Boston, columnist **George Frazier** was a connoisseur of sophisticated nightlife, under which rubric jazz fell for him. He began writing about jazz in the 1930s for publications as different as England's **Melody Maker** and **Mademoiselle.** In the late 1950s and early 1960s, he was a fashion columnist for **Esquire.**

Tribute to Benny Goodman

Jess Stacy
(Atlantic 1225)

It is almost impossible to exaggerate how we felt about the Goodman band in the time of its triumph some twenty tumultuous years ago. We loved it with an eager, sophisticated passion that was probably unprecedented in the not conspicuously unemotional field of popular music. For this was an exultant and vanquishing part of our stubborn and rebellious generation, as bracing and flawlessly-flowing as a mountain stream swollen by a spring thaw and as smooth and honest as the pebbles underneath. It was our darling, this band—our symbol of defiance, our chowder and marching song, our *raison d'etre,* our own very personal *recherché du temps*

Perdido, so that when, on those gallant midnights, it used to keep its rendezvous with destiny at a barricade that had been disputed much too long, it was a little as if spring had come round with rustling shade and apple blossoms filled the air. Or, to put it another way, we dug it the most.

Wherever there were radios—in spiraling, nocturnal cities or in drowsy hamlets with "the sharp names that never get fat" and "the snakeskin titles of mining claims"—there were people who recognized, albeit intuitively, that history was being made at night. This was a fresh and unplatitudinous kind of music, a music of challenge and courage and jubilation, of promise and of protest, with the clarinet like a streak of summer lightning against a darkling landscape, with the reeds a feathery cushion, with the brass as clean and crisp as a slice of Melba toast. This was the Goodman band; this was our special pleasure and when it read its offertory in such tabernacles as the Palomar in Los Angeles or the Madhattan Room in New York City, we listened, so to speak, all kneeling, as is the custom with the Book of Common Prayer. This was our pride and our prejudice, our sense and sensibility, our lares and our penates. This was the sorcerer and his apprentices. This, though, we know. But what is passing wondrous is that their wizardry has neither perished nor become a trifling thing. For it is not often that you can go home again, which is why it is best that auld acquaintance be forget. T. S. Eliot, after all, is not the only one to have seen the moments of his greatness flicker.

Everything considered, it would not have been surprising if the Goodman idiom had been made contemptible by too much familiarity. For when you do something beautifully—uniquely well and with a special grace—you risk vulgarizing it. Popularity is the plague of permanence and a vogue, more often than not, is its own victim. The classy, alas, is forever in imminent grave danger of becoming a cliché—for isn't a cliché a cliché simply by virtue of the fact that it was originally something with special distinction, something with class. This is true of everything creative. Only the tall men, the true geniuses at whatever their trade— whether it be the Spencer Tracy of *Bad Day at Black Rock,* the Bud Redding of *The End of a Love Affair,* the Garbo of *The Flesh and the Devil*—only the truly tall men are inimitable. Not unimitable, but inimitable, and in a way immune to custom's withering and age's staling. The Goodman band was so extravagantly, so outrageously, right that it seemed that there must be a catch somewhere. But there wasn't and now we know for certain that it was not for an age, but for the ages.

In part at least, this is because it was more than merely a band. It was a romantic symbol—and one to which success did not come easily or swiftly. In the beginning, in fact, its admirers were so few that there was a bond among them, a kind of fierce kinship. So that if you suddenly discovered, say, that this swell girl from Smith happened to like Goodman, too—well, it was just sort of wonderful and then and there you had something special going for you—for the two of you. You were sharing a rare emotional experience and nobody, neither Shep Fields nor Lawrence Welk, could ever take it away from you. It was what the members of the band had—the realization that they were together at Mafeking, as it were. Working for Goodman, of course, was a privileged thing, a special dispensation, sort of like playing for the Yankees or dancing with Astaire or being tapped for Bones. It was the top. But above and beyond the obvious matter of talent, quite apart from the fact that a man had to know his instrument, there was a deeper and more abiding bond—the bond of courage and explorativeness and audaciousness, of being in on a noble experiment. For these men were, after their fashion, embattled farmers who needed no rude bridge arching any flood to fire a shot heard round the world and, as we know now, for all the years to come—a shot, for that matter, that is to be heard in this compendium recorded by some of those who raised their muskets some twenty years ago, who were present and accounted for when a tune called *Let's Dance* became the rallying cry of a whole liberated generation.

The pianist-leader on this date was Jess Stacy, a gentle, soft-spoken man who was born in the Mississippi River town of Cape Girardeau, Missouri, on August 11, 1904, and started playing by ear ten years later. Nowadays, it seems to be the fashion for young jazz musicians to explain their work—rather, on occasion, as if they fear it needs annotation in order to be appreciated. Actually, there is nothing calamitous about this, especially when it reveals, as it does on a recent Pacific Jazz album, that an instrumentalist like Jack Montrose has an authentic gift for writing prose. Still and all, one cannot resist the suspicion that some of the modernists do protest too much. For my own part, I prefer Stacy's way, which, in the matter of his own accomplishments, is one of impenetrable taciturnity. His attitude is that his music is there to hear—so make of it what you will.

When the steamer *Majestic* docked at Cape Girardeau one day in 1920, it was looking for someone to replace its pianist, who had drowned while swimming during a stopover at Alton, Illinois. Stacy, who had been studying with a music professor at Missouri State Teachers' College, was hired at a modest salary that was amplified by five dollars a week for manning the steam calliope whenever the boat approached a bend in the river. After two years of being glad to have been aboard, however, Stacy decided to move on to Chicago, where the nights were reputed to be incandescent with the gutbucket grandeur of such unheralded geniuses as Louis Armstrong and Earl Hines. His first noteworthy job was in 1927 as a member (along with his favorite clarinetist the late Frank Teschemacher, and Muggsy Spanier) of Floyd Towne's orchestra at the Midway gardens.

Stacy, who was to win *Down Beat* awards in 1940, 1941, 1942, and 1943, was with Goodman from June 1935 until July 1939. Subsequently, he was for three years with Bob Crosby, with Goodman again in 1943, with Horace Heidt for six tedious months in 1943–44, with Tommy Dorsey for another half-year, and, in 1945, at the helm of his own band, which did not survive long enough to cut much of a swath in jazz history. Since 1950, he has been living in Los Angeles, where he holds gainful and unharrassed employment as a solo pianist with a devoted following.

The high point in Stacy's artistic career—and, for that matter, one of the peaks in the annals of recorded jazz piano—occurred on the evening of January 8, 1938, when the Goodman band gave its now-legendary concert in Carnegie Hall. It came during the extravaganza performance of *Sing, Sing, Sing.* Stacy, who had no idea that he was to take a solo, had been providing Goodman's clarinet with a superb background when the leader suddenly nodded to him. The major miracle that followed is as revealing a picture of Stacy's style as can be heard on records. Swinging irresistibly, it has that big, resonant sound that only he seems able to get out of a piano, a soaring lyricism, unflaggingly exalted inventiveness, and, of course, "the waits," which is his expression for the little pauses, the barely perceptible hesitations, that are the essence of authentic swing. But this has been said before—and in a marvelous way that makes everything else that has ever been written about jazz seem inarticulate. It was said by the late Otis Ferguson in a piece called "Piano in the Band" that appeared in *The New Republic,* for which he was the movie reviewer. Ferguson, who was killed when his ship was struck off Italy during the Second World War, was such an assiduous researcher that he used to sit *under* Stacy's piano when the Goodman band was at the Pennsylvania Hotel in New York. If you would know what magic can be written about good jazz, look up those Ferguson pieces in *The New Republic*—one called "Young Man with a Horn" that was about Beiderbecke, one (the title of which escapes me) about Jack Teagarden that made you hear the burr in that trombone, and, of course, the one about Stacy. It is only appropriate that the blues in this album should be *in memoriam* Otis Ferguson.

Now Jess Stacy's Richard Barthlemess-black hair is turning iron gray, but his touch and invention and lilt are as matchless as on that gallant night in Carnegie Hall. And so, for that matter, are the skills of Ziggy Elman, who is surely one of the most underrated trumpeters in history. Elman felt so deeply about this album that he continued to play long after his lip had begun to bleed. To him, as to Stacy and the others, this was a class reunion of the greatest and most delightful urgency. I think that their enthusiasm will be apparent to anyone hearing them clutch—bravely and with unimpaired talent—at the vanished years. And then, too, this album is significant for another reason: Stacy is neither to be seen nor heard in *The Benny Goodman Story*, an apocryphal confection out of the Universal-International movie studio. He *could* have been in it, but he is, for all his diffidence, a prideful man. When he arrived at the studio one day to discover that he was to play only one number, he was not pleased. What the hell, he thought. And with that, he looked at Goodman and for once it was not Benny who was the Ray. "Good-bye, Mr. Chips," said Stacy and turned on his heel. One lousy number, he thought. Who needs it? As it happens, *The Benny Goodman Story* needs it. *The Benny Goodman Story* could use Jess Stacy very nicely, indeed!

(1956)

BENNY GREEN

Anyone who bought any albums on Norman Granz's Pablo label during the 1970s or 1980s was likely surprised by the consistently high level of writing on the liners. The party responsible was British critic **Benny Green**, one of the finest and warmest jazz writers. His work was always thoughtful and sympathetic to the musicians, the writing of a man with a real love for jazz and nothing to prove.

Sirius

Coleman Hawkins
(Pablo 2310707)

It was during the war years that I first met up with Coleman Hawkins. I was around fifteen years old at the time and beginning to learn my way round the discographies when somebody gave me a record of Hawk playing *Stardust*. I had only been playing the tenor saxophone myself for about eighteen months at the time, and frankly the whole thing was too much for me. Looking back on it, I suppose that what happened to me was some kind of a brainstorm. I played the record over and over and over again, without ever failing to be both deeply moved emotionally and deeply confused technically.

At last, in desperation, I played the record to a professional music teacher I knew, and he, understanding my infatuation, assured me that a day would come when familiarity and sophistication would enable me to contemplate the contents of that record with a clear head and a cool heart. He was wrong. That version of *Stardust* recorded back in the spring of 1935, when Hawk was barnstorming across Europe, still stupefies me, which leads me to the gratifying conclusion that I must have had good taste in saxophone players when I was fifteen.

For all of my life since, Hawkins has been a kind of musical lodestar, as he must have been for thousands of other musicians, an infallible fount of harmonic and melodic wisdom from which issued every now and again the definitive jazz statements of the day. There was a period, in my earlier days as a professional musician, when my fervent evangelizing in the cause of Lester Young, at that time a scandalously neglected player (he received exactly one vote in the 1944 *Esquire* critics' poll), misled some people in to thinking I was rejecting Hawk, which is an interesting illustration of how boneheaded jazz thinking has so often been. The great achievement of Lester was not that he superseded Hawk—nobody human could ever do that—but that he gave jazz an alternative method to Hawk's, a feat which in itself was a stroke of genius.

Probably Hawk performed the symbolic act of his maturity when in 1929 he cut a version of *If I Could Be with You One Hour* with the Mound City Blue Blowers, and eradicated finally and completely the last lingering vestiges of that angularity and brittleness which marks the saxophone jazz of the 1920s. From that point on, his genius ran riot, spilling and splashing all over Europe, producing the superlative 1937 sides with Django Reinhardt and Benny Carter in Paris, the miraculous paraphrase of *Body and Soul* in 1939, and a version six years later of *It's the Talk of the Town,* which is less celebrated than some of the earlier sides only because as the years went by people tended to take for granted Hawk's intuitive grasp of form in the jazz solo.

For the last twenty-five years of his life, Hawk was lionized wherever he went, but even so, it has always been my suspicion that for all the accolades, the princely receptions, the sackloads of superlatives, Hawk remains an underrated and incompletely understood musician.

Not that any of us was dilatory in recognizing his genius. But his vast body of work remains neglected because there has never been enough time to digest it. What Hawk could play in five minutes, it might take a contemplative mind five years to plumb to the very depths, and for my part, although I first heard the Paris recordings back in the war years, have lectured on one of them in particular, *Out of Nowhere,* have written at length about it, delivered broadcasts on it, analyzed it, written it out, even learned to play it parrot-fashion, I am still totally unable to locate the wellsprings of inventive resource which make such a performance possible.

By now it will no doubt have become apparent to the reader that on the subject of Hawkins I am incapable of anything even remotely resembling objective criticism, which is hardly surprising, as no such thing as objective criticism exists anywhere. All criticism of all things is intensely subjective, and mine of Hawkins is nurtured by affection, love, idolatry, whatever the right word is to define the mixed emotions of jubilation, gratitude, and awe with which I receive his music. Although I never met the man till the last days, when the whiskers were white and venerable on his face, in a sense we have been close ever since *Stardust,* and for that reason, when Hawk died, a little bit of my good was interred with his bones. For like so many other aspiring saxophonists, I invested far too much of the emotional capital of my youth in Hawk not to have felt diminished when finally he died, a grand old man in every sense of the word.

To suggest that there is anything on this album to compare with the towering genius of, say, the 1937 *Crazy Rhythm* or the 1945 *Wrap Your Troubles in Dreams* would be not only to inflate the pretensions of Hawk's last works, but also to debase the currency of that criticism which rightly acknowledged the works of his prime as masterpieces. On the other hand, Hawk is one of those jazz musicians, like Louis Armstrong and Charlie Parker, whose every note is vital if we are to form a complete picture of the man. This is the album which none of us ever wanted to hear, the last milestone on that long fascinating road which stretches back to the day in 1922 when, as part of Mamie Smith's Jazz Hounds, Hawk first made his bow in a recording studio. Why a man should want to go on trying for so long is another one of those mysteries like the one embedded in the mysterious contours of *Out of Nowhere*. I only know that in this last version of *Don't Blame Me,* the grave, contemplative beauty of Hawk's opening thoughts is truly reminiscent of the grand designs of his greatest years, that in *Sugar* he is not so senile that he cannot adjust that hoary old chord sequence with a series of descending minor seventh chords here and there, that in *Sweet and Lovely* there are some surprisingly significant shapes being sketched in when Hawk arrives each time at the release, and that tonally in *Just a Gigolo* we can still hear echoes drifting across from the past of a master musician. I remember thinking, when I last saw him play, when he was already a man three-quarters dead, that however frail the husk might be, somewhere inside there remained intact the heart of a lion, a conclusion which, having listened to these last tracks, I will settle for. I believe that Coleman Hawkins was a great artist, and I am sorry he never turned out to be immortal.

(1975)

STANLEY DANCE

For years regarded as one of the premier experts on the career of Duke Ellington, with whose band he traveled off and on for decades, **Dance** came to the United States from England in the late 1950s. Not a fan of modern jazz, **Dance** has contributed much to our picture of the lives and work of musicians from the Swing Era, especially in his books **The World of Duke Ellington** and **The World of Earl Hines**. His tart and elegant writing may still be read in **Jazz Times**.

The Wild Man from Texas

Arnett Cobb
(Classic Jazz CJ 102)

Arnett Cobb is one of the most cheerful, warm, and humorous musicians engaged in the business called jazz. Unlike most of those who sing the blues about the dues they've paid, Cobb has really had a whole lot of pain, bad luck, and trouble, far more than any one man might expect in a lifetime. Yet whenever adversity struck him down, he emerged from the hospital prepared to blow, and swing, and fight again. The

Lord certainly gave him the strength to bear his crosses. Or perhaps a better word for the gift would be *courage*.

Nowadays, he swings across the stage to his chair on a pair of crutches, and lays them down. Most of the time, slightly hunched, he will stand on his own two feet to take his solos. The music that emerges from his horn communicates with equal power on two levels, the lyric and the rhythmic. He likes to play ballads in a breathy subtone, phrasing the melody so that it swings, and then increasing the rhythmic emphasis as his improvisation develops chorus by chorus. If he gets carried away by emotional stress, he will often return to the melody and exit with a quiet theme statement, just as one of his idols, Ben Webster, liked to do. In between, there may well have been some outrageous quotations, apparently delivered deadpan unless you caught the twinkle in his eye.

There has been a great deal written about the "big sound" of tenor saxophonists born or raised in Texas. It is a big state, of course, and a big sound is appropriate to it, but Arnett Cobb offered an explanation of how the sound came into being in his case: "When I was a kid, I used to take my horn, the music, and the music stand out on the prairie back of the house. I'd practice by the hour out there!"

In the earliest beginnings of jazz, the New Orleans musicians who played on the streets were famous for their big, carrying tones. A familiar, possibly apocryphal story tells how Buddy Bolden could be heard clear across the river from Algiers, and on hot, still nights sounds have a freakish way of traveling. But the *basic* model for most of the Texas tenors was the man from St. Joseph, Missouri, the man with the biggest tone of all—Coleman Hawkins. Herschel Evans, Buddy Tate, Budd Johnson, Jesse Powell, Maurice Simon, and even Booker Ervin were all spiritually descended from him, although in later years the younger men would show the influence of Lester Young and others, too. Illinois Jacquet owed something to Hawkins via Herschel Evans, and Arnett Cobb's inspiration stemmed from the same source via Joe Thomas, his close friend in Jimmie Lunceford's band. (For some strange reason, the importance of Lunceford's chief stars—Willie Smith, Trummy Young, Sy Oliver, and Joe Thomas—tends to be minimized by latter-day historians, but these four exerted a widespread influence in the thirties and early forties.)

Cobb's senior by some nine years, Thomas was an exciting and determined swinger, one who really believed, like Ellington, that "It don't mean a thing if it ain't got that swing." Born in Uniontown, Pennsylvania, in 1909, he too was influenced by Hawkins, and also by Lunceford's great lead alto, Willie Smith, just as Ben Webster was first influenced by Hawkins and then by Ellington's alto giant, Johnny Hodges. Thomas simplified the Hawkins style in order to swing to the utmost, and he developed a very personal tone that had an arresting vocal quality. Hawkins' vocalized tone and singing lines were a major inspirational factor in the thirties, but in assimilating it musicians like Thomas and Chu Berry still managed to preserve their own individuality. Despite the pronounced vocal character of his tone, too, Arnett Cobb is always easily distinguishable from Thomas, but in terms of attack the two are truly soul brothers.

The entwining history of the great tenor saxophonists is thus full of surprises. The saxophone, for example, was not Cobb's first instrument. Born in Houston, Texas, in 1918, he was first taught piano by his grandmother and then studied violin, but the look of the saxophone attracted him and by the time he was fifteen he was proficient enough on it to join the local band of Frank Davis. His next step was to Chester Boone's band for two years, and from there he went to Milt Larkins' for nearly six. Larkins had played trumpet with Boone and in 1936 he got the opportunity to take a big band into a Houston ballroom. This band was to prove a remarkable incubator of talent. From it, Cleanhead Vinson went to Cootie Williams, and Illinois Jacquet to Lionel Hampton. Jacquet had been playing alto saxophone with Larkins, but he switched to tenor and was an overnight sensation on *Flying Home,* although it was another Texas tenor, Budd Johnson, who played on Hampton's first record of that number. Meanwhile, Cobb had turned down an offer to take Herschel Evans' chair with Count Basie. The Larkins band was a success, toured the country, played at the Apollo Theater in Harlem, and then secured a long engagement at the Rhumboogie in Chicago. The onset of World War II brought problems, however, and in 1942 Cobb accepted an offer from Lionel Hampton to take Illinois Jacquet's place.

The excitement Jacquet had caused made the fans debate the possibility of *anyone* successfully filling his chair, but in a very short time Arnett Cobb proved he was more than capable. Extending Jacquet's original solo, he was soon creating more excitement than ever, and *Flying Home No. 2* was the recorded proof. He became known as "The Wild Man of the Tenor Sax," his uninhibited blowing making him a major asset of Hampton's band for five years.

He formed his own small group in 1947 and recorded hits like *Dutch Kitchen Bounce* and *When I Grow Too Old to Dream,* but was forced to disband to undergo a protracted period of hospitalization the following year, a result of a spinal injury as a child. He got another group together in 1951 and had more than recaptured lost ground when, in 1956, he had a serious automobile accident and broke both legs. His doctors advised him to give up playing, but he began touring again in 1957, this time with crutches. It made work hard and tiring for him, so from 1958 onward he stayed home in Houston for long periods, playing local gigs, leading his own group, teaching, and sitting in with visiting bands like Ellington's—all between further spells of hospitalization.

In 1973 he went to New York to play in a concert with Illinois Jacquet and his brother, and then on to France for a tour instigated by Jean-Marie Monestier, the sagacious proprietor of

Black and Blue records. The French had never forgotten his work with Hampton, and now they were astonished and delighted to find him playing as well as ever. He was reunited there with his old friend and associate in the Hampton band, organist Milt Buckner, whose career had received a new lease on life in Europe, just as Sidney Bechet's had years before. Cobb returned in 1976, when this album was made, and a year later was the veritable sensation of the Nice Festival. Opportunities for him to be heard were also occurring more often in his own country. At the last night of the 1978 Newport Jazz Festival in New York, he participated in a tribute celebrating Lionel Hampton's fiftieth anniversary in the music business. The Carnegie Hall audience gave him a standing ovation for his solos, which included one on *The Nearness of You* as here. A couple of days later, he was off to Nice again!

In between such jaunts, he can be found in his hometown, more than likely blowing up a storm at the Club la Veek on Blodgett Street, where everybody in the room seems to be his friend, including the tall, lean men who keep their big Texas hats on as they dance energetically with girls half their age. Arnett leans back on his chair while the organist takes a couple of choruses. He is smiling. After all, life is to be lived, and life is to be enjoyed.

This set divides Arnett Cobb's chief musical impulses neatly by putting the more rhythmical material on the first side, the more lyrical on the second. *Smooth Sailing, Dutch Kitchen Bounce,* and *Flying Home No. 2* are three of the numbers for which he is most famous, and they are given definitive, swinging treatment. No matter how often he plays them, Cobb finds fresh ideas as he improvises. Different accompanists result in different routes being taken. Like *The Nearness of You, Smooth Sailing* was effectively arranged by pianist André Persiany. Eddie Chamblee, who was one of Cobb's successors in the Hampton orchestra, plays the bridge in the climactic choruses of *Flying Home,* and the second sixteen bars in each of the first two choruses of *Where or When*. For the most part, however, the band's role is supportive while the stars, Cobb and Buckner, are in the foreground. The latter not only plays organ in his inimitable manner, but also vibes in a sparkling style reminiscent of their onetime leader, Lionel Hampton. A rapport derived from long association is not hard to understand, but what is a little surprising is the undiminished drive and enthusiasm these two veterans still possessed and revealed in the course of this happy encounter. As you will hear, they were cooking, not just going through the motions on old routines.

(1978)

ORRIN KEEPNEWS

Keepnews has had a long and illustrious career in jazz, as one of the editors of the seminal magazine **The Record Changer** in the late 1940s and early 1950s and then as founder, producer, and liner note writer for Riverside Records (and later, Milestone), one of the most important jazz labels of the 1950s. **Keepnews** either discovered or brought into the limelight some of the most important jazz musicians of our time, including Wes Montgomery, Bill Evans, and, above all, Thelonious Monk. He is still extremely active as a producer of reissues.

April in Paris

Thelonious Monk
(Milestone M-47060)

There's a timeworn cliché telling us that "Those who can, *do;* those who can not, *teach.*" I suspect this may be a saying largely kept alive at colleges by students looking to put down their instructors: If the professor were really a master of the subject, he'd be out in the world of action, instead of lecturing about it in academic seclusion.

It is a concept with a certain amount of truth to it,

but like a lot of clever phrases, what it fails to say is probably even more valid. For it ignores a most important category: those who are constantly giving postgraduate courses right out there in the real world, who are able—usually without being aware of it and certainly often without wanting to do it—to teach by example. In effect, great artists and scholars and performers who teach *by* doing.

All of which is one way to lead up to my very strong belief that Thelonious Monk is (or, at least, until he took himself entirely off the scene in the mid-1970s, *was*) among the greatest teachers I have ever known.

To the best of my knowledge, Thelonious has never had a student in the formal sense. Actually, the idea of Monk giving lessons has to conjure up in anyone who knows him a mental picture that is both funny and deeply frightening. Thelonious has never been a verbally articulate man—unless you listen very attentively. He has never been a patient man in the usual sense of accepting the gradual growth of understanding on the part of those around him; he isn't good at waiting for others to grasp slowly (if at all) things that are immediately, perhaps instinctively, clear to him. And he has never been overly tolerant of other musicians: In the liner notes to a 1956 album, I described him as "a hard taskmaster at a recording session...who drives the others as hard as he drives himself—which ... is possibly a little unfair of him."

So he certainly lacks some, probably most, of the major requirements of a teacher. But his influence, both direct and indirect, has been incalculable: through his own work, that of his disciples, and of those who have even unknowingly received a small spark from him and passed it on; and also through the music he has written, and the drastically varying ways in which he and others have performed and recorded it. Sonny Rollins and I have talked more than once on this subject and have come to the same conclusion: Each of us was closely associated with "The

High Priest" at an early and formative stage in our respective careers, and in quite separate ways absorbed extremely different but equally important lessons.

For me, it was first of all a matter of being exposed to a situation I was quite inadequately prepared to handle. I first dealt with Monk in a recording studio setting in the summer of 1955. I was at the time what can only be called a self-described record producer: I was one for no better reason than that I said so. Since I was one of two partners who were the management (and virtually the entire staff) of the fledgling Riverside label, there really was no one to contradict me. In fairness to my younger self, I should note that I was following an established path of the day. As a jazz fan turned producer, I was merely emulating several predecessors, including Alfred Lion of Blue Note and Bob Weinstock of Prestige. But I must also admit, looking back on that scene from the vantage point of today, that I would never consider entrusting so important a session—the debut appearance on the label of a major artist who was also a famous eccentric—to such a novice. In 1955, I had very few sessions under my belt, and working with gentle and totally cooperative people like Randy Weston and Mundell Lowe was certainly not suitably heavy experience.

I did more or less dodge the bullet for a couple of albums. My partner, Bill Grauer, and I had virtually stolen Thelonious from Prestige. (To put it more kindly, the artist wanted out and the company couldn't have cared less—how could Weinstock have known that the move would turn out to be the making of Riverside?) Aware that "The High Priest of Bebop" mystique, originally created as a Blue Note publicity device, had backfired into frightening potential listeners away, we began with two trio albums of standard tunes, the first all-Ellington and the other a mixed bag. It was our reasonably accurate belief that by avoiding both the use of horns and Monk's angular original compositions, we might help bridge the gap between him and the jazz public, as well as demonstrating to certain critics that he really could play piano well enough to execute normal chord progressions and known melodies.

Thelonious accepted the Ellington idea without visible reservation (although he had never previously recorded any of Duke's pieces, and as far as I could tell was still learning some of them from the sheet music as we began the first session). We got through both albums with relative lack of tension, although I am more aware now than at the time that I was being put through various little tests. *Item:* We canceled the very first session when the highly reliable Kenny Clarke failed to show up (when eventually contacted, he insisted Monk had given him the wrong date; and I believed him) and I vetoed the leader's suggestion that we use Philly Joe Jones instead. The point is not that I later came to value Philly's work inordinately (he probably played more Riverside sessions than any two other drummers), but that at the time I didn't know who the hell he was and I declined to be manipulated. *Item:* The aforementioned on-the-scene "learning" of the Ellington music; I've never really known how much of that was real and how much a put-on, but I didn't flip out and didn't climb anybody's back about the passage of costly studio time, and eventually the music got onto the tape as interesting, unstudied, and unique performances, and it turned out to be a lastingly valid album.

Emboldened by surviving the first two albums and getting pretty good response to them from the world—even to having some critics express annoyance because we didn't let Thelonious be himself and play his own far-out material!—I marched bravely into the LP that came to be *Brilliant Corners.* This is well-remembered by me as the album that led my wife to tell me: "Next time you're recording Monk, don't come home; just check into a hotel until the whole thing is over." Meaning that I had begun to learn an important lesson about staying under control during a session: Keep the tensions bottled up inside; you can always blow up when you get home! This was the album on which, at one session, Monk devised an impromptu self-duet, playing piano with one hand and celeste simultaneously with the other. It was also the one on which Monk's uneven bar structure and arranged tempo changes drove such professionals as Max Roach, Oscar Pettiford, and Rollins to such distraction that in four hours of work we never managed a single complete take. (The issued version represents my first real tape-editing achievement.) It's the album at whose last session I was startled to encounter two substitutes for sidemen Monk had fired without telling me. (On the other hand, the replacements were merely Clark Terry and Paul Chambers.) What I was learning, in that tough school, is best expressed as: Once I'd been broken in by an apprenticeship with Thelonious, no way was any other musician ever going to scare me—or any kind of in-studio problem whatsoever shake me up.

There were other valuable things to learn from this man, including one basic law I suspect some producers have never come to understand, that in jazz (perhaps not elsewhere, but certainly in jazz) the artist is what it's all about. His music and personality is what you are trying to express, not your own; so that each leader you work with requires a different kind of approach, a different working relationship. Flexibility is far more valuable to a jazz producer than a specific personal style.

The bebop school in which Monk himself learned was a tough turf: The almost entirely white world of club owners, music publishers, and record companies (and, never forget, the Law) gave jazz musicians very little respect and, on occasion, some possibly slightly inaccurate accountings. The term that cropped up a couple of decades later to describe a breed of country music performers—the Outlaws—would have fit very well for Monk and Bird and their associates. To make matters worse, even musical contemporaries often had a hard time adjusting to the jagged eccentricities of Thelonious' performances and compositions. And when some critics got around to jumping on the new music bandwagon, they insisted on relegating Monk to the back of the wagon. For example, Leonard Feather's 1949 book, *Inside Bebop,* which asserted that "high-powered publicity" had led to Monk's importance being "grossly" overstated. While admitting that he was an "original thinker" and had "written a few attractive tunes," Feather devoted more attention to Monk's "often falling asleep at the piano" at Minton's, to "his lack of technique and continuity," and to the rather bizarre statement that "it cannot be too strongly emphasized ... that he is not a bebop pianist." I quote all this not to scold Leonard (he has long, long since revised his attitude; and God knows *none* of us should be held accountable for three-decades-old statements), but to stress that it took a very long time for most mortals to begin to understand what Monk was all about. A few more-than-mortals (like Rollins, Milt Jackson, Art Blakey) did catch on early, but it is quite understandable that the man could have had a large chip on his shoulder at the time I began working with him. Among the lessons this leads to is: If the artist in the studio is feeling a draft, that's your problem rather than his—*if* you remember that your primary goal is to produce the best possible record.

There is of course a corollary to that lesson, also Monk-taught: Don't roll over and play dead, either. The scheduled first session for my fourth Monk album, the basically solo-piano *Thelonious Himself,* never took place because he arrived at the studio something like an hour and a half late (there *had* been a couple of "He's on his way"-type phone calls) and in no way prepared to work. More in anger than in sorrow, I delivered a fairly pompous lecture about my need to respect myself regardless of how he might feel, and telling him that, while I'd consider half an hour late to be close enough for jazz (and I've held to that time frame ever since), he needn't bother to come to the studio any later than that because I wouldn't be there. We set up a new date; I arrived about fifteen minutes early; and there in the control room sat

Thelonious, waiting for me. He gave me that huge slow smile of his and asked, very quietly: "What kept you?" It was a beautiful session.

I wouldn't go so far as to say that the remainder of my six years of working with Monk were serene, but thereafter I considered myself a well-schooled professional, aware of the kind of severe crises and last-minute major adjustments that are the routine facts of recording life. He and I functioned well together through a total of twelve and a half albums. (The half was the single session that was all I was able to record with the quartet that featured Coltrane, for various contractual and personality reasons touched on in my producer's note to the *Monk/Trane* twofer—Milestone M-47011.) That total does not include the performances reissued here; I had nothing to do with recording this concert. Actually, by the time this material was first released, the relationship between Thelonious and Riverside was over. It was a familiar enough story for that period in jazz: The once esoteric artist grows "popular" enough to be attractive to a giant company, and his advisers feel that a move up to presumably higher status will improve his career. In the 1950s, Prestige had lost Miles Davis to Columbia and the Modern Jazz Quartet to Atlantic under such circumstances, and those maneuvers would certainly seem to have paid off. For Riverside, this was the first such raid (in the same year, 1961, Cannonball Adderley had elected to stick with us), and it hurt. I couldn't entirely blame Thelonious, nor take any satisfaction from the fact that there was no real creative progress displayed in his several albums for Columbia; but I am certain that a lot of good music remained unborn because we had to stop working together.

I've never fully understood the means by which Bill Grauer, who was the business head of Riverside, came into possession of these concert tapes; my best recollection is that either the promoters or French radio had recorded them. In any event, they gave us a viable solution after we complained to the musicians union that Monk's Riverside contract remained unfulfilled—and, somewhat to our surprise, they agreed that he owed us a couple of albums before he could go to work for Columbia. This could have been a rather hollow victory (how do you force a reluctant artist into a studio?), but by paying proper fees to the leader and his sidemen for this Paris concert material and some similar tapes made in Milan, everyone was able to wind up more or less happy.

There is much that is intriguing and rewarding in this music, particularly when considered in the context of Monk's career during the preceding dozen years—but also if you just plain listen to it as good, swinging, "live" Thelonious. It's played by a tight-knit quartet whose tenor player was already well into the longest term of service by far of any of Monk's several notable hornmen. Charlie Rouse was the immediate successor to Johnny Griffin, who had followed Coltrane. He had already recorded with the pianist on three occasions, although this was the first to involve only the working group. [The historic February 28, 1959, Town Hall concert had included three quartet numbers that weren't adequately recorded; the album is made up of seven-horn band versions of Monk classics, with Rouse on tenor. Similarly, an album recorded during an April 1960 San Francisco club appearance added two guest horns to the basic lineup. Both of these have been reissued as the Milestone twofer *In Person*. In between were June 1959 session resulting in an LP by quartet-plus-Thad Jones; that is combined with the *Brilliant Corners* material in the reissue titled *Brilliance*.]

This Paris concert was part of Thelonious' very first European tour. Even considering that his stature didn't begin to be recognized in his own country until the late fifties, and that American jazz artists weren't being booked over there all that frequently in those days, his European debut was pretty disgracefully overdue. That makes it appropriate that the program was on the order of a capsule history of his career. *Off Minor* and *Well, You Needn't*, for example, were first recorded for Blue Note by a trio including Art Blakey. The date was October 24, 1947, and it was only Monk's second recording session as a leader. *Epistrophy* and *I Mean You* were made the following July by a quartet with Milt Jackson. By 1961, all four had of course become staple items in his repertoire, but they had not remained static. While preparing these notes, I did some comparative listening (all four are also on earlier Monk Riverside albums), and rediscovered that the alterations in approach and performance are fascinating. I recommend the procedure as a good course in Monk-listening.

Noting that Frankie Dunlop is the drummer in this unit (he had been with Thelonious for about a year at the time and stayed with him for several more), I was reminded of a conversation with Tony Williams during a mid-seventies McCoy Tyner trio date that also included Ron Carter. They were about to do a Monk tune, and Tony spoke of listening, as a teenager in Boston, to this very quartet. He recalled being fascinated by the way Dunlop literally played melody on *I Mean You,* catching every accent along with the piano. That was how Monk wanted it, Carter told us from experience; he had subbed with them on a couple of occasions, and so he also knew that playing it that way was extremely rough on the bassist. The result was a decision to have McCoy and Tony play the piece as a duet, which is how it appears on Tyner's *Supertrios* album—yet another example of the all-pervasive influence of Thelonious!

Of the remaining six selections here, two were first recorded during Monk's early-fifties Prestige period (*Hackensack* and *Just a Gigolo*). The other two standards on Side 1 (*April in Paris* and *I'm Getting Sentimental Over You*) can both be heard in solo form on the *Pure Monk* reissue (M-47004); they were originally part of the Riverside *Thelonious Himself* project. Monk wrote *Rhythm-a-ning* for a 1957 date with Gerry Mulligan; and the youngest composition here, *Jackie-ing,* first appeared on the 1959 album with Thad Jones. The previous comment about the artist's changing approaches to his material of course applies, in varying degrees, to all of the above.

As of now—early 1981—Thelonious has in all probability not touched a piano key in nearly four years and I'd have to guess he's unlikely ever to perform in public again. The fact that school is no longer in session is a great loss, but those who did get to study with the master will always be grateful. And it should not be forgotten that, as long as the records remain available, there is no shortage of textbooks.

(1981)

*Straight
No
Chaser*

Thelonious Monk
(Columbia CL 2651)

This is a new album by Thelonious Monk, and therefore it is an important event—because everything musical that Monk does is of real importance.

This is not a matter of choice, but of inevitability. It would no more be possible for Thelonious to be trivial or casual or superficial than it would be for the sun to decide some morning to rise in the West. It is true that there is nothing specifically new or startling here: Monk is working in his customary quartet context, with tenor saxophonist Charlie Rouse, his constant associate since the start of the 1960s, and with a bassist and drummer who have also long been at his side. The repertoire includes three Monk compositions that are more than a decade old (although the very fact that two of them have not been re-recorded until now is in itself highly intriguing and promising). However, one does not look for new ground to be broken every time Picasso paints. The comparison is, of course, inexact, as are all comparisons in art, but the point is surely valid: A master has produced here a further example of his unique and valuable work, and that is quite enough reason for us all to be pleased and to hasten to treasure and enjoy it.

These opening remarks may seem rather extreme. That is exactly the way they are intended; after having heard and known Monk for nearly two decades, I have extreme feelings on the subject. I first met Thelonious in 1948 and was awed by his earliest records; subsequently, I have written about him, and produced about a dozen of his albums on another label. And I continue to listen to him avidly. As a result, I have long been thoroughly convinced of his abiding importance. It is not just that he was a founding father of modern jazz and has for twenty years been a vast influence on so many musicians. This is accurate, but it is not the essential truth. That truth is that Thelonious is important because he *exists*, because he and his music form an immense, unavoidable, and inevitable presence, like an Alp or the Mississippi River or summer.

Many people believe that Monk is a musical "revolutionary." But this is simply not the case: Such a revolutionary takes part in a deliberate overthrow or change of regime; by doing so, he inaugurates a chain of events that will almost certainly lead to further stylistic upheavals and render him passé. But mountains do not overthrow anything; nor do they ever become obsolete. Thelonious began to play in his own way at a particular time—about 1940—and a revolutionary new form of jazz called bebop eventually grew up around him. By now, bebop is rather old hat; but immutable Monk, who still sounds much as he did in the forties, is entirely alive and fresh. In a way, you might say, he has always had old-fashioned roots, deriving from the Harlem *stride* pianists of the thirties. (There's a lot of that feeling in the unaccompanied Monk treatment of Harold Arlen's 1931 *Between the Devil and the Deep Blue Sea;* in particular, he brings to my mind that other great musical humorist, Fats Waller.) But it is equally true that he is of the avant-garde: John Coltrane is close to being the patron saint of today's newest jazz wave, and many people, including Coltrane, readily grant how much the tenor player owes to a late-fifties period spent in Monk's quartet.

Yes, Monk can be quite a paradox. More accurately, by being so completely himself, he is often a source of confusion to would-be analysts, leading them to stumble into paradoxes. His work has been described by adjectives like *harsh, lean, angular,* which are accurate enough—except, what about the fact that he is also the composer of the incredibly lovely *'Round Midnight,* or that he can play as tenderly as he does here on Duke Ellington's *I Didn't Know About You?* It has been said that he lacks a sense of form and structure—and he often does seem to be attacking notes and even phrases at random. But it's also true that so many of his solos are remarkably faithful to the melodic line. And, to choose one arbitrary example, what could be more strikingly well-constructed than his accompaniment to Charlie Rouse's solo on *Straight No Chaser,* the album's title tune—complex at first, then progressively simpler, and finally silent for a few choruses before surging in to make his own statement.

As initially noted, there is some not-new music here. The *Japanese Folk Song* is new; it may be an original number inspired by a recent tour of Japan, or it may actually be a native folk tune (but no one's going to discover which by any such simple means as directly asking Thelonious!). Also, the two standards have not previously been done by him.

But *Straight No Chaser* dates back to the late 1940s and a Monk recording quintet featuring Milt Jackson and Art Blakey, while both *Locomotive* and *We See* were first presented in the early 1950s by a group that also included Blakey. However, one of Monk's most intriguing musical characteristics is his ability to adapt the performance of a number to fit specific instrumentation and personnel. Thus, all three are quite different from the original models—as good as new, and, in the case of the "neglected" two, perhaps even better, representing as they do the uniquely crosshatched mosaic created by superimposing mid-sixties performance onto earlier composition.

(1967)

The Freedom Suite

Sonny Rollins
(Riverside RLP 12-258)

> America is deeply rooted in Negro culture: its colloquialisms, its humor, its music. How ironic that the Negro, who more than any other people can claim America's culture as his own, is being persecuted and repressed, that the Negro, who has exemplified the humanities in his very existence, is being rewarded with inhumanity.
>
> —*Sonny Rollins*

One of the most exciting characteristics of the growing creative artist is that he seems to be in a constant, dynamic state of flux. His work is marked, above all, by an urgent sense of ferment, motion, change. Sonny Rollins is at this time clearly in this position.

It is already quite generally recognized in the jazz world that he is an artist of huge and as yet unbounded importance and potential. But it is far from easy to guess what Sonny will be up to next. (It isn't even *safe* to guess: Reviewers who first dogmatically pigeonholed him as a hard-bopper with a raw, harsh sound then had to listen as he developed a considerable ability to express a deep, if quite unique, sense of melodic lyricism.) He is not an infallible or even performer: that limited form of perfection cannot be one of the goals of the innovator and creator. It is of much more consequence to say that he is virtually never dull, and usually unpredictable. For example, while it probably remains accurate to label him a "blowing" musician, Rollins demonstrates on this LP (in the remarkable *Freedom Suite*) that that term can mean vastly more than just taking a loose string of choruses on a standard tune or routine original.

Sonny is working here with the instrumental format—a trio consisting of himself, bass, and drums—that has recently appealed most strongly to him. On one side he is concerned with the adventurous reworking of pop tunes, past and present: two waltzes (*Someday I'll Find You* and *Shadow Waltz*) to which he applies his own personal standard of lyricism; a new ballad from Meredith Willson's score for the Broadway hit, *Music Man;* and one of Matt Dennis' most melodic and most lasting tunes, *Will You Still Be Mine*. But the heart of the record is unquestionably the work that takes up all of Side 1: *The Freedom Suite*. Representing something that Sonny has never before attempted and that very possibly no one has ever attempted in precisely this way, it could turn out to be a jazz work of massive and lasting significance. And at the very least it must be judged a rare listening experience and a vivid proof that flux and change and the unexpected are among the most exciting qualities a creative artist has to offer.

The Freedom Suite is Sonny's first venture into extended composition. Just as Rollins' approach to his instrument and, for that matter, to the entire structure of modern jazz has been characterized by departures from accepted procedures and conventions, so is his concept of a long jazz piece a highly personal and unusual one. The suite is built on a very simple musical basis: It consists, fundamentally, of a single melodic figure, which is developed and improvised upon through several different phases. The difference between one of its separate sections and another may be a matter of tempo or of rhythm, or simply of mood. But these differences are actually secondary in importance to an overall feeling of unity of expression: The suite makes up a single complete whole, so that it is very much to the point and very much a part of the writer-performer's intention that it is presented here unsubdivided—as a full, uninterrupted record side, not as a series of separate tracks.

Precisely what this unity consists of is none too easy to describe; but having heard the piece several times, and having discussed it with Rollins, I feel that some understanding of its meaning is an important part of listening to it. Not completely essential, perhaps: It is probably possible to enjoy the suite very much merely as nineteen minutes of fascinating variations on a theme by a superior improvisor and two of the finest rhythm men in jazz. But that approach puts undue emphasis on the virtuoso aspects of the performance. True, it is no small matter for a single horn to carry nineteen minutes of music without ever becoming trite or repetitious. But if you stop with that, you are missing a great deal.

For this is, as very few pieces of jazz writing even attempt to be, music *about* a specific subject. It is, by title, about "freedom," but just as that one word itself means many things, so does its application here have many facets. In most fields of music, a composition that is about something is concerned with a concrete picture, is "program music." But in jazz, which is so much a music of personal expression, "program music" is more fittingly about some*one*. This suite, then, is "about" Sonny Rollins: more precisely, it is about freedom as Sonny is equipped to perceive it. He is a creative artist living in New York City in the 1950s; he is a jazz musician who, partly by absorbing elements of Bird and Monk and many others, has evolved his own personal music; he is a Negro. Thus the meaning of freedom to Rollins is compounded of all this and, undoubtedly, much more. In one sense, then, the reference is to the musical freedom of this unusual combination of composition and improvisation; in another it is to physical and moral freedom, to the presence and absence of it in Sonny's own life and in the way of life of other Americans to whom he feels a relationship. Thus it is not a piece *about* Emmett Till, or Little Rock, or Harlem, or the peculiar local election laws of Georgia or Louisiana, no more than it is *about* the artistic freedom of jazz. But it *is* concerned with all such things, as they are observed by this musician and as they react—emotionally and intellectually—upon him.

The suite is, then, in essence a work dedicated to freedom: It is dedication and homage and resentment and impatience and joy—all of which are ways that a man can feel and that this man does feel about something as personal and basic as "freedom"— and all expressed through the medium he best commands. Someone else, having something like this set of feelings, might write an essay or a novel or paint a picture, or, being artistically inarticulate, might ride a train to another city or get into a fight without knowing why. Sonny Rollins, being who he is, writes a musical theme and plays it. And (without ever talking about it in this way) communicates to two fellow musicians so that they support him most sympathetically and, in specific instances, create their own apt solo expressions of it. This, as closely as I can get to it, is what *The Freedom Suite* is.

Sonny Rollins is by now, to use the toastmaster's cliché, "a man who needs no introduction." For the record, he was born in New York in September 1929, has been playing tenor sax since 1946, first came into prominence playing alongside the late Clifford Brown in Max Roach's quintet in 1955, has most recently been leading his own small groups. It should also be noted in case anyone hasn't been listening lately, that Sonny has been the most sensational new jazz force of recent years, and that his impact has quite literally revolutionized jazz tenor playing. Max Roach and Oscar Pettiford have not needed introductions for many years: Let us just say that Max is the major jazz drummer and Oscar has comparable status among bassists of the past decade, and merely add that here they are up to the standard that their own past performances have set for them.

(1958)

FRANK KOFSKY

One of the militant jazz critics of the 1960s, **Kofsky** was a spokesman for the jazz avant-garde of the time. His work is a good example of the ways in which politics became an overt part of the discourse about jazz in the 1960s. His notes for this reissue of Sonny Rollins' **The Freedom Suite** make an interesting contrast to Orrin Keepnews' annotation of the original.

The Freedom Suite

Sonny Rollins
(Riverside 3010)

This record was originally released by Riverside, first under the name *The Freedom Suite* and then issued as *Shadow Waltz*. That small fact, seemingly innocuous, can be most instructive when properly interpreted.

I don't have my copy of *The Freedom Suite* at hand at the moment, but even though I haven't been able to look at it in months, I still recall that on the back cover there was a boxed color photograph of Sonny Rollins showing his head and the top third of his torso, naked; and also a brief statement by Sonny to the effect that though Afro-American art was at the basis of America's

220

popular humor and music, ironically the Afro-American himself had never been permitted to attain his freedom. *The Freedom Suite* was meant as his musical response to the enslavement (only the enslaved require liberation) of the black man in this country, formally before 1865 (the date of the Thirteenth Amendment's ratification), informally thereafter. It was at once both protest against the past and affirmation of the future—and perhaps more than anything, a statement of pride in the heritage of being born black.

For all of that, when the album was issued by Riverside for a second time, it was under the heading *Shadow Waltz* (the second-shortest track on the album) and *The Freedom Suite* had been considerably de-emphasized. Indeed, Orrin Keepnews, who wrote the notes for the second album and, if my memory serves me correctly, produced it originally, went to great pains to deny that Rollins' extended composition was primarily involved with the question of being a black man (or woman) in this country in the twentieth century—even though in so doing he directly contradicted what Rollins himself had written on the notes for the *Freedom Suite* LP.

I go into this matter now, first of all, because I assume that some knowledge of Rollins' motivation in recording *The Freedom Suite* is helpful, if not absolutely essential, in understanding it; and secondly, because Riverside's decision to reissue this album under a different title is, as I wrote in the opening paragraph, illustrative of the way in which the jazz world works.

In a moment of candor, the remarkable young tenor saxophonist Archie Shepp (who does not have many uncandid moments in any case) offered a pithy description of how jazz music is produced: "You own the music," he said, "and we make it." The "you," of course, refers to whites, and the "we" to blacks.

To an intelligent and unbiased observer—a man from Mars would do nicely—it would appear that Shepp's laconic statement is unexceptionable. Speaking generally (which means that there are some exceptions, but they are few in number), whites *do* own the clubs, control the recording companies, and publish the magazines that are involved with jazz; they also comprise the major portion of the jazz audience. The musicians, on the other hand, have been mostly black, and the significant innovators—from Louis Armstrong to Charlie Parker to the late John Coltrane—almost exclusively so. The latter state of affairs is hardly secret, as a glance at any of the myriad polls conducted by this or that magazine will readily attest.

This peculiar division of labor has some curious results. For one thing, many whites active in the jazz world do not like to have it pointed out to them that the bulk of the economic benefits from the music have been reaped by whites, while the bulk of the music itself has been created by blacks. Thus they tend to resist statements such as that by Shepp, or Sonny Rollins' assertion (in the notes to the original *Freedom Suite*) to the effect that Afro-American contributions are at the root of American popular culture. Even though such propositions would be regarded as unmistakably true by our mythical man from Mars, some whites seek to discredit them by labeling them manifestations of "Crow Jim" (implying that blacks are attempting to suppress whites by employing the same methods that have been used on them, which is absolutely and demonstrably false) or, more recently, of black nationalism. The same line of thinking also produced the metamorphosis of an album initially called *The Freedom Suite* into one blandly labeled *Shadow Waltz,* which is one reason why I have gone into the matter at such length here.

Very well, then, suppose we concede that *The Freedom Suite* was at least partially inspired by black nationalistic sentiments. Is this necessarily A Bad Thing? I do not think so at all. The people who employ "black nationalist" as an epithet to discredit anything of which they disapprove would have you believe that black nationalism is to be equated with hatred of anything white. To anyone who takes the trouble to look at nationalism, black or otherwise, objectively, however, such an implication is absurd (even the most militant nationalists do not reject out of hand joint action with whites for common goals). There are, of course, some types of nationalism—such as the nationalism of the Nazis in the Second World War and its latter-day successors—that are virulent and ultimately have to be extirpated. But not every nationalism need be of that stripe. Nationalism exists in all sizes and shapes; it may be nothing more than the determination to assert the positive values of one's cultural-social inheritance.

In that sense, black nationalism has long flourished in jazz, regardless of what its detractors would have you believe. When Miles Davis chose to drop the final *g* and title his composition *Walkin';* when the pianist Bobby Timmons attempted to capture the pattern of Afro-American speech by calling one of his pieces *Dis Hyeah* rather than *This Here;* when Charles Mingus evoked the spirit and feeling of a black working-class church with his *Better Git It in Your Soul;* when John Coltrane wrote works with names like *Dahomey Dance* and *Africa,* and Sonny Rollins authored one called *Airegin* (spell it backward)—all these were acts which affirmed the unique worth of blackness, of the contributions to mankind made by the Afro-American. Which means that such actions were inherently nationalist in character, as much of jazz is likely to be, consciously or otherwise, until we arrive at that Utopia where distinctions of social class and "race" no longer are a matter for concern.

If I have gone to great lengths to point up the nationalist sentiments which underlie Sonny Rollins' *Freedom Suite,* it is solely because I believe that one must take such sentiments into account before we can gain a full understanding of what Rollins aims at accomplishing in the *Suite.* To delve into this background, however, need not preclude our dealing with the *Suite,* and the other tracks on this album, in musical terms as well.

To begin with, there are Rollins' accompanists—on drums, Max Roach; on bass, the late Oscar Pettiford. Both men had proven, even before this recording was made late in the 1950s, that they were consummate masters of their respective instruments and a source of inspiration for younger musicians. They work closely and sympathetically with Rollins here, especially Roach, who was familiar with Rollins' idiosyncratic phrasing from the many months that the latter spent during the 1950s in the Roach–Clifford Brown quintet (and who has always been more or less explicitly a nationalist himself).

As for Rollins' solos, it ought not to be necessary to say more than that they are sterling examples of a kind of playing that he has made famous in jazz, one that has become thoroughly identified with him. Writing in the now-defunct *Jazz Review,* composer-musicologist Gunther Schuller first described Rollins' solo style as *thematic improvisation,* meaning that Rollins erects his solo edifices on a few simple phrases which serve as the basis for increasingly complex variations and elaborations. That mode of playing is much in evidence here, both on the shorter selections and on the extended *Freedom Suite.* The *Suite,* in fact, is for Rollins primarily a collection of short, related phrases that function as jumping off points for more prolonged improvisations.

Such is my overall interpretation of *The Freedom Suite,* which forms the core of this recording. It is not the most bland one I could have formulated and for that reason will probably not be universally accepted; but it is as close to the truth as I believe I can get. In any event, my hope is that it will prove of use to you as you dig ever deeper into the consciousness of its author, Sonny Rollins.

(1968)

AMIRI BARAKA (LEROI JONES)

A major poet, playwright, and political activist, **Baraka** was also an active writer about jazz during the 1960s, and a special champion of the black avant-garde players of the time. His book **Blues People** is one of the most widely read books on African American music.

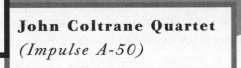

Coltrane Live at Birdland

John Coltrane Quartet
(Impulse A-50)

One of the most baffling things about America is that despite its essentially vile profile, so much beauty continues to exist here. Perhaps it's as so many thinkers have said, that it is because of the vileness, or call it adversity, that such beauty does exist. (As balance?)

Thinking along these lines, even the title of this album can be rendered "symbolic" and more directly meaningful. *Coltrane Live at Birdland.* To me Birdland is only America in microcosm, and we know how high the mortality rate is for artists in this instant tomb. Yet, the title tells us that John Coltrane is there *live.* In this tiny America where the most delirious happiness can only be caused by the dollar, a man continues to make daring reference to some other kind of thought. Impossible? Listen to *I Want to Talk About You.*

Coltrane apparently doesn't need an ivory tower. Now that he is a master, and the slightest sound from his instrument is valuable, he is able, literally, to make his statements anywhere. Birdland included. It does not seem to matter to him (nor should it) that hovering in the background are people and artifacts that have no more to do with his music than silence.

But now I forget why I went off into this direction. Nightclubs are, finally, nightclubs. And their value is that even though they are raised or opened strictly for gain (and not the musician's) if we go to them and are able to sit, as I was for this session, and hold on, if it is a master we are listening to, we are very likely to be moved beyond the pettiness and stupidity of our beautiful enemies. John Coltrane can do this for us. He has done it for me many times, and his music is one of the reasons suicide seems so boring.

There are three numbers on the album that were recorded *live* at Birdland: *Afro-Blue, I Want to Talk About You,* and *The Promise.* And while some of the nonmusical hysteria has vanished from the recording, that is, after riding a subway through New York's bowels, and that subway full of all the things any man should expect to find in some thing's bowels, and then coming up stairs, to the street, and walking slowly, head down, through the traffic and failure that does shape the area, and then entering "The Jazz Corner of the World" (a temple erected in praise of what God?), and then finally amidst that noise and glare to hear a man destroy all of it, completely, like Sodom, with just the first few notes from his horn, your "critical" sense can be erased completely, and that experience can place you somewhere a long way off from anything ugly. Still, what was of musical value that I heard that night does remain, and the emotions...some of them completely new...that I experience at each "objective" rehearing of this music are as valuable as anything else I know about. And

226

all of this *is* on this record, and the studio pieces, *Alabama* and *Your Lady* are among the strongest efforts on the album.

But since records, recorded "live" or otherwise, are artifacts, that is the way they should be talked about. The few people who were at Birdland the night of October 8 who really *heard* what Coltrane, Jones, Tyner, and Garrison were doing will probably tell you, if you ever run into them, just exactly what went on, and how we all reacted. I wish I had a list of all those people so that interested parties could call them and get the whole story, but then, almost anyone who's heard John and the others at a night-club or some kind of live performance has got stories of their own. I know I've got a lot of them.

But in terms of the artifact, what you're holding in your hand now, I would say first of all, if you can hear, you're going to be moved. *Afro-Blue,* the long tune of the album, is in the tradition of all the African-Indian-Latin-flavored pieces Trane has done on soprano, since picking up that horn and reclaiming it as a jazz in-strument. (In this sense, *The Promise* is in that same genre.) Even though the head-melody is simple and songlike, it is a song given by making what feels to me like an almost unintelligible lyricism suddenly marvelously intelligible. McCoy Tyner too, who is the polished formalist of the group, makes his own less cautious lyri-cal statements on this, but driven, almost harassed, as Trane is too, by the mad ritual drama that Elvin Jones taunts them with. There is no way to "describe" Elvin's playing, or, I would suppose, Elvin himself. The long tag of *Afro-Blue,* with Elvin thrashing and cursing beneath Trane's line, is unbelievable. Beautiful has noth-ing to do with it, but it is. (I got up and danced while writing these notes, screaming at Elvin to cool it.) You feel when this is finished, amidst the crashing cymbals, bombarded tomtoms, and above it all Coltrane's soprano singing like any song you can re-member, that it really did not have to end at all, that this music could have gone on and on like the wild pulse of all living.

Trane did Billy Eckstine's *I Want to Talk About You* some years ago, but I don't think it's any news that his style has changed a great deal since then, and so this *Talk* is something completely different. It is now a virtuoso tenor piece (and the tenor is still Trane's "real" instrument) and instead of the simplistic though touching note-for-note replay of the ballad's line, on this performance each note is tested, given a slight tremolo or emotional vibrato (note to chord to scale reference), which makes it seem as if each one of the notes is given the possibility of "infinite" qualification, i.e., scalar or chordal expansion, "threatening" us with those "sheets of sound," but also proving that the ballad as it was written was only the beginning of the story. The tag on this is an unaccompanied solo of Trane's that is a tenor lesson-performance that seems to get more precisely stated with each rehearing.

If you have heard *Slow Dance* or *After the Rain,* then you might be prepared for the kind of feeling that *Alabama* carries. I didn't realize until now what a beautiful *word* Alabama is. That is one function of art, to reveal beauty, common or uncommon, uncommonly. And that's what Trane does. Bob Thiele asked Trane if the title "had any significance to today's problems." I suppose he meant literally. Coltrane answered, "It represents, musically, something that I saw down there translated into music from inside me." Which is to say: Listen. And what we're given is a slow delicate introspective sadness, almost hopelessness, except for Elvin, rising in the background like something out of nature . . . a fattening thunder, storm clouds or jungle war clouds. The whole is a frightening emotional portrait of some place, in these musicians' feelings. If that "real" Alabama was the catalyst, more power to it, and may it be this beautiful, even in its destruction.

Your Lady is the sweetest song in the album. And it is pure song, say, as an accompaniment for some very elegant uptown song and dance man. Elvin Jones' heavy tingling parallel counterpoint sweeps the line along, and the way he is able to solo constantly beneath Trane's flights, commenting, extending, or just going off on his own, is a very important part of the total sound and effect of this Coltrane group. Jimmy Garrison's constancy and power, which must be fantastic to support, stimulate, and push this group of powerful (and diverse) personalities, is already almost legendary. On tunes like *Lady* or *Afro-Blue,* Garrison's bass booms so symmetrically and steadily and emotionally, and again, with such strength, that one would guess that he must be able to tear safes open with his fingers.

All the music on this album is *live,* whether it was recorded above the drinking and talk at Birdland, or in the studio. There is a daringly human quality to John Coltrane's music that makes itself felt, wherever he records. If you can hear, this music will make you think of a lot of weird and wonderful things. You might even become one of them.

(1963)

Lady-Love

Billie Holiday
(United Artists
UAJ-14014)

The Dark Lady of the Sonnets

Nothing was more perfect than what she was. Nor more willing to fail. (If we call failure something light can realize). Once you have seen it, or felt whatever thing she conjured growing in your flesh.

At the point where what she did left singing, you were on

your own. At the point where what she was was in her voice, you listen and make your own promises.

More than I have felt to say, she says always. More than she has ever felt is what we mean by fantasy. Emotion, is wherever you are. She stayed in the street.

The myth of blues is dragged from people. Tho, some others make categories no one understands. A man told me Billie Holiday wasn't singing the blues, and he knew. Okay, but what I ask myself is what had she seen to shape her singing so? What, in her life, proposed such tragedy, such final hopeless agony? Or flip the coin and she is singing *Miss Brown to You*. And none of you cats would dare cross her. One eye closed, and her arms held in such balance, as if all women were so aloof. Or could laugh so.

And even in the laughter something other than brightness, completed the sound. A voice that grew from a singer's instrument to a woman's. And from that (those last records critics say are weak) to a black landscape of need, and perhaps, suffocated desire.

Sometimes you are afraid to listen to this lady.

(1962)

J. B. FIGI

Chicagoan **J. B. Figi** was an early and vocal supporter of the avant-garde players of the 1960s, especially of the members of the AACM (Association for the Advancement of Creative Musicians). His notes for Roscoe Mitchell's **Sound** are a fascinating document of the time.

Sound

Roscoe Mitchell
(Delmark DS-408)

The Roscoe Mitchell Sextet is armed and dangerous, out to steal your mind. Not merely with names (Roscoe, Bowie), or even the metaphorical mortar of McIntyre's tenor, but with *inner armaments* of self and soul: insistent dignity, purposeful pride, the determination to fulfill themselves as creative beings. You can hear it in the music. All you really need know of these men is the music, the way they play together, the way they play their *selves*. The predatory levitations of Alvin Fielder, hovering like a hawk, demonstrating a drumming that is as much about sounds as rhythm, a Chinese calligraphy written across the music. Malachi Favors' autumnal pungence, wood and earth, dark and dry, dramatic bass structures that become an amen-choir. The big-throated voice of Lester Lashley's trombone, and the magic sewing machine of his cello. Sly extroversion from Maurice McIntyre, a lip-smacking Buddha; his sound—the roar of a moldy bronze lion come somehow to life, or the lonely iron croon of a buoy. Lester Bowie's horn, handled like the knife that shares his name, with keen edge and weight, cutting close to the bone. His appearance is particularly gratifying since only a half-handful of trumpeters have done well by the new music. Where most rip along in formless freedom, or cast careful statements which never gain motion, Bowie has excitement *and* a fine sense of running architecture. Roscoe Mitchell, the informing presence of the group, has driven the vocal cry and sudden structures of today's horns into a new intensity, and is one of the very best of them, an uncautious player who'll jump right out at you, take your throat, and shake. He'll surprise you, and so will the sextet, coming whole and unexpected as it does, but, even so, this phenomenon is only part of a larger phenomenon.

The *holy artistic family* that dances through the daydreams of certain seers of New York (where the climate of rampant ego would alone void such visions) is not a mirage. It does exist. In Chicago. Where musicians already pressed together by the frustrations of scuffling and sharecropping, of having their fates overseen by others, and by their own growing need to create a strong, daring music which would remain in the rightful hands of its makers, have drawn even closer together to shape a common answer. Their answer, their family, the Association for the Advancement of Creative Musicians, is the healthiest organism at work in jazz today. A large and benevolent family, it encourages individuality and freedom, yet has a remarkable spiritual unity. Its actions and attitudes have achieved an imposing communal dignity, offering its people the perfect framework for the accomplishment of their art. By producing its own concerts (all details handled by the musicians), the AACM has escaped the insensitive evils of the entertainment arena and afforded a positive setting for the member-units of Roscoe Mitchell, Joseph Jarman, Richard Abrams, Jodie Christian, Troy Robinson, the Artistic Heritage Ensemble, and the Experimental Band. Those concerts have been the ultimate vindication of the alliance. From them has come a music of such compelling strength and beauty, richness and diversity, as to shout down any doubts that this must eventually become the answer for serious jazz musicians everywhere.

As with any vital organization, the AACM is a convergence of individual voices and directions, toward the furtherance of a large goal. Many trains issuing from one roundhouse. Among them, Roscoe Mitchell has been a prime mover from the start, and, even earlier, was an important part of the Richard Abrams experimental band which laid so much of the track for the present Association. Lashley's virtuosity on three instruments (his bass is not heard on this album) has led him to work with most of the AACM groups. Fielder and Favors have been with Roscoe right along. Maurice's tenor burst upon us during the latest concert series, when he was heard in three of five concerts. Bowie, recently arrived from St. Louis, showed up as part of this sextet during the same series.

Ornette opens like a jack-in-the-box. Roscoe springs out, urging himself immediately on to a plane of cultivated hysteria, where *the tongues* are talked, whistled, and shrieked. Bowie slices in, notes falling as deftly as a tap dancer's steps, then powers ahead. Maurice indulges in belly-rubbing r&b drolleries, made abstract by the funhouse mirror of his mind. Then an incestuous dialogue of cello and bass, and back to the theme, the lines of which, along with the title, are self-evident marks of Mitchell's deep respect for Ornette Coleman, though Roscoe is quick to point out his awareness that respect must never be exaggerated into worship.

He explains *The Little Suite* as a "suite of colors," in which the instruments represent different and modulating colors. Colors, in this case, synonymous with moods. The listener may hear more definite human imageries. A rural Halloween, ritual march of children on the way to mischief, which becomes decidedly more devilish as it goes along. Although the playing throughout is beautiful (the puckish theme of Bowie's harmonica, his trumpet and mellow flugelhorn, McIntyre's honkings, the insertions of cello, bass, Roscoe's sax, clarinet, recorder, and whistle, drum clusters, and the playful gourd, maracas sounds), there are no solos as such; rather, a patchwork quilt of staggered statements, ever-shifting, Roscoe's own wild kind of warlock's brew.

Sound is something else again. Roscoe presents it as an exploration of the possibilities of unorthodox, yet meaningful, sounds inherent in the instruments. But it is far more than mere experimentation; a total piece of music, wholly shaped, sustaining a mood while varying it in pitch and intensity, a tour de force, each solo seeming to feed from the others. The stately lament of the theme invokes the dignified, deep melancholy of a dirge, a convocation of priests chanting a ceremonial death-song. The plaintive bells, mournful strikings of a half-filled water can, add to this feeling. Each priest steps forward from the circle to take his turn at elegy, at preachment. Bowie moans and mutters, lowdown nasty sounds reminiscent of Rex Stewart (*Menelik, The Lion of Judah*), while cymbals chatter and shimmer behind him. Maurice's message is a marvel of abstract construction, of off-center balance, of bent symmetry, his horn a heavy hammer, lusty and plangent, gathering earthly backtalk from the bass. The trombone edges in with slurs and soft whoops and groans, then opens into respectful rowdiness. Roscoe pipes his entrance. His mad, gnarled solo is that of the high priest, the exorcisor at work with strings threading and squealing at his side. Spirits speaking together. Malachi Favors has an impossible, wild-eyed, head-tossing bowed solo. You can almost smell his bass going up in smoke. A short cymbal summation recalls the theme. Somehow the same notes have now transcended anguish, have metamorphosed the occasion into something positive, subtly but firmly rejoicing an affirmation of life.

This album is the first of a series Delmark will issue as evidence of the music and musicians that have come tumbling from the cornucopia of the Association for the Advancement of Creative Musicians. In the future, there will be not only more Roscoe Mitchell, but recordings by Joseph Jarman and Richard Abrams as well. For now, hear the Roscoe Mitchell Sextet.

(1966)

ROBERT PALMER

Robert Palmer was the jazz, pop, and blues—he labels them all American vernacular music—writer for **The New York Times** during the 1970s and one of the most gifted and insightful music writers of the last thirty years. His book **Deep Blues** is a classic of American music writing.

Outer Thoughts

George Russell
(Milestone M-47027)

George Russell is approachable along many avenues. One is his theoretical masterwork, *The Lydian Chromatic Concept of Tonal Organization,* and the effect that this super-textbook has had on several generations of musicians. The MJQ's John Lewis called it "the most important theoretical contribution to come from jazz." Ornette Coleman said that "The Concept surpasses any musical information I have ever been exposed to." The Norwegian composer Kare Kolberg wrote that "The Lydian Chromatic Concept has previously been called a philosophy—one could just as well call it poetic, demanding without being binding, open without being anarchistic, precise without being petty. It tells you something about melodies and chords, which can be in-going and outgoing, but it also says something about an attitude to music generally, and about a human attitude."

Kolberg's comments suggest another avenue of approach. Russell the theoretician is important, but Russell the humanist is more immediately engaging. Russell the humanist titled some of his compositions *Lydiot, Takin' Lydia Home,* and *Oh Jazz, Po Jazz.* He directed his musicians into areas which can only be described as "pan-tonal dixieland," "free-form bebop," "21st-century soul music." He fashioned for two great jazz soloists—saxophonist Eric Dolphy and vocalist Sheila Jordan—arrangements which remain among their most effective vehicles, the stunning versions of *'Round Midnight* and *You Are My Sunshine* which are included in this album. He spoke directly, warmly, and eloquently in all of these performances, recorded by his various sextets and septets between 1960 and 1962.

A "New Thing," radical in its rejection of the bebop conventions of the forties and fifties, was being proposed by Coleman, Cecil Taylor, and other players during those years. Russell's music was more an expansion of bebop than an assassination of it; he proclaimed himself "an evolutionist, not a revolutionist." But his overhauling of previous procedures was so conceptually profound and operationally thorough, and his effect on most of the soloists who passed through his bands was so pronounced, that he effectively created a "New Thing" of his own. His thing juxtaposed playfully affectionate uses of jazz tradition with an occasionally austere formalism, blues and church roots with influences from serialism and *musique concrète.* The closest parallel is probably the music of Charles Mingus, but there was a crucial difference, namely Russell's invention and application of "a missing link that unites tonality with chromaticism." This brings us back to where we started, to Russell the theoretician, but in reality this forbidding creature and the humanist are inseparably one and the same.

The one and only George Russell has composition in his blood; his father was a professor of music at Oberlin. And his appreciation of early jazz derives from his childhood, when he heard the legendary Fate Marable's band playing on a riverboat. This was near Cincinnati, where Russell was born on June 23, 1923, and where composer-arranger Jimmy Mundy, then writing for Benny Goodman, was a neighbor and early influence. As a youngster, Russell played the drums in a Boy Scout Drum and Bugle Corps and, after age fifteen, in nightclubs. In 1940 he was a scholarship student in music at Wilberforce University and then, at age nineteen, he contracted tuberculosis and was forced to spend several months in a sanitarium. Those months were among the most important of his life, for he picked up the fundamentals of arranging from a fellow patient.

Soon after his discharge, Russell joined Benny Carter's big band as the drummer, and it was this group that played his first big band arrangement, aptly titled *New World*. Russell charts for Earl Hines followed and then, inspired by his first hearing of Monk's *'Round Midnight*, the young musician left the Midwest permanently for New York. There Charlie Parker asked him to join his quintet, again as a drummer, but another illness incapacitated him. It was during this second extended hospitalization, which lasted sixteen months, that Russell began his researches into tonality. On the street again, he lost no time putting his developing theories to work. He wrote and arranged *Cubano Be, Cubano Bop* for Dizzy Gillespie's big band—it was premiered in December 1947—and additional pieces for Claude Thornhill, Charlie Ventura, and Artie Shaw. His most ambitious work from this period, *A Bird in Igor's Yard*, was a remarkably successful synthesis of the harmonic and rhythmic innovations of Parker and Stravinsky. It was recorded by Buddy DeFranco and a studio big band in 1949, but the density and rhythmic daring of its opening blasts must have frightened someone at Capitol Records, for it remained unreleased until Dutch Capitol put it on an LP during the sixties (*Crosscurrents,* issued in the United States as Capitol M-11060). Another bristling Russell theme, *Ezz-thetic,* fared better. Charlie Parker and Lee Konitz performed it during the early fifties and in 1961 it became the title tune on Russell's second Riverside LP.

By 1953 Russell had completed *The Lydian Chromatic Concept of Tonal Organization,* a massive thesis which currently retails for $25.00. To be (necessarily) simplistic, the Concept attempts a redefinition of the idea of tonal gravity or *key.* The thesis that the melodic tone with the most repetition or duration in any given line is the true *key center* of that line, whether or not the key signature of the whole piece is the same, had been around for a while. Indeed, the soloists of the bebop era had improvised in, say, C while bassists and pianists fed them F♯ chords, capitalizing on the enharmonic relationship between F♯ as flat fifth in the key of C and C as flat fifth in the key of F♯ and thus creating a *de facto* polytonality. Russell began by extrapolating a "Lydian scale" (C, D, E, F♯, G, A, B) from this crucial intervallic relationship, laid it out as a cycle of fifths (C, G, D, A, E, B, F♯), and proceeded to build various other Lydian scales (Lydian diminished on C being C, D, E♭, F♯, G, A, B, and Lydian augmented being C, D, E, F♯, G♯, A, B) on each new key center in his cycle. The system extended from this basis until the improviser using it was able to think in terms of a Lydian Chromatic Scale having, quite naturally, twelve possible tonics or key centers. Once he had mastered this theory, he was able to (in Russell's words) "superimpose a sequence of scales (their modes or modal chords) upon a single chord or upon a horizontal sequence of chords ... When a single Lydian Chromatic Scale is imposed upon a sequence of chords, it (rather than each single chord of the sequence) becomes the center and conveyor of tonal gravity."

In other words, the improviser using Russell's Concept is able to utilize the expanded melodic vocabulary inherent in twelve-tone music *within the harmonic structures* of blues, standards, and other traditional forms. The result is a musical language to which Russell refers by using various words beginning with the prefix *pan*. Thus the Concept is "pan-tonal" as opposed to atonal, because (quoting Russell again) "jazz is a music that is rooted in folk scales, which again are rooted strongly in tonality. Atonality . . . is the complete negation of tonal centers . . . It would not support, therefore, the utterance of a blues scale because this implies a tonic. But pan-tonality is a philosophy which the new jazz may easily align itself with."

Bill Evans and Art Farmer were among the first jazzmen to "align" themselves with the Lydian theory, on Russell's 1956 RCA Victor LP and in the extended composition *All About Rosie*, performed with Evans as soloist at the 1957 Brandeis University Festival of Fine Arts. It was left to the composer to take the next significant step in the propagation of his approach and in August 1960, at the age of thirty-seven, he formed his first working group. In October the band recorded *Stratusphunk*, Carla Bley's *Bent Eagle*, and four other pieces for its first Riverside album. "I never really had my own means of direct expression as far as my music is concerned," Russell told annotator Chris Albertson. "You might say that I felt I needed an instrument, so there was no choice but to get a band." The players had all been students of Russell's at the summer School of Jazz in Lenox, Massachusetts, and saxophonist Dave Young, trumpeter Al Kiger, and drummer Joe Hunt had worked together previously in the University of Indiana Jazz Orchestra, directed by trombonist Dave Baker. Bassist Chuck Israels was from Stockbridge, Massachusetts, and had performed with Bud Powell in Europe.

Five of the six tunes on Russell's second Riverside LP, *Ezzthetic*, are included in this package. Two new and notable presences, Eric Dolphy and trumpeter Don Ellis, add considerable brilliance and depth to the music. Dolphy was along only on this session, but Ellis played on all the subsequent Riverside dates. Other major additions were bassist Steve Swallow (later a Gary

Burton mainstay) and, on the final date which yielded *Au Privave*, *Zig Zag*, *The Outer View*, and *You Are My Sunshine*, the excellent, underrecorded drummer Pete LaRoca. The music maintained an astonishingly high level of adventurousness and creativity throughout these continuing personnel changes. As Joe Goldberg observed in his notes to *The Outer View*, Russell "neither writes nor thinks in one groove. He likes to work in many ways: One piece may use old techniques and references, another may be entirely new." This refusal to be "bagged" kept the music fresh and appealing and provided an unpredictable but always intriguing counterbalance to the theoretical implications of some of the pieces, as did the contributions of the sextet /septet's best soloists.

These were undoubtedly Baker, Ellis, and (briefly but incandescently) Dolphy. The trombonist, who later became one of the most influential black music educators in America, displayed a fluid style which entailed ripping off streams of sixteenth notes like Jimmy Cleveland and, often in the same solo, delving into inflections and effects introduced by the likes of Joe Nanton and Jimmy Harrison. This style-mixing approach was also reflected in the trombonist's writing. *Honesty*, for example, takes the old idea of introducing each chorus of a blues with stop-time figures one step further; each chorus is introduced by a section in free time. Russell's chording on this piece suggests a sanctified church service, and Dolphy contributes some of his most moving blues playing.

Baker missed the *Outer View/Sunshine* sessions because of a dislocated jaw. His replacement, Garnett Brown, was then and is now an assertive original, equally at home recreating older styles with the New York Jazz Repertory Company and blowing with Billy Cobham's jazz-rock recording groups. Trumpeter Don Ellis had been leading an avant-garde trio in New York when he joined Russell's group, but his background included stints with Maynard Ferguson, Woody Herman, and Lionel Hampton, and he subsequently led a successful big band of his own. His work with Russell ranged from the tentative (*Ezz-thetic*), to the self-conscious (*The Outer View*), to the assured and highly distinctive (*Pan Daddy, The Stratus Seekers*). At his best, Ellis was an acutely sensitive and very witty style-mixer. His solo on *Honesty,* for example, pays homage to Rex Stewart and Henry (Red) Allen even as it hints at polytonality.

Eric Dolphy was subjected to frequent and often pointless criticism during his all-too-brief career, but his fellow musicians recognized his worth. When pressed to define it, they mentioned first the singularly vocal way he handled his horns and, second, his incredible rhythmic vitality. Yet his harmonic ear and melodic sense were no less extraordinary. In the present album, his solos on *Ezz-thetic* and *Honesty* raise the energy level of the tracks by quite a few notches—as Dolphy solos always seemed to do—but it is *'Round Midnight* that stands out. From the *musique concrète* sounds (played on acoustic instruments) which open the work to the almost terrifyingly vivid images of the final saxophone cadenza, this homage-to-Monk qualifies as a masterpiece.

The other masterpiece in the set is, of course, *You Are My Sunshine.* According to Joe Goldberg, "the arrangement...had its genesis when Russell and Miss Jordan were singing and playing for their own amusement in a small tavern in her home area, the coalmining region of Pennsylvania...The resulting treatment mirrors his impression of the humanity of the people pitted against the cold, bleak, often brutal demands of the region." Sheila's three choruses build to a pitch of guileless emotion which is quite unlike anything else in the jazz of the period, and the shifting voicings and rhythms of the arrangement, signaled by Russell's piano punctuations, are so evocative you can see and feel the Appalachian landscape.

Another lady figures prominently in this album. Carla Bley was a composition student of Russell's for a time during the early sixties and contributed the memorable *Zig Zag* and *Bent Eagle* to his Riverside sessions. During the early seventies, her *Escala-*

tor Over the Hill included sections written especially for Sheila Jordan.

Russell himself had become discouraged with the situation for creative musicians in America by the mid-sixties. He spent several years in Scandinavia, where his work was much more enthusiastically received and he was able to experiment with electronic music and write and direct performances of works for very large orchestras. He was also instrumental in shaping the styles of several of Europe's best young jazz players. His return to the United States in 1972 was announced by Columbia's release of the album-length work *Living Time,* featuring Bill Evans, and by the formation of Concept Productions for the dissemination of his writings, and of such recent recordings as his *Othello Ballet Suite* and *Electronic Sonata for Souls Loved by Nature.* The seeds of Russell's continuing, still-expanding creativity are very much in evidence in this reissue collection of courageously eclectic, ingeniously integrated, thoroughly enjoyable early-sixties performances.

(1975)

*Dogon
A.D.*

Julius Hemphill
(Arista 1028)

The Dogon of Mali are among the most remarkable and mysterious people in all of Africa. Most of them live in spectacular cliffside villages which are scattered along 125 miles of rocky escarpment to the southwest of the Niger bend. According to the French anthropologist Marcel Griaule, who studied them for nearly twenty-five years, "The Dogon live by a cosmogony, a metaphysic, and religion which put them on a par with the peoples of antiquity, and which Christian theology might indeed study with profit." Germaine Dieterlin, who accompanied Griaule on many of his expeditions, wrote that the elaborate cosmology of the Dogon "inspires, directs, and permeates all their activities. It is in this perspective that, through the forms, colors, and even the materials used, the manifestations of their art—which is essentially symbolic—are seen to be linked with the system of the world as they conceive and live it... Music, which is associated with these same manifestations, seems to occupy a preeminent place. It was to the sound of a drum that speech, which was to distinguish man fundamentally from other living creatures, was revealed to the first men in mythical times by God, the creator."

The systematic world-view of the Dogon has been linked to Ancient Egypt through a variety of correspondences both in thought and in the artifacts which express it. Dogon sculpture, masks, and architecture have long been prized by Africanists, though these artifacts all have complex symbolic aspects which only Dogon initiates comprehend fully. The fascination of these people is that the more one understands, the more one realizes how much is hidden. Perhaps it was this quality which attracted Julius Hemphill to them, for in his music, his poetry, and his works for the stage, Hemphill presents a multiplicity of incantations, symbols, and ritual actions which express an underlying unity—the unity of one world of black culture and of the word or sound or drumbeat which created this world and best expresses it.

Hemphill produced *Dogon A.D.* himself in 1972 and released it on his own Mbari label. Since that time it has become an authentic underground classic, and reviewers in various publications have compared it to the finest works produced by improvising musicians during the past decade. Part of its attraction was its uniqueness, for until late last year, when Arista/Freedom released Hemphill's *Coon Bidness,* there was nothing remotely like it in anyone's discography. The title tune in particular is a strikingly original, fully formed vision. The cello-drums rhythm section lays down a loping, rocklike ostinato-with-a-backbeat, and the spacing of the horn lines is rocklike as well. But there is a starkness to the music that separates it decisively from all the glib fusions perpetuated in the name of jazz rock, and Hemphill and trumpeter Bakaida E. J. Carroll do not deliver fashionably funky solos but instead testify at length, with a fervor reminiscent of some of the Southern and Southwestern shouting preachers recorded by the Library of Congress during the thirties.

Here we have a key to the strength of the music. It is so deeply rooted in back country preaching and ring shouts and string band music and blues, especially blues, that it sounds, on first hearing, almost primitive. That Hemphill is no stranger to this bedrock of American music goes without saying: He played with Ike Turner and with a number of Southern and Southwestern blues bands before joining the Black Artists Group of St. Louis in 1968. But he shares this background with a number of his contemporaries. The remarkable thing about Hemphill is that he is able to use his roots so lavishly and with such feeling while allowing himself and his musicians a great deal of exploratory latitude. *The Hard Blues,* which was recorded during the sessions which produced this LP and released on *Coon Bidness,* illustrates this accomplishment well, but it does not quite measure up in terms of hypnotic power, terseness, and emotional weight to *Dogon A.D.*

But what does all this have to do with the Dogon? These cliff dwellers never influenced American music directly. Their region of Mali is far from all trade routes and is a difficult journey from any urban center in the region. When the slave raiders came, the

Dogon pelted them with rocks from their cliffs and drove them away. But the Dogon are also part of a larger culture, an African savannah culture which is dominated by their relatives the Mande peoples. And the savannah contributed much to American music. It contributed the banjo, and the frailing style in which white American mountaineers and a handful of very old Afro-Americans still play it. It probably contributed to the predisposition of the earliest black Americans toward fiddle music, for banjo-like instruments and fiddles are prominent throughout the West African savannah. So the earliest Afro-American string band music, the music which certain whites learned from slave orchestras on the plantations and parlayed into the peculiar institution of minstrelsy, was essentially a savannah music. And the English blues authority Paul Oliver has suggested, in his book *Savannah Syncopators,* that insofar as the blues owes its identity to origins in Africa, those origins are largely in the savannah.

Through some alchemy of inheritance, conscious will, and, perhaps, ecology (for Hemphill's home territory, Fort Worth, is flat and dry, like much of the savannah), the music on this record ended up resembling savannah music in several significant respects. Listen to the dry, crackling sound of Hemphill's alto saxophone, and to the slightly overblown, almost parched tone of his flute. Listen to the spare textures and deliberate ceremonial rhythm of the first piece, which sounds at times like an excerpt from a funeral on the French LP *Les Dogon* (Ocora OCR 33). Listen to the collective furor of *Rites,* which resembles the climax of the Dogon funeral on the same recording. Just why and how did this happen? The only answer must be that things as magically generative and sustaining as music, and especially music this powerful, can never be entirely explained. As with the cosmology of the Dogon, the more one discerns, the more one realizes how little he really knows.

Nevertheless, a few things are certain. This LP contains some of the most gripping improvisational music to be recorded dur-

246

ing the past ten years. Its appearance on a label with national distribution is a welcome event, and one which was long overdue. And if, in whatever sense, *Dogon A.D.* marks the beginnings of a Dogon age of music, in which the unity of sounds, their roots, and their potentiating energy are stressed, Julius Hemphill will play a decisive part in the developing culture of that age.

(1978)

STANLEY CROUCH

Stanley Crouch arrived on the New York scene from California in the mid-1970s and quickly established himself as a perceptive jazz critic with a florid, combative, and extremely literate style. His books **Notes of a Hanging Judge** and **The All-American Skin Game** have established him as one of the most visible and interesting social and literary critics of our time as well.

The Freedom and Space Sessions

Booker Ervin
(Prestige P-24091)

Though these recordings were made in the early 1960s, they do not sound very old at all, nor in the least bit dated. Much of that has to do with the fact that by 1963 Booker Ervin, Jaki Byard, Richard Davis, and Alan Dawson had each achieved a level of emotional, intellectual, and technical sophistication equal to that of the top-shelf performers of the classic past and of the generation that has since evolved. The control each musician had not only of his instrument but of the art of improvising made these very important albums at the time they were released, and the present reissue shows them to be among the best of the many examples of the richness of jazz captured in studio sessions over the last half-century.

Like more than a few bands that have produced superb recordings, this unit existed only in the studio, yet its playing shows that a great deal had taken place since a Charlie Parker, Sonny Rollins, or John Coltrane had gone before the microphones in the early and middle fifties with the same saxophone/piano/bass/drums instrumentation. The concept of group playing had shifted quite a bit and the distance between "soloist" (always a misnomer unless unaccompanied) and rhythm section had pretty much dissolved. In more than a few ways, the New Orleans conception of collective playing was being reiterated in the language of the day. Of course, remarkable years should produce remarkable music, and the 1960s were some of the most remarkable in American and world history, primarily because convention—aesthetic, social, and political—was being challenged, for better and for worse. And since, regardless of how great a reservoir of fine compositions exists, jazz remains an improvisational music based in the skills and sensibilities of its players, the texture of the times may be more precisely expressed within that art than any other (except perhaps a great work of fiction or a great film). Within these performances one can hear not only the sound of liberation but the sound of deliberation. These players are never content to reduce a musical situation to the level of primal scream therapy. There are continual displays of joy, tragic sorrow, adventure, optimism, ambition, wit, and that extremely exciting combination of relaxation and almost barbaric intensity that epitomizes hard swing. This music contains no such thing as *background*. Each player is working on the front line as an orchestrator who places the color, range, and texture of his instrument in improvised melodic, harmonic, and rhythmic relationships to the rest of the ensemble. Paraphrase, anticipation, contrast, and counterpoint are used by everyone. Their intent was obviously to sustain the high standards of performance that had been passed on to them by the tradition and by their individual mentors. They succeeded remarkably.

Texas tenor saxophonist Booker Ervin, dead July 31, 1970, exactly three months short of his fortieth birthday, exemplifies the sweeping tragedy comprised of an inexplicable lack of recognition and an early death that has defined far too many jazz musicians of exceptional talent. He was a superior performer possessed of his own sound in a time when the sonic direction of John Coltrane overwhelmed most who were not already under the sway of Sonny Rollins. Yet paradoxically his originality would seem to have proved a liability. Unlike, for example, Thelonious Monk in *his* period of unfair neglect, he never inspired the wrath of the jazz critical establishment. Quite the reverse: he was often hailed as precisely what he was—passionate, original, and very swinging. Ervin made very fine recordings (a few of them, in some opinions, classics) and was highly appreciated by his peers. Nevertheless, he found himself moving to Europe, the haven for scuffling American artists, shortly after the last notes of these sessions were played.

It is possible that the lack of recognition could be related to the fact that he never worked for the star-making bandleaders of the day—such as Miles Davis, Cannonball Adderley, Horace Silver, or Art Blakey. He made many public appearances and some excellent recordings with the rarely appreciated pianist-composer Randy Weston and the controversial Charles Mingus, but even working with the great bassist and conceptualist and adding much to his music did not bring Ervin the kind of audience interest one might expect. It is also true that, as Ira Gitler has reminded me, he was not a bandstand personality who entertained with banter, nor was he lucky enough to build a charismatic personal mystique that could make him widely known through jokes and gossip. He simply played the tenor saxophone, and brought with him a song and a cry.

I first heard him on record with Mingus. I knew I wasn't familiar with the sound and, therefore, I was hearing someone new to me. His notes had their own projection and a personal saltiness, or grit. The saxophone was played with great vocal emphasis and captured the essence of the shout and the chant, of the blues and the church, that recognition—through memory, desire, expression, and imagination—of pleasure, ambivalence, pain, and deliverance. I knew that at times I was hearing an unnamed joy and an unnamed agony. In that sense, Booker Ervin was one of the most perfect reflectors of his age.

But above all, Booker Ervin was an exceptional saxophonist and one who had studied the instrument and the tradition with great astuteness. His phrasing and inflection sometimes recall Coleman Hawkins; the motion from joyous yowls to sudden pathos puts me in the mind of Ben Webster; while his relaxation and freedom of phrasing show that he heard loudly and clearly the messages of Lester Young, Dexter Gordon, and Sonny Rollins. It also seems to me that somehow John Handy's saxophone color worked its way into Ervin's sound and gave it more of a soaring quality—particularly on ballads—which made the total blend of influence and individual personality extremely distinctive.

While Ervin represents the rawness, lyricism, and swing of the big-toned Texas tenor tradition, these recordings bring together figures who represent two other very important areas in jazz. Richard Davis is from Chicago, that Midwestern buckle of the blues belt that has served as greenhouse and pressure cooker for more than a few major figures in modern American music. Unlike Ervin, Davis has had more than a modicum of recognition of his great talent, having worked in literally every context from pop jingle to superb jazz ensemble of any style, as well as under the batons of Leonard Bernstein and Igor Stravinsky. Both Jaki Byard and Alan Dawson, however, share with their leader here the paradox of being an original with exceptional knowledge and control of his instrument without having achieved the attention and rewards one would think such craft and artistry would bring. Both are part of the extremely influential Boston jazz community that has included musicians of the caliber of Roy Haynes, Sam Rivers, Cecil Taylor, Clifford Jarvis, and Tony Williams (the last two students of both Dawson and Rivers).

These were men who had experienced, or even helped to initiate, so many of the new ideas that by 1963 were readily available to modern musicians. Jaki Byard is one of the players responsible for establishing mastery of the entire range of African American musical styles as the new level of virtuosity. Prior to the work of men like Mingus and Byard, jazz musicians (excepting only those in the Duke Ellington Orchestra) tended to master only the style their generation was responsible for bringing to the fore, or the one that had the most contemporary currency. Previous styles were looked upon as outdated, square, or corny—regardless of the technical problems they may have presented.

Byard would have none of this. He amalgamated the past with the most adventurous new harmonies and rhythms, evolving a style that *always* offered the possibility of numerous improvisational perspectives. His playing rumbles and waddles, often summoning the dark tremolos of the church, the spank and kick of stride piano, and the nearly seamless blisters of sound in Tatum and Powell. And all of this periodically careens into new musical worlds where some of Europe's harsher harmonic responses to modern life are given a lilt even as they curse the age. A style such as this obviously calls for the superior command of the keyboard that Byard has. Quite aware of the importance of changing his touch and the color of his articulation, he is capable of moving from the fastest notes played one on top of the other to airy lines in which bebop is enunciated in the flat-footed fashion of a Monk. Through subtle use of the pedals, he is capable of making a note or a chord glimmer or seem to spring into the air. His rhythm is extremely unusual: Well aware that pianists don't have to take breaths or shape their phrases around lung power, Byard tends to let his ideas run past—or stop short of—the regular points of rest. And he has learned his percussive lessons from Basie, Ellington, and Monk, so that the piano sounds like tuned drums as often as anything else, particularly when a horn is also improvising.

Richard Davis is an indication of what the American musician of the future may be, a virtuoso who is highly respected in any jazz style, and also has mightily impressed those who work in European art music forms. He seems to me one of the first African American bassists to have taken seriously what Charles Mingus gave to the instrument in terms of glisses, large interval leaps, extended melodic lines, multiple-stops, and an expressive range that parallels that of Segovian guitar. It is clear here that Davis is also fond of the ideas of Eric Dolphy and a concept that makes it possible for the bass to drive a band whether playing time, ostinatos, ongoing melodic obligatos, rhythmically independent thematic vamps, or walking chords. Most importantly, he contributes musically in an orchestral fashion; for anyone can disdain to play time or can produce odd effects for their own sake without achieving anything musical, but Davis's forte, as often as not, is the creation of that pleasurable or provocative tension which is the essence of syncopation. Also highly significant is his ability to vary the timbres of bass notes and plucked chords, so that the broad array of colors and inflections jazz wind players and singers have long been using is applied to the pizzicato bass technique. Obviously a master of the instrument and the moments of decision that make a significant improviser.

Upon listening to Alan Dawson, one can conclude that there is something close to a Boston style of post–Kenny Clarke–Max Roach drumming that seems to have developed from the ideas of Roy Haynes—in terms of looseness, precision, variance of the cymbal beat, superb control of texture, and a witty approach to surprising rests and syncopations. Yet Dawson is much more than an imitator or duplicator of Haynes. His students, Tony Williams and Clifford Jarvis, both suggest a specific sound and approach (as with New Orleans drummers or Texas tenors) that has plenty of room for inspired individuality. Dawson himself is one of the most articulate drummers I have ever heard; he is always playing the song, supportively orchestrating the phrases, accents, and rhythms of his fellow players, or proposing directions in much the way a comping pianist does. (During one of his unaccompanied improvisations here, he plays exactly the same notes that Richard Davis uses to introduce the melody!) What he brings to time in the up-tempo selections is quite often amazing: dislodging the beat, setting up brief rhythmic vamps in response to Davis, rhythmically paraphrasing the ideas around him, and using the sock cymbal for a variety of accents and metric superimpositions that are gone almost as soon as you notice them. And more than a few rock drummers could learn from what he does near the end of his solo on *The Second #2* or the way he plays during all the vamps of *A Lunar Tune*. Along with Williams and Jarvis, he was one of the most important drummers to emerge during the sixties.

All told, what impresses me most about this unit is that it came up with a group concept that was an alternative to the sounds of the Thelonious Monk and John Coltrane quartets, the two most profound working units of the same instrumentation during the early sixties. Had it ever been able to perform regularly, to travel, to appear at the major festivals, there is no telling what this Booker Ervin band could have achieved. But the fact is that those four men performed for an audience made up only of microphones, technicians, and whatever associates might have been on hand. That they created such extremely fine and vitally passionate art is a tribute to the magnitude of the basically unnoticed gifts America and the world so often receive from those creators known as jazzmen. Let us hope that the Booker Ervins of the present and the future will not also become part of the tragic and voluminous underside of the music's history. Hope so, but don't count on it.

(1979)

At the
Five
Spot

Thelonious Monk
(Milestone M-47043)

Though Thelonious Monk's stature is very clear now, his historical relationship to the music was for quite some time a very curious one. In many ways, he was one of the founding fathers of the Bebop Revolution of the forties, but more as a theoretician and instructor than a lickmaker. Dizzy Gillespie admits to having learned a lot from him, Miles Davis went over to his house to learn chords as did so many others, he composed songs that many played, worked in a band with Coleman Hawkins, and maintained enormous respect among the makers of the then-new music. Part of it had to do with the fact he was capable of teaching musicians inroads to a music he himself wasn't interested in playing. He was, to use Regis Debray's phrase, conducting a "revolution within the revolution." Where men like Charlie Parker, Gillespie, Navarro, Powell, and others were inventing styles that called for new levels of instrumental control in terms of rapid tempos, passages dense with eighth notes and complex syncopations, Monk was repudiating it all.

It is almost as though Monk understood more quickly than anyone else how the bebop style could be reduced to mannered chord-running and rhythms that were far less varied than those of the musics that had preceded it. He seemed intent on forging a music that could make use of a variety of elements, including the call-and-response energy of New Orleans, the updated antiphonal relationships between soloists and riffs or thematic backgrounds heard in Ellington and Basie, the percussive nature of the African American piano tradition, Jelly Roll Morton's dictum that a jazz pianist should sound like a jazz *band*. And all of this telescoped through the syncopations, polyrhythms, and flirtations with tempo of the African American dance tradition; whether professionals (like the Nicholas Brothers, Bill Robinson, the endless chorus lines with soloists that were the visual counterparts of the large and small bands), or the amateurs in the audience whose elegance, slides, twirls, bumps, and grinds had sparked and inspired more than a few bands. In other words, the problem that Monk presented was one of thoroughness: What made him avant-garde was his determination to sustain the *power* of the tradition rather than reduce it to clichés, trends, novelties, or uninformed parodies. Because of that decision, he had to wait almost twenty years before he could be heard in person on a regular basis rather than by what must have been the incredibly painful proxy of hearing his own songs played by others in clubs which would not hire him because he was "too bizarre."

Much of the problem Monk has presented has to do with the fact that he is the first Picasso of jazz, the first African American musician to develop a style that willfully shunned overt virtuosity in favor of a control of the elements of the music in fresh ways. Monk may be a great aesthetic chef, but he is not a waiter:

256

He may cook the food, but you have to get up and serve yourself. That is: Just as Picasso demanded that the viewer *do* something other than peruse a painted photograph or an *impression* of a photograph, Monk demands that the listener play the song along with him, fill in the holes he leaves, figure out where he is, understand what he's doing with the beat, or at least *sense* more than the ordinary. He understood early that jazz requires each of its artists to develop his own version of four-four swing—fast, medium, slow; his own version of the blues, of ballads, and of the Afro-Hispanic rhythms misnomered as "Latin." All these things Monk did, but in such an original manner that many did not think he could play at all.

Actually, Monk has totally rethought the tradition. He has a great love for the whole legacy of African American music as it has been translated through the piano keyboard and through guitars as well (there is more than a little mutuality to his manner of drive and relaxation and that of Charlie Christian, even to some of his dissonances echoing the tone and the attack of the great guitarist). In his playing, one can hear everything from the most sophisticated to the most "primitive." It is almost as though he (as Ornette Coleman was to do later) took everything he learned when playing with a revivalist or listening to the country blues players, amateur or professional, and used that material as a screen through which he would strain the florid aspects of bebop, removing the bejeweled scabbard (to alter our metaphor) and presenting the constant jumps and jerks or lyrical glints of light on the blade. Replete with a profound understanding of motion, texture, weight, balance, and contrast. But that is to be expected, for Monk is the third man in the chain of major American composers working outside European concert hall forms, the first two being Jelly Roll Morton and Duke Ellington.

It is as a composer on all levels—themes, improvisation, accompaniment thick with thematic abstractions, riffs, percussive grunts, startling shifts of register and polyphonic provocation—

that Monk was to have his say and make his mark. In many ways, he taught musicians *and* listeners *and* critics how to *think*. Though he is a past master of subtlety, he never wanted you to miss anything he was playing or forget what the theme was once the improvising started. Oh, yes, Monk was in pursuit of the most virtuosic of possibilities: authority. He seemed to have realized that jazz was a music constantly at war with the overdone and the sentimental and that it was always in danger of being reduced to maudlin mannerisms, whether through ineffectual vibrato, obviousness, or clichés. Even the new technical levels of bebop could find themselves being shunted through quasi-European graveyards of gangrened pretension (as with those who thought "bop" was a Negroid mispronunciation of Bach). It was not that he was particularly at war with European expertise but simply that it was irrelevant to what he did. With Monk's determination to fuse the victories of Ellington, Basie, and Christian into a perceptible form that could give the small group the orchestral complexity that had not existed since New Orleans, he brought about a movement within a movement, with Miles Davis being his first great pupil. And not only did Monk inspire musicians but he provoked some of the finest critical writing and some of the bitterest fights between schools of writers and fellow practitioners. His performances scandalized pianists of every school and confounded listeners—not to mention the fact that his demeanor and dancing in front of the bandstand when he was finally "accepted" convinced some that he was no more than another flam artist embroidering the emperor's new clothes; or, at best, inept.

Monk's music was so far inside the tradition that he seemed to demand that the listener have a thorough enough knowledge of the African American legacy to appreciate how he was playing around with it, off it, and through it. What he was after was to make a small band take on the force of a big band, and two big bands in particular—Ellington's and Basie's, furthered by the riff power of Christian. What Ellington had was a thorough translation of the entire tradition through his band, including soloists like Barney Bigard who could take you from New Orleans to New York in the course of eight bars; while Basie had an understanding of the power of the musical rest so that the force of the rhythm section's motion could set up almost excruciatingly delicious anticipation and suspense in the mind and emotions of the listener; then Christian could have everything in motion in two bars. Also, it would seem that Monk understood the importance of a leader's organizing his soloists for contrasting melodic, rhythmic, timbral, and harmonic styles. Both Ellington and Basie had players who provided them with a collage of improvisational styles and both were cunning enough to have them play in sequences that would light things up. In answer to this, Monk developed a piano style that could emulate brass, reeds, guitars, and drums and that was capable of carrying you from the barrelhouse to the penthouse and *back*, for his intent was to do as he had heard Ellington do: to address ongoing thematic development rather than merely arrange "backgrounds." If you need references, listen to Ellington's *Skrontch* and *Chatterbox*, recorded in 1937 and 1938, respectively. The accents and the continual concern with the themes are clear antecedents to Monk compositions like *Evidence, Coming on the Hudson,* and *Rhythm-a-ning.* But to understand their relationship to Monk, one must listen to the performances on *all* levels. For he quite possibly was the first musician of his generation to realize that he could reverse the process of taking solos down and orchestrating them by taking powerful syncopated accents (such as the brass figures on *Chatterbox*) as germs to be spaced with powerful notes into themes as stark and beautiful as *Evidence,* with intricate counterpoint provided either by his own runs or the interjections of his drummers. (This is why thematically oriented drummers like Haynes, who magnificently reiterates the melodic rhythms of *Evidence* under Griffin's solo and extends them as well, are so necessary to the fruition of Monk's music.)

Just as fascinating as Monk's relationships to the two greatest bandleaders is his relationship to Christian, a man whose talents were only glimpsed, however profoundly they affected the history of the guitar. I find Monk's solo on *Coming on the Hudson* particularly Christian-like in the way the eighth notes are spun out, the starts and stops, the sustained tones, the percussive chords, the badgering of the rhythm. But that is not the only one. On *Rhythm-a-ning*, he seems to have found a brilliant abstraction of the striding *furioso* of Basie and the booting, meddling, even rageful and simultaneously joyous strumming and plinking of the great guitarist, all undercut and measured by Monk's genius for rearrangement and startling sound-blocks. For those who would investigate, try *I Got Rhythm, Stardust,* and *Tea for Two* by the Charlie Christian Quintet, recorded in Minneapolis in 1939 (Columbia G-30779). Listening to these makes it clear that Christian's spirit and sensibility pervade much of what Monk does and are beautifully redefined for the uses of an extremely unique and priceless musical mind.

By the time the recordings reissued here were made, Monk had been at the forefront of New York music for almost twenty years and had been lucky enough not only to have survived in mind, skin, and spirit, but to have continued growing in confidence and boldness. He had also been well-documented on Blue Note, Prestige, and Riverside recordings, which gave his live performances a backdrop of one of the most significant bodies of musical work composed and performed this century. His songs, such as *'Round Midnight, Straight, No Chaser,* and *Well, You Needn't,* were being played by more than a few bands and three of his best students—Miles Davis, Sonny Rollins, and John Coltrane—were beginning to be looked at as major or important figures. Davis' subtle, spare, and non-European way of playing the trumpet was undoubtedly the result of having perceived the weight of Monk's conception. Rollins' fascination with endless timbres, percussive phrasing, rhythmic trickery, thematic improvisation, irony, and humor go without saying. Coltrane discovered the value of the whole-tone scale and was to tell A. B. Spellman that the "sheets of sound" had in part come from his attempts to imitate Monk's runs while working with him at the Five Spot in 1957. And I would add that the shape and rhythm of Monk's composition *Trinkle Tinkle* was more than a bit helpful. Monk had observed it all and had had one chance, on *Swing Spring* on the famous session with Miles Davis in 1954, to show who the boss really was. In order to tell Monk that he loved him, even though he wouldn't allow him to play while he was soloing, Davis quotes some Monk licks in the trumpet section that precedes the piano solo. The rankled giant responds by taking the lick and building an incredible solo of virtuosic colors, turns, harmonies, and rhythms that seems to say, "Excuse me, young man, but if you intend to piddle around with my shit, see if you can ever get to *this!*" By no means was Monk to be undone or outdone. He was ready and had been ready for a long, long time.

The Five Spot had begun its music policy in 1956 with the band of Cecil Taylor, a vanguard pianist whose linear rhythmic style can be almost totally traced to *Work,* a composition performed by Monk in the early fifties. The following summer Monk came into the club with a quartet that included John Coltrane, tenor saxophone; Wilbur Ware, bass; and Shadow Wilson, drums. The group played to packed houses and the engagement was considered a major event. Unfortunately, it was never recorded in public performance, but three studio tracks exist (reissued on Milestone M-47011). It is equally sad that the two records in the present reissue set were met with critical derision when they were initially released (probably because Johnny Griffin and the rest of the members constituted a *different* band). To my ears, these recordings are excellent and every member of the band

261

rises to the opportunities provided, particularly what must be called the reed and percussion *sections*.

With a quartet that included a tenor saxophonist with the intellectual, emotional, and technical skills of Johnny Griffin, Monk was able to realize his orchestral desires by using the entire range of the horn, pivoting the motion of the band off the bass, with the piano and trap drums creating an ongoing arrangement of textural, harmonic, and melodic development. Griffin could give Monk the clarinet, alto, tenor, and upper baritone ranges, often suggesting in tandem with Monk's particularized and sonorous voicings more than one horn (as had been done brilliantly elsewhere by Gigi Gryce's alto on *Gallop's Gallop*, a Monk performance and composition that still looms over contemporary music). Malik gave first-class bass from start to finish, walking the chords with a melodic direction and a powerful, steady swing that could get hankty and tricky on tunes like *Rhythm-a-ning*. Roy Haynes, one of the all-time giants, played as if in training for the belt every second, with poise, class, fire, and taste, underwoven by superb execution. Each cymbal and each drum is used something like a dancer in an extremely complex fabric of sonic choreography—elaborating, paraphrasing, shifting the beat, giving it different ranges by use of timbral variation and often working up to a magical one-man ensemble in which the drums function as a big band would, filling the roles of chanting brass and weaving, feathery or double-timing reeds—replete with plungers, mutes, and alternate fingerings! A superb orchestrator of the musical ideas as they are extemporized about him, Mr. Haynes is arguably as great—if not greater—than any drummer in combination with Monk. All in all, obviously one of Monk's finest working groups. Again: a four-man orchestra.

Without the precedence of Duke Ellington's *The Mystery Song* of 1931, I cannot imagine compositions like *Light Blue* or *Coming on the Hudson* existing, each of which is one of the "mood" or "blue" numbers that, as Gunther Schuller has pointed out, Ellington invented as categories. The manner in which Ellington uses the piano throughout both takes also prepares one quite well for the way in which Monk works as an under- or counter-voice in the rhythm section. *Light Blue* as performed by this quartet is a stripped-down, elegant, and unsentimental ballroom number of great romance, wisdom, and dignity. As with all the performances, there is a powerful dance feeling to it. In the improvisation, Griffin is very melodic, songful, attentive to the line's contours and weights, its joy and emaciated lyricism. Monk's solo jags, darts, and dangles over the dancing cymbals of Haynes and Malik's Braud-like solemn beauty, creating a masterful composition-within-a-composition and an arrangement-within-an-arrangement. *Coming on the Hudson* is full of despair, pain, and a perseverance of stoic dignity. Griffin brilliantly organizes his arpeggios with thematic and Monkish ideas, rounding out a fusion of Coleman Hawkins, Lester Young, Charlie Parker, and the big blue shout of the Chicago tenor school. Monk's thematic rearrangement seems a paean to courage and responsibility, taking care of the business of being one's self, regardless of the odds and the sorrow. Although *Rhythm-a-ning* is more than strongly related to a passage in Lawrence Brown's opening solo on *Ducky Wucky* (an observation passed on to me by Gary Giddins), at least in terms of certain notes, its rhythmic character is more about Charlie Christian. There is a joy to the statement of the line, the interjections of Griffin that are echoed by Monk and the improvisation that epitomizes the sensibility of swing. Griffin and Haynes really stretch out in the long tenor solo, always listening to each other and buoying the music up over the driving bass line. Monk's solo was spoken of earlier. Malik carries the music into a solo by Haynes that is not only melodic, but is a *good* melody. *Epistrophy,* the band's closing theme, ends the first side as it does the second, each side of the original album having been intended to suggest a club set.

Blue Monk is a classic blues theme which receives a fine rendition. One of the interesting structural aspects of the improvisation is how Monk begins his section with a variation on Griffin's last phrase and fades his own solo into an accompaniment for the bass improvisation, thereby avoiding a break in musical feeling. Excellent musician that he is, Haynes begins his drum solo with a variation on Malik's last phrase. Other notable aspects are Griffin's blue authenticity and Monk's ability to capture the essence of the form and sensibility without relying on clichés.

Evidence achieves great power and Griffin's range on his horn allows the melody to build with extreme tension. Griffin's melodic imagination, his arpeggios, and the excellent ways in which he uses the ideas presented to him by the rhythm section keep a focus on the theme that belies facility for the sake of exhibition. Monk is, again, cogent and muscular, creating a spare melody of acidic colors before submerging his thematic arabesques into the environment for Malik. Haynes takes another solo that is as well thought out as one of Monk's.

Nutty, Blues Five Spot, and *Let's Cool One,* are all very interesting Monk themes. *Nutty* takes on a lyricism at Griffin's hands that makes it an affectionate portrait of something while maintaining the rhythmic surprise and genius, with Monk's paraphrases and satiric asides seeming on occasion to descend through the meter. The control of Monk's solo and the motion of the band is outstanding. *Blues Five Spot* is an example of how an exceptional musician can take a very traditional phrase and get the feeling of more than one horn by subtle shifts of register. Griffin overflows with ideas and notes, then eloquently plays the last two choruses *a cappella* before Monk's entry with the rhythm section. Just as the band sound has been varied before by Monk's laying out and letting Griffin stroll with bass and drums, the whole rhythm section's leaving him out there does the same thing and extends the conception of the break as well. Monk is especially skillful in his solo as he reiterates the theme in abstraction and builds in complexity to then contract the melody to a series of oddly syncopated jabs that are marvels of implication because, before one knows it, one is filling in the rest of the theme on his own. As with his solo on *Blue Monk*, Haynes gives the sound and feeling of hand drums but builds an original percussion melody that illustrates his imagination and his personalizing of things that Art Blakey would seem to have begun bringing to the drums in the early fifties. *Let's Cool One* begins almost as a march in abstraction before developing in rhythm and line to a beautiful melody with a supremely sophisticated bridge tinted with blues. Griffin holds on to the theme throughout his improvisations, with and without rhythm section, playing particularly beautiful bridges and, in his unaccompanied two choruses, giving possibly his best playing of the record. The composer's playing is another splendid thematic venture characterized by bittersweet and jolting harmonies.

In Walked Bud is one of the best selections of the entire two volumes. First, it is a fascinating example of how well Griffin had captured Monk's ideas and transmuted them for his own devices, as when the trills, oblique scalar melodies, thematic paraphrases, and register leaps come off sounding more Monkian than anything else. But Griffin is doing more than aping Monk, for the swing, the drive, the sound, and the juggling of the dense runs over the wonderful rhythm section is definitely his. When Monk enters, the fire is way up and he proceeds to push the smoke button on his own, rippling and building a solo that drives and drives, breathes, makes fine uses of repetition, and builds, again, a new composition. Malik takes his finest solo of the recording, deftly anticipating the later popularity of Eastern musical approaches. Haynes bats a beautiful clean-up and the bouncing, swinging theme burns its way out. The rendition of *Just a Gigolo* has recently struck me as a Monkian recasting of the piano solo that appears on an Armstrong version of the song done in the thirties. On *Misterioso,* another classic blues that closes the recording, Griffin's lovely and biting blues melodies are shouting, sophisticated, and powerful, yet free of the hysteria of imitation or spiritual mimicry. Monk's last solo of the package is quite a fitting one: It shows off the resources of a musical master who can take the most basic of forms and bring a range of moods and techniques that gives it freshness while refusing to sell it out.

In closing, I would like to say that you have in your hands the documentation of a wonderful musical unit and some of the best improvising ever captured in performance. It is part of the legacy of one of the finest of American and world artists, a man whose gifts to the spirit, the mind, and emotions of the mass of strangers all over the world who listen to him have been given unselfishly. The work of Thelonious Monk personifies one of the closing passages in Albert Murray's masterwork on African American music, *Stomping the Blues:*

> What it all represents is an attitude toward the nature of human experience (and the alternatives of human adjustment) that is both elemental and comprehensive. It is a statement about confronting the complexities inherent in the human situation and about improvising or experimenting or riffing or otherwise playing with (or even gambling with) such possibilities as are also inherent in the obstacles, the disjunctures, and the jeopardy. It is also a statement about perseverance and about resilience and thus also about the maintenance of equilibrium despite precarious circumstances and about achieving elegance in the very process of coping with the rudiments of subsistence.

For those who would experience the wisdom, courage, and clarity of a great twentieth-century artist, listen closely.

(1977)

TOM PIAZZA

The compiler of this collection began writing for **Down Beat** at the age of sixteen, in 1972. Apart from occasional pieces for **The New York Times** and elsewhere, I concentrate on writing fiction these days.

Giant Steps

Jaki Byard
(Prestige P-24086)

aki Byard, to borrow a phrase James P. Johnson used in describing Fats Waller, is *all* music. He is also a man of parts and his music changes shape and mood unpredictably. Or, rather, it seems to have many shapes and moods at once. Allusions spanning the history of jazz surface unexpectedly in his playing like fish breaking water in different parts of a lake.

The recurrent theme of all the writing about Byard seems to be: "Why isn't this man a 'star'?" A star, presumably, is one who is easily recognized by large numbers of people, makes more money than he needs, and has more demands on his time than he can meet. Such a life has blunted the talents of more than a few of America's most sensitive artists; it is hard to survive as a complex or self-contradictory human being in a culture that must reduce everything to the quickly recognizable images and catchwords with which our media manipulate taste and values. Jaki's personality, both as a musician and as a man, resists this sort of treatment. He is unclassifiable.

Byard was born in 1922 and grew up around Boston. He took piano lessons briefly, as a child, but spent his teens teaching himself and listening avidly to the bands that came through town. He played piano with several bands in the area, and also played trumpet, which he learned with some help from his father. He was drafted just as his career started rolling, and spent the years from 1941 until the end of the war in the service, bunking, for a time, with drummer Kenny Clarke and pianist Ernie Washington. Here he learned trombone, which he played in the Army band.

After the war, Byard freelanced in Boston for a couple of years before going on the road with Earl Bostic in 1947. Then he spent some time in Canada, studying saxophone while there. He returned to Boston, where he was becoming something of a local legend, and, besides playing piano regularly at several local clubs, played tenor next to the great baritone saxophonist Serge Chaloff in Herb Pomeroy's big band. He also began teaching in earnest, and influenced a number of younger musicians, among them Don Ellis and the fine, short-lived pianist Dick Twardzick. In 1959 he joined Maynard Ferguson's band and began working regularly in New York. It was at about this time that he met Charles Mingus; when he left Ferguson, it was to join that great bassist and composer.

Byard spent a significant period with Mingus, after which he freelanced around New York and recorded an extraordinary series of group performances for Prestige. But despite the enthusiasm of fellow musicians and a few of the more perceptive critics, he never seemed to receive notice from the jazz public commensurate with the size of his talent. The sixties were a time for partisans, in and out of jazz, and for the most part the new players who gained the most recognition were those who aggressively asserted a *new* approach to playing. It was a bad time for an individualist with a predilection for history and no axes to grind.

Byard started teaching at the New England Conservatory of Music in 1969. He still teaches there, dividing his time between Boston and his home in Hollis, Long Island, where he lives with his family. Jaki maintains active playing and private teaching schedules as well.

In the late spring of my senior year at college, I drove with some friends to a concert in Bennington, Vermont. There, from the loft of an old carriage house, we looked down and watched Jaki Byard, trumpeter Jimmy Owens, bassist Chris White, and drummer Warren Smith. I no longer remember what they played, but I remember how it felt, which was very close to the spirit of some of Fats Waller's small group recordings. The music kept changing shape, molded largely by Byard with dissonant chords, facial expressions, and shouted remarks. It was exhilarating, and the glow stayed after they finished playing. We offered the pianist a ride back to his hotel, and when we got there he invited us in. We had some sandwiches and a jug of wine; Jaki had a can of small sausages and some cheese. We put it all in the middle of the floor and ate and drank until three-thirty in the morning, listening to Byard expound on nightclubs, the American educational system, the dangers of hero worship, and lots of other things. I remember how comfortable he made us feel; we might have been in a dorm talking to an exceptionally alive, witty friend.

Later that summer, I attended a jazz program at Bennington College for a couple of weeks; Jaki was one of the faculty members there. Late one night, while wandering out by a cornfield, just soaking up the evening and the country, I heard, faintly, a Bird-like alto coming from the direction of the arts complex. As I got closer, I could hear a rhythm section; they were playing the changes to *Half Nelson*. I walked in and saw Jaki in a chair in the middle of the room, wailing away on alto with a student rhythm section at midnight just for kicks.

Byard is a natural teacher; his endless enthusiasm for playing and his real concern for younger players is a great inspiration. In 1976 Jaki played with a trio on Sunday evenings at a Greenwich Village restaurant called Willy's. I spent a few nights there listening and occasionally sitting in. Many young musicians came to play, and Jaki was gracious to everyone, always introducing the sitters-in from the stage and making sure everyone got a chance to blow. When we weren't playing, we sat at a table behind Byard; from time to time he would play big, rumbling, train-wreck chords and look over his shoulder at us and give us monster-movie eyes and break us up.

What comes through, I hope, in these glimpses of the man is some of his generosity of heart, his enthusiasm and openness. Ordinarily, it is dangerous play to look for parallels between an artist's life or personality and his work. Jazz is, however, a unique form which, by fusing the creator with the thing created, by making the work of art an *act*, turns that work into evidence for all kinds of existential inductions about the artist. From this comes the peculiar sort of hero worship that surrounds many players, the same kind that surrounds many athletes.

Some musicians enjoy playing the public figure role to the hilt, and seem to suffer little inner conflict from it. Many who find themselves in that role are never sure whether their audience sees them as artists or as dancing bears. Some of these kill themselves, quickly or slowly; some emigrate to Europe; some are able to keep a perspective and continue creating despite the contradictions and disproportions of their position. Byard belongs with the latter group. He is in no way reticent about performing, or less than generous when he appears. He is, in fact, a most witty and entertaining presence, but he is unwilling to focus all his disparate moods into a consistent, recognizable persona. That is, he is unwilling to fashion an image for himself and thereby become fixed, predictable, packageable, and consumable by a society with little use for artists but an insatiable craving for romantic heroes and, especially now, messianic father figures. His music is the most important part of him, and mirrors his absolute individuality.

Byard's version of the jazz continuum is like a web; everything in his musical personality suggests breadth and simultaneity. A reference to Erroll Garner is sounded, resonates, and brings Fats Waller to the surface, followed quickly by Monk. Within one chorus his piano might suggest bells, fog horns, Bud Powell, or a riffing big band. He has performed or recorded on piano, tenor and alto saxophone, guitar, violin, drums, trombone, and trumpet.

Half the tunes here are Byard originals showing a real diversity of mood and approach. The other half are from composers as different as Thelonious Monk, Randy Weston, James P. Johnson, John Coltrane, and George Gershwin. Byard plays Weston's *Hi-Fly* with a lope and spareness that, by having a little more to do with Monk than with Weston, reminds us of Randy's roots in Monk's playing. He treats *'Round Midnight* in a very unMonklike fashion. And if we are aware of Thelonious' roots in the stride piano tradition in which James P. held such a towering place, it will not be too surprising to find an excerpt from Johnson's large-scale work *Yamekraw* on the same album with the Monk and Weston selections. Jaki might take an old Basie big band tune and rip it apart and reassemble it (as he did once on a memorable recording of *Broadway*); flip the coin and he might play *Giant Steps* in stride.

So it would be inappropriate to place Byard within a stylistic category, or at the front of a movement. His work *is* illustrative of a certain tendency in playing, however, which explains why he is usually grouped with "modern" players. Bebop was the peak of the art of the soloist-with-rhythm. After Charlie Parker, the major contributors to the music have been people who thought as orchestrators, who heard the *total* sound in their heads (think of Miles, Mingus, Ornette, Zawinul, and Shorter...). Bird's melodic innovations pointed the way to this later approach by demanding a new vocabulary of the rhythm section, a vocabulary that began to seem more and more like an improvised counterpoint to the soloist's line. Consider that the early "modernists" were fascinated by Latin-American music. In Latin and African-based musics, simple rhythms combine to form compound rhythms which are heard not merely as the combination of two distinct rhythms but as entirely new rhythmic shapes. Many early bebop recordings (Bud Powell's *Un Poco Loco;* Bird's contrapuntal lines *Ah-leu-cha* and *Chasin' the Bird;* Dizzy Gillespie's *A Night in Tunisia*) seem partly to be studies in how one rhythm may trick another to the surface. You can hear this also in the way Bird would echo and play against his favorite drummers, particularly Max Roach and Roy Haynes. Harmonically, too, his music demanded a more subtle and equal interaction between pianist, bassist, and soloist. Each member became a more flexible part of the total group, and no part could be taken for granted.

It is this approach to music that Byard carries forward in his playing and composition. The recordings reissued here, made shortly after he began playing regularly in New York, show an approach to piano trio music that was rare at the time. Rather than being a series of piano statements with rhythm accompaniment, they are as varied in shape and mood and texture as a series of paintings by Paul Klee. Ron Carter and drummers Haynes and Pete LaRoca perform different roles from tune to tune, but always they are present as equals with Byard in performances which add up to more than the sum of their component parts.

Our sense of justice tells us that great talent ought to reap great material rewards but justice, in this respect, is cheated as often as fulfilled. Posthumous fame is, as Hannah Arendt said, "the lot of the unclassifiable ones, that is, those whose work neither fits the existing order nor introduces a new genre that lends itself to future classification." Stardom is a mixed blessing; Jaki Byard's music bears the signs of one engaged in endless pursuit of form and beauty, rather than shallow recognition. Let us end with a quote from another individualist, e. e. cummings, from the little self-interview that serves as an introduction to his novel *The Enormous Room:*

> If people were interested in art, you as an artist would receive wider recognition—
> Wider?
> Of course.
> Not deeper.
> Deeper?
> Love, for example, is deeper than flattery.

(1978)

LOREN SCHOENBERG

Saxophonist and arranger **Loren Schoenberg** brings a sophisticated musical knowledge and a warmly appreciative yet healthily critical intelligence to his writing about music. A close musical and personal associate of both Benny Goodman and Benny Carter, he has conducted the jazz orchestras at the Smithsonian Institution and at Lincoln Center, as well as the American Jazz Orchestra. He is also the leader of the Loren Schoenberg Big Band.

Music for Loving

Ben Webster
(Verve 31452774-2)

Many of the musicians included in this collection were close friends and shared many professional connections. At a time when both the jazz world and the musicians' community seem prone to define themselves by their differences, this assemblage is eloquent proof of the interchange of musical ideas that flowered during the music's so-called "Golden Age."

Both Ben Webster and Harry Carney had distinguished themselves as members of Duke Ellington's saxophone section and throughout their careers were always associated with that specific sound. It was a stroke of genius on the part of producer Norman Granz to feature them in expansive settings in the early fifties that placed them outside of the "Ellington sound." Although many of the tunes and players involved were Ellingtonian, the results were different.

Ben Webster was born on February 27, 1909, in Kansas City, Missouri. As his close friend Rex Stewart succinctly recounted in *Jazz Masters of the Thirties* (New York: Macmillan, 1972; Da Capo, 1982), Ben was the only male in the house he grew up in and was pampered as a child. This led to the brusque facade that he presented to the world at large, although many who knew him well remember him a sensitive man, easily moved to tears. Music entered his life early on. Webster: "When I was a kid growing up around Kansas City, I studied the violin. But I finally had to put it down 'cause I could never get the right sound that I was always after. So I turned to the saxophone for what I had to say musically." Ben established himself as a bandleader-pianist and even played for the silent movies. In the late twenties, he encountered Budd Johnson of Texas and the Young Family Band (specifically their son Lester)—and they taught Ben how to play the saxophone. As Stanley Crouch has noted in his essay on Ben (included in *The Ellington Reader,* edited by Mark Tucker, New York and Oxford: Oxford University Press, 1993), elements of Young's style may very well have found their way into Webster's. This may have been the beginning of Ben's fascination with the expressive potential of sound. Coleman Hawkins, however, remained Ben's main source of inspiration, and it must have been a thrill when Ben was asked in 1934 to take Hawkins' chair in the Fletcher Henderson band after Young's heroic but short-lived effort. Henderson had an uncanny ability to glimpse yet-unrealized brilliance in players, and this was certainly the case in Webster's instance; if the 1932 recordings he made with Bennie Moten's band are any indication, Webster was miles away from the coherence already being realized on his instrument by the likes of Bud Freeman and Bob Carroll (well known at the time as Don Redman's tenor man). The first real glimpse of Ben's subsequent development came not in the recordings made that fall with Henderson, but during a session with Benny Carter a few months later. On the kind-of-Dukish *Dream Lullaby*, Teddy Wilson (brought to New York by Carter the previous year) plays an almost verbatim Ellingtonian introduction, but the real magic comes during Webster's sixteen-bar solo. Something in the way Carter voiced the chords and framed Webster brought out a new maturity that was to lay dormant for the rest of the thirties. And the two recordings made in 1935 and 1936 on which Ben sat in with the Ellington band contain no glimpses of what lay ahead. Besides Hawkins and the pianists Art Tatum, Willie (The Lion) Smith, and Fats Waller, Ben always credited two altoists with being his main inspirations—Johnny Hodges and Benny Carter. And strangely, in 1936, Carter recorded a tenor saxophone solo on *Nightfall* that sounds more like the Ben we know than Ben did at the time.

Webster spent the rest of the thirties in the best bands— Willie Bryant, Cab Calloway, Henderson again, and, in 1939, joined Wilson's newly formed ensemble. He also participated in many classic studio sessions with Wilson, Billie Holiday, and Lionel Hampton. But it wasn't until he joined the Ellington band in January 1940 that he entered his first period of greatness. Two things contributed to this metamorphosis: the extended exposure to Johnny Hodges and the immersion in the unique and challenging universe of Ellington's music. In turn, the band and those who were inspired by it were influenced by Ben's warmly rhythmic phrasing and attitude toward improvising.

New and exciting sounds were emanating from many sources in 1940: Besides Ellington, there was the Basie band with the futurist Lester Young and a new level of ensemble perfection, due largely to the presence of lead trumpeter Al Killian; Benny Goodman's Sextet (featuring Young's leading disciple Charlie Christian and Lionel Hampton) and big band, just heading into new musical territories, courtesy of Eddie Sauter; and trumpeter Roy Eldridge, drummers Sid Catlett and Kenny Clarke, pianists Art Tatum, Nat Cole, Ken Kersey, Thelonious Monk, and Nat Jaffe were comingling and finding new avenues of expression. Up in Boston, the eighteen-year-old Ralph Burns' ears were wide open.

Ralph Burns was born on June 9, 1922, into a large Irish family in Newton, Massachusetts. The piano had attracted him from an early age, and he had been working as a professional pianist since his early teens. Ruby Braff, the eminent cornetist, encountered Burns in the late thirties: "I first heard him at a session run by Joe Dixon's brother, Gus, in Lynn, Massachusetts. This little kid sat down—Ralph looked like a faun, he was a baby—and played the piano with the genius and maturity he was to display later in life. It was twinkling with joy, sure enough, and it wasn't too long after that he was on his way." Classical lessons had paid off in making Burns musically literate, and he supplemented his income by transcribing Ellington, Basie, and Goodman records for local bands. It was also at this time that he became a lifelong fan of Louis Armstrong.

Burns came to New York in 1941 with a Boston band led by Nick Jerrett that also featured vocalist Frances Wayne. They were the relief band at Kelly's Stables on 52nd Street, and Burns rubbed elbows with many of his musical idols. His first recorded arrangement, *Flo-Flo,* was recorded by Sam Donahue's band in 1942, but it was when he joined Charlie Barnet's band (through Wayne's recommendation) that he hit his stride. Barnet's band was known for its devotion to the music of Duke Ellington. It was considered the hardest-swinging of the white bands at the time, and was an excellent atmosphere for Burns to grow creatively as a writer. Several months later, Wayne, along with bassist Chubby Jackson, left Barnet for Woody Herman and took Burns along. This was a period of transition for Woody. Arranger Dave Matthews had transformed the band from "The Band That

277

Plays the Blues" into a more contemporary Ellington-inspired unit. Burns created a new sound for the band with his innovative scores. They combined the formal aspects of the big bands with the new, fresh sounds being heard along 52nd Street.

One of the first Burns' arrangements that Herman recorded was *I Get a Kick Out of You,* which featured guest Ben Webster. The saxophonist had recently left the Ellington band and was freelancing with Herman occasionally. It is clear that even at this early stage in his writing career Burns knew exactly what to do with Ben. One Burns piece, a rhumba entitled *Bijou* that was a solo vehicle for trombonist Bill Harris, had caught the ear of Igor Stravinsky. This culminated in the great man's *Ebony Concerto,* which the Herman band premiered at their 1946 Carnegie Hall Concert, along with Burns' extended composition *Summer Sequence.* When the band went on the road, Stravinsky sent his protégé, Alexis Haieff, along to conduct. He eventually became Ralph's composition and orchestration teacher. In the Barnet band, Burns had begun as pianist-arranger and eventually let go of the playing to concentrate on the writing. The same thing happened with Herman, and after a spell, Burns decided to settle in New York. Billy Strayhorn had a similar deal with Ellington, which allowed him to spend large amounts of time in New York. Burns: "I had admired Billy since I heard his *Chelsea Bridge* back in 1941. In New York we became real good buddies. He was a great cook and threw great parties for his friends that would last two or three days. I spent many happy evenings at his apartment uptown. He was also a marvelous human being, in addition to his great talent." By the time of these sessions, both men had already worked on ambitious and artistically successful projects with strings for Norman Granz.

Starting in 1953, Granz had been recording Ben Webster in various settings and was struck by the development of his ballad playing. The quartet session with Teddy Wilson included in this package was the first time Ben had recorded exclusively ballads and may have inspired the commissioning of the first strings date with Strayhorn.

As Lester Young noted, necessity is a mother, and when confronted with the challenge of writing for strings, Billy Strayhorn came up with four simple yet interesting settings for Ben. Clarinetist Tony Scott, a dear friend and musical associate of both Ben's and Billy's, was present to add tonal color. In the original liner notes, Ben was quoted as saying: "The violin is a wonderful instrument. If a man plays the violin well, nothing can be compared to it for sweetness and purity. There is no substitute. Strings create a special atmosphere and this atmosphere makes me feel better and it makes me play my horn better, too." This is made manifestly clear from the first notes of *Chelsea Bridge*. Strayhorn supports Ben with encouraging pianistic commentary and a classic half-chorus. As Albert Murray has noted, a true virtuoso, once he gets past the more superficial feats of velocity and range, begins to get to the real work, which is the development of nuance. Louis Armstrong, Pee Wee Russell, and Coleman Hawkins had incorporated a breathy attack into their solos by the late twenties, but it remained for Ben to place a strong emphasis on air. Strayhorn was also nothing if not subtle. A lifelong devotee of Art Tatum, Strayhorn picked up early on Tatum's mastery of allusion and played that musical card brilliantly by transforming the bridge of *It Happens to Be Me* into the *King Porter Stomp/Ole Miss* tag that Ben loved so much. (It was no accident that Duke featured Ben on the similarly derived *Bojangles* back in 1940.) You will find many more exquisite musical treasures on each of the other selections, too.

Several months later, Granz commissioned another session for Webster and one for Harry Carney. The baritone saxophonist was the sonic anchor of the Ellington Orchestra for over forty-five years, and his importance to Ellington's composing style is reflected in Duke's scores—his part was always written on a separate musical staff from the rest of the band. His strength lay in

melodic presentation and embellishment, and the most successful titles on his date let him do just that. Known for his friendly
demeanor and cavernous sound, Carney was an inspiration to
many. Baritone saxophonist Danny Bank: "The sound he got was
unique. If he would miss a set, it sounded like a different band
without him, absolutely. He was built for the instrument—big
nostrils and a big head. I used to follow Duke's band around and
one night at a dance hall in Harlem, it must have been around
1937, Duke came over and said, 'A boy your age shouldn't be
around here'—so he put a chair under the bandstand so I could sit
right under Harry and nobody would see me. Later on, when I
was with Benny Goodman—Teddy Wilson was also in the band—
both Harry and Duke would come around and tell Benny I
sounded like an organ. Even Coleman Hawkins told me that
Harry's sound had inspired him back in the twenties. He never
stopped studying, and in later years Harry took flute lessons from
me. At the time of these dates, Jimmy Hamilton and I were both
studying with Leon Russianoff, and we used to get together and
play clarinet duets." Fellow Ellingtonians Ray Nance and Jimmy
Hamilton add their sophisticated sounds to the proceedings and
have a few solos. Clarinetist Hamilton was the most brilliant of
Benny Goodman's disciples. His first major engagement in New
York, with Teddy Wilson's band at Café Society, featured him in a
tribute to the Goodman Trio every set. He was also a facile
arranger: *Ghost of a Chance* is his. Burns contributed four titles to
Carney's session, and all the music for the Ben Webster date the
next day. The reed duties were split between Bank, on flute and
clarinet, and Al Epstein, on English horn, clarinet, and bass clarinet. Epstein, a fine tenor saxophonist and arranger, had known
Ben for years: "I first met Ben at Charlie's Tavern. I came in with
a tenor and he says, 'What you got there?' He looked mean—and
he said, 'Can you play that thing? Take that out and play *Tenderly*
for me.' I thought he was going to hurt me or something. I tried
to play it like him, and he liked it and bought me a drink. All that

meanness must have been a coverup. It was one of the joys of my life to be around him."

By the mid-fifties, Ralph Burns had already begun his hegira from jazz into more commercial ventures. The opportunity to work on a project he had some emotional ties to, however, must have inspired Burns, for he responded with some of his most inspired writing. Burns: "Ben was one of my early idols. I loved his record with Duke of *Cottontail*. It was a great thrill to meet him later in New York and we became great friends and drinking buddies. We would usually wind up at either my place or his, listening to records." This resulting music studiously avoided all of the usual pitfalls of the jazz with strings genre. The years of studying with Haieff had paid off, as had hundreds of commercial assignments, through which Burns learned the true potential for intelligent string writing. There are virtually no repeated sections—Burns through-composed each title, freeing the music from the empty repetitions endemic to so much of arranged jazz. Each story is patiently told, with one beautiful counter-melody building upon another. These melodies linger in the listener's ear long after the CD is over. The slightest musical motion suggested by one of Burns' inspired lines presented several options, and it's a delight to hear Ben, with his keen ears and his own compositional talents, make his choices as to where to take his variations. He plays with a delicacy that Rex Stewart had once glimpsed when he visited Ben at home and watched him gently combing his grandmother's hair.

The piano chair was split between Teddy Wilson and Hank Jones. Wilson, whose playing had always had the feeling of chamber music, fit like a glove, and each of his solos is a gem. This collection marks the first release of a second session with Teddy, done after his first and several months before the Jones date. Among the new titles is *Some Other Spring*, written by Teddy's first wife, Irene. Although Billie Holiday made the definitive version, it was also a feature for Ben in Wilson's short-lived 1939 big band. Hank Jones' special gifts were noted by Coleman Hawkins early on, and they are displayed on these sessions in all their glory. Gifted not only as a soloist, Hank could comp in both blowing sessions and arranged dates such as this with an uncanny prescience. There were no rehearsals for these recordings, and it's almost beyond belief how gorgeously Jones undergirds everything, after only a cursory rundown. Artie Shaw, with whose group Jones was working around this time, has said that Hank's left-hand chords sounded like cellos, and it's a perfect analogy. Some of the most beautiful music on these recordings comes straight from Hank's hands: The block-chorded solo on *Early Autumn* and the comping on *Until Tonight* are good places to start.

Burns didn't let one harmonic progression slip by without linking it functionally to both Ben and this specific context. The spinning of keys, replete with a handful of simple yet thrilling modulations and the unexpected inversions of chords, are like a breath of fresh air. A few favorite moments: the seemingly inevitable but original move to the subdominant during the last eight bars of *Blue Moon;* the haunting counter-melodies throughout *There Is No Greater Love;* the descending bass lines that support both *Until Tonight* and *My Greatest Mistake* (both of which had been vehicles for Ben with Ellington); and the otherworldly introduction to the aforementioned *Early Autumn,* which is at least the equal of the original Woody Herman–Stan Getz recording.

For many years, intelligent string writing as far as jazz was concerned was an oxymoron. These Ralph Burns–Ben Webster sessions, along with Paul Jordan's work for Artie Shaw's 1941 band and Eddie Sauter's 1961 *Focus* featuring Stan Getz, are high-water marks in the evolution of jazz composition for strings. I envy the listener who is hearing these recordings for the first time—you've just made a friend for life.

(1995)

FELICITY HOWLETT

Like Loren Schoenberg, **Felicity Howlett** combines real writing ability with deep musical knowledge. The subject she has set for herself—the work of piano genius Art Tatum—could not be more formidable, but she brings grace and light to her incisive and clear exploration of his approach.

> *20th Century Piano Genius*
>
> **Art Tatum**
> *(Emarcy 826 129-1)*

With this issue, these very special Art Tatum solo interpretations are released intact and complete for the first time, produced directly from uncut tapes of the original performances. All but two of the performances were taped during a private party on July 3, 1955, at the Beverly Hills home of Ray Heindorf, then musical director for Warner Bros. (*Memories of You* and *Mr. Freddie Blues* are believed to have been taped at Heindorf's home on April 16, 1950.) The July 3 festivities were in celebration of the completion of the movie musical *Pete Kelly's Blues*. Heindorf had been in charge of the music for the production, which featured Jack

Webb as a jazz musician up against the mob. The atmosphere was convivial, the piano was superb, and Tatum was surrounded by a receptive and appreciative audience. Individual expressions of surprise and delight and various grunts of approval can be heard during Tatum's performances as listeners are caught here and there by an unanticipated melodic swoop or the charm of a perfectly placed phrase or thrilled by an unanticipated harmonic flurry.

For listeners today, the collection offers a rare opportunity to step into the atmosphere and share in the excitement and plea-sure of the gathering. A special aura envelops these interpreta-tions, perhaps most clearly expressed in the nature of the melodic lines. Even among tunes bursting at the seams with ex-tra-melodic materials, Tatum uses his fingers to give voice to the lyrics of the songs, to dramatically enunciate important words. We can even hear Tatum humming along with his fingers during some of the performances. Is Tatum perhaps "singing" the phrases for the benefit of singers who were present at the party? Does the festive atmosphere elicit a special voice from his inter-pretations?

For the most part, Tatum's selections are standards of the pe-riod, songs that in fact continue to live in the American popular music tradition. Most of the guests attending the party knew these tunes well enough to sing or whistle them, and many peo-ple also knew the lyrics. Some knew the basic harmonies of the tunes, and a few were well acquainted with previously recorded interpretations of some of the selections Tatum performed that evening. While never stepping out of his own character, Tatum warmly responds to the character of the gathering by interspers-ing musical morsels that will have an overall effect no matter what the level of attention of the listener. To the guests who are listening intently, Tatum does not offer his traditional crowd-pleasing variety numbers such as *Elegie* or *Humoresque,* nor does he play high-flying showpiece numbers such as *Tiger Rag,* specifically designed to blow any would-be competition out of the window and out of town. Rather, he provides an evening of state-of-the-art Tatum: shreds of the familiar interlaced with fresh insights, new ideas, and a unique mood.

Tatum is obviously at ease in the surroundings. Los Angeles had become his place of residence. A veteran of its clubs and recording studios, Tatum had ample experience playing private parties in the homes of celebrities and aficionados. During his first lengthy visit to the West Coast in 1936, he had appeared at the Paramount Theatre, the Melody Grill, Club Alabam, the Trocadero, and had played private parties for Irving Shulberg, Aileen Pringle, and Mary Pickford. During 1942–43, he had spent considerable time at the 331 Club, the Streets of Paris, and the Swanee Inn, and it was at this time the Art Tatum Trio was formed. Later on, there were substantial engagements at Billy Berg's (1946), the St. Francis Lounge (1949), and the Surf (1950), and many recording sessions.

This collection represents the last large set of solos recorded in Tatum's lifetime. He passed away only sixteen months later on November 13, 1956, at the age of forty-seven. These performances can be seen as a summation of Tatum's achievement, yet they are equally illustrative of the artist in the very midst of the creative process. The musical statements preserved here contain direct and indirect references to ideas Tatum had already introduced and examined. They lunge into the future as well with tonal, rhythmic, and textural combinations that are still being explored.

Well-documented anecdotes and reports from musicians of all ages attest to the profound impact Tatum had and continues to have on their musical development. His intricate rhythmic combinations opened up new vistas to tap dancers and to drummers. Tatum single-handedly elevated the level of technique in improvised piano performance and set new standards for what could be expected from ten fingers on a keyboard. His harmonic explorations provided new opportunities, new perceptions of space for melodic instruments, and his unique ability to stretch and compress time while never relinquishing a solid sense of beat was a gift for all musicians. And, with all that he accomplished and explored during his lifetime, his greatest gift is perhaps that his performances are still in motion, still traveling toward the beyond, and they are very actively providing fresh insights and creative inspiration to musicians today.

Heindorf had excellent recording equipment in his home, and, contrary to previous assertions about the occasion, Tatum was aware that a tape was running, although both men may have supposed that the tapes would go no further than Heindorf's private collection. A snippet of conversation contained on my audition tape provides proof of Tatum's awareness that he was being recorded during a revealing interchange: A listener requests *Without a Song.* Other voices join in agreement. Tatum replies, "Oh, no! I can't play the thing anymore." After vigorous coaxing, Tatum comments, "I'll have to bring that record out and let Ray hear it." Then a voice, presumably Heindorf's, says, "I want to have it on my tape, Art." Tatum gives in to the request but adds, "I'll just run over it...I mean, I won't play it like the record." Without further ado, he launches his "run-through," a crystalline two-chorus study in lyrics, harmony, clarity of concept, and the intermingling of on-the-beat movement with motion impelled by the lyrics, by forces set off from the placement of single important notes or chords, or by other mysterious means. The "record" that Tatum refers to is the only other published recording of the tune, a nearly six-minute modulatory contemplation recorded during one of his sessions for Clef on December 29, 1953. Tatum's performance here is utterly different and fascinating on its own terms.

Just Like a Butterfly is another miniature, a two-chorus version of a tune also recorded only once previously, at the solo session mentioned above. In earlier recordings, Tatum often played an introductory *rubato* chorus followed by a series of choruses displaying a more strictly metronomic beat. In this performance, as in *Without a Song* and other interpretations in this collection, the distinctions between the luxurious expanse of a *rubato* approach and an "in-tempo" chorus are slightly blurred and intermingled. Perhaps Tatum's greater attentiveness to the lyrics partly explains how this takes place. Another contributing factor may be his meticulous attention to the bass lines, especially in the slower performances. Even when everything is in motion, there seems to be time to perceive and appreciate the carefully drawn legato connections and soft breaks in the walking left-hand activity. Single bass notes seem to set up their own, sometimes major, waves of rhythmic force. Tatum's emphasis on the contrapuntal potential of the inner voices, especially the tenor as a melodic possibility separate from the bass, adds to the collection of areas from which pulses are derived.

One of the charming pleasures afforded by this collection is the opportunity to hear Tatum doodle himself into position. *Don't Blame Me, Sweet Lorraine,* and *My Heart Stood Still,* for example, each have rather extended preliminary matter which gives the listener little idea of what is about to transpire. The *Don't Blame Me* intro fiddles around until it positively identifies a shred of *Body and Soul,* and lo and behold, the ear has already arrived at the second beat of the real tune. The *Sweet Lorraine* intro and its flow into the first phrase of the body of the tune is strictly high-class comedy and a real play on past performances. Tatum merrily alludes to other tunes while carefully setting up the ear for the key of G. Suddenly he is on the road with *Sweet Lorraine* but in the key of G♭. Before his listeners can really catch their balance, he teases their ears twice more with suggested modulations back to G before settling firmly on G♭. Typical of many of the interpretations in this collection, *Sweet Lorraine* is a tune that Tatum had recorded on many different occasions. Yet, this performance is fresh and clean and different than all other recordings. Continuity with past interpretations is maintained through shapes, gestures, and fragmentary connections, yet this performance is new and stands on its own. *I Cover the Waterfront,* though with many fewer recordings for comparison, is similarly reworked, receiving its most extended solo treatment in this collection.

Performances like *Sweet Lorraine, Begin the Beguine, Someone to Watch Over Me, Memories of You, Willow Weep for Me, Body and Soul,* and *Danny Boy*—tunes that Tatum recorded several or even many times over the years—provide an immense amount of material for pleasure, for study, for contemplation. Some change more dramatically than others do as time goes by, and the changes take place in different ways. The intermingling of harmonies and phrase shapes of *Memories of You* with *To a Wild Rose,* which Tatum played with for a long time, is removed from the body of the present interpretation. *To a Wild Rose* appears only briefly as a reminiscence in a little codetta. Tatum is faithful throughout his performances to those left-hand beating rhythms of *Begin the Beguine.* People familiar with Tatum would probably recognize his attack on those notes, even before the entrance of the right hand, in any of his performances. Yet the character of the notes produced here is utterly different than, for example, that of the 1939 Standard transcription. *Danny Boy* is laced with familiar trills and other faithful references to past performances. The unexpected occurs in new harmonic placements, right-hand swoops, and left-hand/right-hand combinations. *Willow Weep for Me* and *Yesterdays* are built on opening motives that have come to be identified with Tatum's interpretations of those tunes. Many interpretations carry familiar sounding shapes and phrases that function as foundation stones for new matter that is interwoven, used for expansion, and sometimes bursts the seams of the previous concept. And yet, even in those performances where perhaps the only recordings for comparison are contemporary—from the 1949 Capitol issues or the Clef solo recordings—the difference in the atmosphere of the recording situations, the obvious interplay between Tatum and his audience in 1955, and the very different qualities of the two pianos used in these sessions contribute to the strikingly different results.

The carefree quality of the *My Heart Stood Still* introduction disappears in a flash with the first enunciation of the melodic line. This performance and others, such as *The Jitterbug Waltz,* are so tightly worked that they have the quality of written compositions. The magic is that so many of the carefully crafted combinations are reworked, reentangled with the onset of each new phrase. In *My Heart Stood Still,* the melodic line begins with a descending three-note passage and within and below it a chromatically descending faster line unravels. This is used as a kind of motive within the structure of the tune—other descending passages take on significance in relation to this combination beginning. There are other treasures in the performance, but the opening phrase lines are enough to stop the heart. The roots of *The Jitterbug Waltz* performance can be heard in its earlier Clef recording. How branches grow out from these roots, how the interpretation develops, and how even the most tiny detail is subject to new timings, placements, and juxtapositions is a matter of continuous fascination. Within a fairly rigid structure, left-hand lines continue to wander, never really repeated identically. *In a Sentimental Mood* provides another example of Tatum's careful working out of an independent left-hand motive, combined, in this case, with great affection for Ellington.

There is a great variety of texture and intensity among the performances. Melodies are especially clear within the easygoing and congenial atmosphere of *I'll Never Be the Same* and *September Song.* In August 1932, Tatum had first recorded *I'll Never Be the Same* as part of an ensemble accompanying Adelaide Hall during his first tour with her to New York City. He recorded it occasionally as a solo after that time, always with a certain warmth. Despite the clarity of the melody in *September Song,* an ongoing process of expansion at the fringes is reworked in the middle registers and interwoven with new musical ideas throughout. Especially interesting are the organlike tones Tatum produces in his bass lines, and the soft staccato left-hand chords of the last half chorus. The extreme resonance of the piano Tatum is playing and the rich bass structures he works with produce an awesome combination in *Moon Song*. When Tatum links the thick bass chords to full right-hand chords, the listener can nearly feel the vibrations produced in the room. For contrast, Tatum pokes certain bass notes softly, as if he were adding an invisible fiddle to his piano for the performance. In fact, there are three contemporary ensemble performances of *Moon Song*. Tatum recorded it with Louis Bellson in 1954, with Roy Eldridge in 1955, and with his own trio in 1956. Other tunes, such as *Body and Soul*, are available in several solo and ensemble versions.

Climax points appear in different locations: *Wrap Your Troubles in Dreams* begins happily and lyrically with a little modulatory leap in the first phrases that one begins to anticipate. It disappears. The listener is suddenly in the midst of a tremendous surge of single-note rapid chatter, as if Tatum were giving us a thousand reasons why troubles are not so easy to wrap. He balances the end, returns to the reassurance of the lyric, and soothes the commotion with a simple conclusion. In contrast, *Someone to Watch Over Me* and *Tenderly* present a careful but determined intensification of materials from beginning to end. *Love for Sale* is a more dramatic example of this intensification. Starting with a mood set in the intro and rather tersely stating the lyric in the first chorus. The registers and the textures expand as the pulse quickens to the end.

Of the two performances in this collection that were not recorded elsewhere, *Little Man, You've Had a Busy Day* is a smooth, streamlined interpretation, so lyric that one can hear a bit of one voice that could not resist humming along, as well as a few musical grunts from Tatum. Its simplicity is only in its overall effect. However, the effect is so powerful that the performance can slide by easily on the pleasure of its lyric qualities. The interpretation is abubble with internal material, available whenever it is possible to penetrate the silkiness of its outside texture. Tatum plays *Mr. Freddie Blues* to jostle the memory of one of his listeners. He gives him nine choruses of old-fashioned *Mr. Freddie* in combination with what sounds like an etude for the left thumb. The thumb line is part of a rhythmically funny and intriguing bass line consisting of broken, gallumphing tenths, split bass/tenor or tenor/bass, which skip up and down a chromatic line. Into this rather complicated mix, Tatum inserts a chorus of straightforward poker-faced comping that feigns oblivion to the antics surrounding it.

Too Marvelous for Words is for the most part a soft-spoken interpretation that evades time—that seems to have time in abundance—and retains an air of simplicity even while tickling the ear with seemingly impossible combinations and rocking between a left- and right-hand melodic command. *You Took Advantage of Me* has a lush left-hand chordal accompaniment which in this interpretation occurs in combination with soft staccato rhythmic pokes and a higher-register placement generally than, for example, *Moon Song*. The result is an up-tempo, lighthearted performance that joyfully defies its own complexities.

Tatum offers something for everyone in this collection and some of the best of himself. Here's to your continued pleasure in enjoying a great master who speaks directly from his piano and his heart on these recordings.

(1986)

PART FOUR

The Musicians Themselves

MICHAEL BROOKS

Michael Brooks pioneered a fascinating approach to liner note writing with his oral history montages for Columbia's late-1970s twofer reissues. The first volume of their monumental Lester Young series is a classic; the voices of Young's contemporaries, especially drummer Jo Jones, come through in elegant counterpoint.

The Lester Young Story, Vol. 1

Lester Young
(Columbia CG 33502)

For most of us, those few words written on a gravestone are the only tangible things we leave to posterity. We all come into the world kicking and screaming, some of us depart the same way, while the time in between is spent justifying our brief existence, usually to the complete indifference of present and future generations. And maybe we're the lucky ones. Those birds of paradise who flutter through life surrounded by a swoon of idolators have a way of becoming the clay pigeons of tomorrow. Who, for example, still regards Rudy Wiedoeft as a great jazz saxophonist? How many people buy the novels of such former literary "giants" as Sir

295

Hall Caine and Robert W. Chambers? And does anyone consider the pre-Raphaelites as anything other than practitioners of charming Victorian kitsch?

Conversely, Lester Young was ignored during his lifetime. A few people loved and believed in him, and stuck by him until the end, but it wasn't enough to counteract the corrosive effects of racial intolerance, thousands of mindless humiliations, and general public indifference. He died at forty-nine: The official verdict was alcoholism and overall debilitation of the system, but those words were a mere bowdlerization for the slow ritual murder of a black man who knew his own worth, but who didn't know his place.

So now we're back to the gravestone, and the way that Lester justified his particular existence between the two stark lines of birth and death. He was undoubtedly the single most important jazz musician of his generation, as his contemporaries will testify. My own comments will be purely subjective, for I never knew him, never met him, never even heard him in person. But that is totally unimportant. A million face-to-face interviews could not capture in words the essence of the 122 tracks he recorded for ARC and Columbia between 1936 and 1941.

The Reverend John Gensel once described Lester Young as the "the most profane man I'd ever heard." Lester's speech and attitudes merely reflected the filth that had been dumped on him during his lifetime, like a stately marble building exposed to years of city pollution. The real soul of the man is heard on these records and there isn't a note of hatred or ugliness on any one of the tracks: just the purest beauty and love of life.

Lester is one of those very rare people who has left us something that will not be diminished by time. Who knows what even greater heights he might have achieved had the world accepted him as the consummate artist that he was, instead of relegating him to the back of their consciousness as a second-class citizen.

LESTER YOUNG: "I was born in Woodville, Mississippi. I was born there and then I was taken to New Orleans, where I was raised. We lived in Algiers, just across the river, where Henry Allen was born. I didn't even know I had a father until I was ten years old: just me and my mother and my sister (Irma) and my brother (Lee).

"In New Orleans they had these trucks that went 'round advertising for a dance that night and the band would be playing on the truck and it just excited me. I got to act as handbill boy: I'd be running around, giving out handbills, and I loved that music so much that I'd be running until my tongue was hanging out. Every time I heard some music playing, I'd stop whatever I was doing—*boom!*—and run and see what was happening. I got so I knew all the places the trucks would stop and I'd be there. At that time I didn't even know my father was a musician with his own band. He played all instruments, but he liked trumpet the best.

"When I was around ten, we went from New Orleans to Memphis, then from there to Minneapolis, where I was raised mostly. They tried to get me to go to school there and all that bullshit, but I wasn't interested.

"I first started playing drums because I liked the guy who played drums on the truck. My father had a touring band and I played alto in it, 'cause he got the motherfucker out of a pawnshop, so I just picked it up and started playing it. I'd get close to my sister when she was playing and I'd pick out the parts, marches and all. Then one day my father goes to each one in the band and asks them to play their part and I knew that was my ass, because he knew goddamn well that I couldn't read. Well, my little heart was broken, you know; I went in crying and I was thinking, 'I'll come back and catch them, if that's the way they want it.' So I went away all by myself and learned the music. And then I came back into the band and played and all the time I was copying what I'd heard on records, but I knew the music, too,

297

just so I could fuck those motherfuckers completely, you know? I threw out all those goddamn marches and everything was great. And the rest of the band, they all laughed when I was thrown out, and now they came up to me and said: 'Won't you show me how to play like that?' And I showed them. I showed them shit!"

Lester was probably in his early teens when that incident occurred, but already his passionate belief in himself and his refusal to knuckle under to his detractors is evident. He possessed the type of qualities that enabled many a white man to rule empires—and got many a black man lynched!

Lester toured with his father's band during the late twenties, covering Minnesota, Kansas, New Mexico, Nebraska, and the Dakotas. The break came when the leader proposed going south, as he did most winters. Lester was eighteen: a very street-wise eighteen. He balked at the prospect of even more racial humiliations, and quit the band in Phoenix, Arizona. He next surfaced at the Wiggly Cafe, Salina, Kansas, where the following incident probably took place.

LESTER YOUNG: "I gave up drums because of chicks. Well, one chick did it for me. She was kinda one too many. Well, this night I was playing someplace and I had my eye on this nice little bitch and her mother kept saying: 'Come on, Mary, let's go.' Comes the end of the date and I'm trying to pack my kit and her mother's calling her, once, twice, and all the other guys are walking out with their fucking clarinet cases and trombone cases and finally she splits. So I say, 'Shit! I'm through with drums.'"

The world owes a debt of gratitude to Mary. And to her mother.

JO JONES: "Do you know that for twenty years after he gave up drums Lester Young played more drums than fourteen other drummers?"

It was while he was in Salina that he teamed up with Art Bronson.

LESTER YOUNG: "After that I switched to alto. I was playing with Art Bronson's Bostonians. It was a nice little group, about eight or ten pieces. Art Bronson played piano. But we had this evil-assed motherfucker in the band who played tenor. Oh, boy! He had a good background, mother and father with money, and we were always having to wait around for him. Then one night this cat starts up as usual: 'Wait for me. I've got to put my tie on. Help me find my coat'—all that kind of shit, and all the guys are standing around, mad as hell. So I told the bossman, I said, 'Listen, let's not keep going through this. You buy me a tenor saxophone and I'll play this motherfucker.' So Art went to the music store, bought me a tenor, and we split. As soon as I got my mouth 'round it, I knew it was for me. The alto was a little too high."

Lester gigged around with Bronson for two years, rejoined his father briefly, and reteamed with Bronson until the latter's group broke up in Wichita in 1930. He then moved back to Minneapolis and worked at the Nest Club under the leadership of Frank Hines and Eddie Barefield.

JO JONES: "I first met Lester at the Nest in Minneapolis. I was playing with a guy named Bert Patrick around Nebraska. That would be August 1930. I heard about Lester through a wonderful entertainer by the name of Clarrie Cammell. There were three entertainers: Clarrie, Genevieve Stearns, and Arcola Coles. These three had Chicago, Kansas City, and the rest of the Midwest all sewn up. You couldn't bring anyone else in there, from Ethel Waters on down. Anyway, she said: 'I want you to hear something,' and she pulled out this silver record. And after I heard it I had to see Lester in person. I'd find out enough of an individual through friends or relatives, so that when I met them I could hold a conversation, then I'd hop a car or freight and go there. Anyway, I reached Minneapolis, met Lester, knew he was as great as I heard, then we went our separate ways for a while."

In 1932 Lester forged his first link with the Basie band, joining the Blue Devils led by the legendary bass player Walter Page.

JO JONES: "Without Mr. Page, you would never have heard of Count Basie, Jimmy Rushing, Lester Young, Hot Lips Page, and certainly not Jo Jones. He was my father and my son."

The next two years were brutal and never remembered with any accuracy by Lester. The Blue Devils played for a while in Oklahoma City, toured extensively, had their instruments impounded in West Virginia, and finally decided it was every man for himself.

LESTER YOUNG: "We were sitting around with all these hoboes and they showed us how to grab a train. We made it—with bruises—and we hit Cincinnati with no horns, all raggedy and dirty, and we were trying to make it to St. Louis or Kansas City."

Then came a job with the great King Oliver—the nadir of his young career.

LESTER YOUNG: "I was with King Oliver for about a year. He had three brass and three reeds and four rhythm. He was old then and didn't play all night, but his tone was full when he played. He was a nice fellow, a gay old fellow, and it wasn't a drag playing for him at all. Shit, that was so long ago. People are always coming up to me, asking me questions about the past."

We have a few sketchy accounts of that King Oliver band, but even if we hadn't it would not be too difficult to reconstruct the picture. King Oliver was then in his late forties, his gums and teeth ruined by pyorrhea, a has-been in the music business, only able to hire burned-out veterans and green kids. The tour embraced some of the poorest areas of the South, impoverished even before the advent of the Depression. Audiences of three and four were not uncommon, and when there was a decent take at the box office he was more often than not gypped by unscrupulous bookers and managers. Oliver had the reputation of being a sexual athlete and it's not hard to see that this man, broke, at the end of his rope, his once formidable musical talents shot to hell, would draw increasingly on the one remaining symbol of his manhood, leaving the band and the business to disintegrate around him.

Somehow or other, Lester made his way back to Minneapolis and there he heard Count Basie broadcasting out of Kansas City.

LESTER YOUNG: "Now, Earl Hines had eyes for me, but I wanted to join Count Basie, 'cause I heard him all the time on the radio. He had a tenor player I couldn't stand."

COUNT BASIE: "I first met Lester Young in Kansas City. Guys who'd heard him play in Minneapolis used to tell me about him, then he wrote to me, saying he didn't like my tenor man [Slim Freeman] and that he'd like to play with my group."

LESTER YOUNG: "So he sent me a ticket."

This was in late 1933 and it heralded the start of one of the happiest periods in Lester's life. He was also to join up with his great friend and rival, Herschel Evans.

JO JONES: "I joined Basie on St. Valentine's Day, 1934. By that time, Lester and Herschel were twins."

COUNT BASIE: "I'll always remember when I first heard Lester. I'd never heard anyone like him before. He was a stylist with a different sound. A sound I'd never heard before or since. To be honest with you, I didn't much like it at first."

JO JONES: "Lester had style—like the shape of a Coca-Cola bottle—or a Rolls-Royce."

Lester alienated a lot of good musicians when they first heard him play, just as he baffled and enraged people who like to see jazz's family tree neatly pruned and cultivated—and no cross-breeding! The more dogmatic critics have always backed away uneasily when faced with the specter of Lester's sole inspiration—a part American Indian C-melody sax player who came out of the Midwest and who never played with blacks in any band.

JO JONES: "Lester hated critics and always jived them. The only time he talked straight with them was when they asked him

301

who his inspiration was. They thought he'd say Coleman Hawkins or someone like that, and he said Frankie Trumbauer. I don't think they believed him, but they didn't understand the influence that man had on musicians until after World War II, because half the time they don't listen. Trumbauer had all the technical knowledge and individuality in the world—so much that he was forced out of the music business and had to go into the airplane industry."

LESTER YOUNG: "Frankie Trumbauer was my big influence. I had to make a decision between him and Jimmy Dorsey. I wasn't sure which way I wanted to go, you dig? I had these records and I'd play one of Jimmy's and one of Tram's and all that shit. I didn't know nothing about Hawk then, but I knew of all the guys who were telling stories those two had it. Finally Trumbauer was my man. Did you ever hear him play *Singing the Blues*? That tricked me, right?"

MITZI TRUMBAUER: "Tram was playing with Paul Whiteman and sometimes after he'd finished for the evening we'd go up to Harlem and hear Count Basie and Lester Young. Tram was always interested in hearing good new musicians in town—I think all the boys were. I think sometimes Lester would recognize him, because he'd look over and give a funny little movement of his head and Tram would smile and nod back. But I don't think they ever spoke. Lester seemed very shy and Frank was part Indian and never used two words where none would do, but they seemed to understand and respect each other."

That was later, when the Basie band was established in New York. But Lester had worked in New York two years earlier, which proved to be a traumatic event.

LESTER YOUNG: "The Henderson band came to Kansas City and I ran a million miles to hear Coleman Hawkins play, but Hawk wasn't with the band that night, so Fletcher went around saying: 'Ain't you got any tenor players in Kansas City?' and that sort of shit. Now, Herschel was out there, but he couldn't read.

302

So they said: 'Red'—they called me Red then—'Red, come up here and play this saxophone.' So I went up and played Coleman's saxophone and all the parts, clarinet and all, then I had to run ten blocks to where I was playing and there were all of thirteen people waiting to hear me."

But it seemed Hawkins turned up later. Certainly, he appeared with Henderson at the Cherry Blossom, where the Basie band was playing.

JO JONES: "I wasn't with Basie then"—(he was with Tommy Douglas, playing piano and vibes)—"but I was there. Everyone was. It was December 18, 1933."

MARY LOU WILLIAMS: "The word got 'round that Hawkins was at the Cherry Blossom and within an hour there were Lester Young, Buddy Tate, Ben Webster, Herschel Evans, Herman Walder, and one or two unknown tenor men piling in the club to blow. Ben Webster woke me up at about 4 A.M. and told me Hawkins had his shirt off and was still blowing, trying to compete with Ben and Herschel and Lester. Lester always took about five choruses to get warmed up, but no one could handle him in a cutting contest."

JO JONES: "That was the first night Hawkins was really challenged. But when I say 'challenged' it was respectful. These sessions were held for the joy of playing. Anyway, when Hawk left to join Jack Hylton in England, he recommended Lester to take his place with Fletcher. Fletcher wanted Chu Berry, but Hawk said, 'Get Lester Young.'"

JOHN HAMMOND: "Fletcher had been to Kansas City. He came to me and said: 'John, I heard a band out there that is so great that I'd like to fire everyone,' so I asked him if it had a good tenor player because that was what he was looking for, and he answered: 'Absolutely the best.' So I gave Fletcher the money to bring Prez in."

LESTER YOUNG: "I went to Little Rock with Basie and I got this telegram from Henderson asking me to join him. I showed it to Count and he said, 'Ain't nothing I can do,' so I split and went to Detroit first."

Those are the bare facts. But the actual details were quite different and very revealing of Lester and his attitudes.

JO JONES: "I had to put a pistol on Lester Young before he would go to join Fletcher's band, because he didn't want to go—no way! Imagine, we were in Little Rock and here he gets an offer for seventy-five dollars a week, plus a uniform. We were getting fourteen dollars a week and when I joined I had to wait three weeks to get five dollars and the reason I got it so soon was that I took Mac Washington's place and he had drawn twenty-five dollars, so Basie was ahead. If Basie had said, 'No, you can't go,' Lester would have stayed, I know that."

JOHN HAMMOND: "Prez came to New York and stayed with the Hendersons. Now Prez practiced a lot and there was a pretty good piano in the apartment, but Leora [Henderson] couldn't stand his sound."

LESTER YOUNG: "Fletcher's wife would take me down to the basement where they had an old wind-up phonograph and she'd play me Coleman Hawkins records on it and she'd ask me: 'Lester, can't you play like this?' Every morning that bitch'd wake me up at nine o'clock to teach me to play like Coleman Hawkins. And she played trumpet herself—circus trumpet!"

JOHN HAMMOND: "Fletcher's band was supposed to go into the Cotton Club—this would have been March 1934—and they called a rehearsal about two days after Prez hit town. As soon as they heard Prez, the whole sax section rebelled. They said that he sounded like another alto, that the section didn't have anybody: They hated him! And Fletcher was too weak to stand up to them. I was absolutely entranced. Prez would get up and I had never heard anything like it in my life. And I'd say to Fletcher: 'He's the best saxophone player I ever heard,' and Fletcher would reply: 'I know, John, but nobody likes him.'

"I think he lasted about ten days and during that time the band had perhaps a couple of one-nighters."

LESTER YOUNG: "I wasn't happy with the band. The motherfuckers were whispering about me every time I played. So I went to Fletcher and asked him if he would give me a nice recommendation if I went back to Kansas City, and he says: 'Oh, yeah!' right quick. Then I went and joined Andy Kirk's band and had a nice time."

During 1935, Lester returned yet again to Minneapolis, where he played with Boyd Atkins and Rook Ganz. In the following year, he teamed up with Count Basie at the Reno Club, Kansas City.

JOHN HAMMOND: "The next time I saw Lester was in Kansas City in 1936. I'd been in Chicago with Benny Goodman's band and I'd heard the Basie band broadcasting from the Reno Club over a very powerful car radio. I'd never heard such a great sound in my life. They were absolutely electrifying."

John Hammond's enthusiasm won over Williard Alexander of MCA. A contract was drawn up and arrangements were made for the band to come East. However, while Hammond was trying to negotiate a deal with the American Record Company, Decca sneaked in by the back door and signed Basie to a three-year recording contract—with no royalties. It also stipulated that he enlarge his group to a minimum of twelve or thirteen pieces. Herschel and Jo Jones had rejoined the Count in the fall of '36 and he had also brought in Buck Clayton to replace Hot Lips Page.

JO JONES: "When Joe Glaser thought Louis' [Armstrong] lip had gone, he took Lips Page from us and when Louis got better Glaser gave Lips crumbs from the table: crumbs from a crumb!

"We weren't going to come to New York without Walter Page. We begged his wife to let him come for just one month. All he wanted was to be home with his wife and family, but without him we wouldn't have come for a thousand dollars a week each. He was the 'Big 'Un.' 'Big 'Un, what shall we do?' As late as 1947, we were playing in Atlantic City and the sax section was having a problem. He walked around, grabbed Jack Washington's baritone, moved him slightly, walked back, and sat down. Everything was jim-dandy after that."

John Hammond wanted to get the band's original sound on wax before Decca took them over. The group had a month's date at the Grand Terrace in Chicago on their way to New York, and it was here that Lester made his first recordings, under the illicit title of "Jones–Smith Inc.," Jones and Smith being the plebian names of the drummer and trumpet player, respectively.

COUNT BASIE: "John asked me if I wanted to record. I didn't have my library and didn't know what the heck we were going to do. So we just sat down and came up with four tunes and had a nice little ball on the session. John was always figuring out little things like that and I think those sort of dates go a lot better than when things are written out and planned in advance."

JO JONES: "The Jones–Smith session upset the recording world. We had worked at the Grand Terrace from 10 P.M. until 4 A.M., then we left there and went to the Cafe de Lisa. John went over to the studio and got things set up early, because he was used to New York musicians, but we were there on time.

"The books always give October 9 as the recording date, but they're wrong. It was the day after my birthday—October 8, 1936."

Shoe Shine Boy #1

Lester was twenty-seven when he made his recording debut, comparatively late for a major jazz musician at that time. Rarely can anyone have had such a stunning initial impact. From his opening sixty-four-bar chorus to the closing two-bar break he is in complete command of the situation. Solos: Count Basie, Lester Young (sixty-four bars), Carl Smith, Basie, Young (two bars),

Smith, Basie, Young (two bars), Smith, Basie, Young (two bars), Jo Jones, Young (eight bars in ensemble), Basie, Young (two bars), Basie, Walter Page, Smith.

Shoe Shine Boy #2

This was the rejected take which lay in the vault until it appeared on a European bootleg LP in the early seventies. Now, for the first time, collectors have a chance to compare both takes, back to back. Solo sequences are identical, but this version is slightly more raggy and loose. Oddly enough, the original file card says this tune came out of *Hot Chocolates of 1930* but the tune wasn't written until 1936. Solos: As #1.

Evenin'

A somber showcase for the band's vocalist, Jimmy Rushing. Jo Jones: "It was very cold that day. Jimmy came in with his overcoat on and kept it on right through the session." Solos: Basie, Young (eight bars), Basie, Jimmy Rushing, Basie (obligato), Smith (obligato), Young (eight-bar obligato), Smith (obligato), Basie, Rushing, Smith and Young (eight-bar obligato duet).

Boogie-Woogie

Jimmy Rushing at his shouting best. Lester comes in like a bouncing ball then rolls, as smooth as a bearing, through twenty-four bars. John Hammond: "Buck had a split lip that day, so we used Tatti [Smith] instead." Solos: Basie, Smith (Young interpolating), Basie, Smith (Young interpolating), Rushing, Young (forty-eight-bar obligato), Young (twenty-four bars), Smith (Young heard faintly in background), Basie, Smith (Young interpolating), Basie, Smith (Young interpolating).

Oh Lady Be Good

The final cut of this date. If only some other rejected takes existed from the session. This tune was featured in a Fred Astaire musical of the same name and Jo, who used to be a great tap dancer, sounds as though he is dancing on his drums. Lester romps like a high-spirited racehorse who hasn't been given enough exercise—this, after being up all night! Jo Jones: "We made these records in one hour. All the time I was looking out of the window, watching a man playing with his dog over by the lake. We were all through by 10:05." Solos: Basie, Young (sixty-four bars), Smith, (Young thirty-two bars in ensemble), Basie, Page, Smith (Young eight-bar riff).

Because of the Decca contract, John Hammond was unable to record the band for the ARC labels, Brunswick and Vocalion. But he quickly found a way around the situation. Although Basie himself couldn't be featured on any other label, there was nothing to stop the star soloists of the band from freelancing and the perfect format was there on ARC: the Teddy Wilson–Billie Holiday records that were produced for the Negro jukebox market. I intend to discuss the Wilson–Holiday setup in greater detail in Volume 2 of *The Lester Young Story*.

JOHN HAMMOND: "In January 1937 I started recording the Basie guys with Teddy Wilson and Billie Holiday and I'll never forget the first session. The electricity between Billie, Prez, Jo, Buck, and Freddie was amazing."

Teddy Wilson was working with Benny Goodman's band as a featured artist and one of the stipulations of the deal was that Benny should work a number of sessions as a sideman for Wilson's recording dates—at sideman's rates. Benny was never happy with the arrangement and didn't get to record as many sides as he should have. But he was on this first, memorable session.

JO JONES: "We came into New York and started recording with Miss Billie Holiday. Before us, the only recording of Billie's that made any sense was *I Cried for You*. Prior to that, they had no system, no format—here we come, two mikes. It was either Teddy Wilson featuring Billie Holiday, or Billie Holiday featuring Teddy Wilson.

"Benny Goodman was on this one. He was with Victor at the time and there had to be some subterfuge. Claude Williams, the guitarist and violinist with the band, was about to quit. He'd just been down and embarrassed Stuff Smith with his playing, but we couldn't pay him enough money and he had a lot of other things going—we won't go into that—and didn't need to be a sideman. John took us all down to the Black Cat to hear Freddie Green play."

JOHN HAMMOND: "They always had good strippers at the Black Cat, so it was never any trouble getting them to go."

JO JONES: "The next time I see Freddie Green he's in the studio for this date and none of us had ever played with him before. I'm recording without a bass drum and Benny Goodman asks me where it is. I say: 'I don't keep time for you. A whole note gets four beats; a half note gets two; a quarter note gets one. That's enough for anybody. All I use is a sock cymbal and a snare drum.' Well, John smooths things over and we start to record with the King of Swing."

Usually, a minimum of two tunes out of the four were dogs, just dumped on them by publishers, but on the January 25 session they had two good new Irving Berlin numbers, plus two classic pops from the late twenties.

He Ain't Got Rhythm

This and the following song came out of a Hollywood musical *On the Avenue*, starring Dick Powell and Madeleine Carroll. It was a dull movie, redeemed by a brilliant score, which also included *You're Laughing at Me, The Girl on the Police Gazette, Slumming on Park Avenue,* and *I've Got My Love to Keep Me Warm.* Billie sings the cynical lyrics in a very flip fashion, Lester bounds along merrily, and Goodman seems very much in command, as befits a star. Little did he know what was going to happen. Altogether, a very auspicious debut for the Lady Day–Prez partnership. Solos: Teddy Wilson, Benny Goodman, Wilson, Goodman, Billie Holiday (Buck Clayton obbligato), Lester Young (eighteen bars), Clayton.

This Year's Kisses

It seems incredible that this group had never played together before. Billie's vocal has the right note of poignancy and Lester's solo acts as the perfect foil. Solos: Wilson, Young (twenty-eight bars), Holiday, Wilson, Clayton, Young (eight bars in ensemble).

Why Was I Born?

A Broadway show tune (from *Sweet Adeline*) written for Helen Morgan. There is a case for omitting this from the set, as Lester's obbligato is so underrecorded that it is virtually inaudible, but he does make his presence felt and Billie's vocal would be the poorer without him. Besides, then we'd be denied Buck Clayton's stunning muted solo. BG seems to be aware of what's happening around him and his solo has a note of sour aggression, quite unsuited to the mood of the piece. Solos: Clayton, Holiday (Young obbligato), Wilson, Goodman.

I Must Have That Man

The pièce de resistance. Billie's rendering of Dorothy Fields' lyrics sends shivers up your spine and I cannot imagine a second take of Lester's solo, because it just couldn't be done any other way. Goodman seems like the man in the grip of a nightmare, a supreme technician relying on his craft to see him through. John Hammond: "I have never seen Benny so much at a loss as he was on this one." Solos: Wilson, Holiday, Wilson (obbligato), Clayton (obbligato), Wilson (obbligato), Young (sixteen bars), Goodman, Clayton.

Sun Showers

This marks the second of the Holiday–Young collaborations and although it isn't as noteworthy as the first session it does have the added attraction of the peerless Johnny Hodges. Both this and the next song came out of the movie *Broadway Melody of 1938*, starring Robert Taylor and Eleanor Powell. (Although *Sun Showers* was cut from the final print of the film, it was later featured in a Judy Garland film, *Thoroughbreds Don't Cry*.) Billie could always transform good songs into great ones, but it's astonishing how she could bring out the hidden qualities in a mundane number such as this. You're not aware of the words, because she uses her voice as another musical instrument. Lester comes in for the last sixteen bars and he's like a giant cat, the lightness of his tone in no way concealing his strength and grace. Solos: Young (four bars), Clayton, Johnny Hodges, Holiday (Buster Bailey obbligato), Wilson, Young (sixteen bars, last four joined by ensemble).

Yours and Mine

Not one of my favorite tunes. A rather jerky construction doesn't help and Buck Clayton, who rarely puts a foot wrong, seems to be straining for effect. Lester, however, takes it all in his stride. Jo Jones: "I wasn't on this one, but it doesn't matter. You say the clarinet player is unknown? Well, I know who he is. Who do you think it is? Remember, you weren't there, either, so be careful. You're right, it is Buster. How could it be anyone else? Unknown, shit!" Solos: Wilson, Hodges, Clayton, Holiday (Bailey obbligato), Wilson, Young (sixteen bars, last four in ensemble).

Mean to Me #1

This was the original 78 issue. Lester phrases "da-da" at the beginning of the second eight bars of his first sixteen-bar chorus, Buck plays open horn and Lester is like a voluptuous woman stretching on the eight bars after the bridge. Solo Wilson, Young (sixteen bars), Clayton, Young (eight bars), Holiday (Hodges obbligato), Wilson, Clayton.

Mean to Me #2

This was first released on microgroove. The most obvious difference is that Buck plays muted horn and Johnny Hodges is more subdued behind Billie's vocal. Lester's last eight bars before the bridge are more languid than take #1, while the eight bars after the bridge are phrased more intricately. Solos: As #1.

Fooling Myself

I'm prejudiced in favor of this one, because it was the first Billie record I ever bought. Lester plays the melody straight, yet still puts a completely different emphasis on its structure. Listen to how Billie's voice tails off on "affair." Heartbreaking! Solos: Wilson, Young (sixteen bars), Wilson, Clayton, Holiday (Bailey obbligato).

Easy Living

They played this behind the credits of a wonderful iconoclastic Preston Sturges movie of the same name. The lyrics are intelligent and way out of the Tin Pan Alley rut and the middle eight always makes my spine turn to water—or maybe that's because of Lester, Billie, and Buck. Catch Buck's muted obbligato, or if you're a trumpet player who thinks he knows how to accompany vocalists, better skip it! Solos: Wilson, Bailey (subtone clarinet), Young (sixteen bars), Wilson, Holiday (Clayton obbligato).

I'll Never Be the Same

This was originally called *Little Buttercup,* but I think that title would even defeat Billie. Teddy Wilson takes an outstanding thirty-two-bar chorus. Lester's intro is like a charcoal fire, quiescent on the surface, but glowing with heat underneath. Billie tells the truth when she sings, for she never was the same after she teamed up with Lester. Solos: Young (four bars), Wilson, Holiday (Young thirty-bar obbligato).

I've Found a New Baby #1

This is the original 78 issue. It's a free-for-all jam session with no holds barred. Buck comes tearing in with Eldridge-like ferocity and Lester is in a swaggering mood. Solos: Wilson, Jones, Bailey, Clayton, Wilson, Young (sixteen bars), Jones, Bailey, Jones, Young (eight bars).

I've Found a New Baby #3

The difference between the two takes are very noticeable, but I would like to mention that Teddy Wilson's intro is reminiscent of *That's A Plenty*, Buck is quieter and Teddy's solo swings more than #1. Solos: As #1.

Me, Myself and I Are All in Love with You #1

This is the first Holiday–Young session under Billie's name, issued on the thirty-five-cent Vocalion label. Actually, this take never appeared on 78, making its debut on a ten-inch Columbia LP. Instead of Teddy Wilson, we have the obscure James Sherman on piano. Sherman only worked in New York for a couple of years. Most of his career was spent in his native Pennsylvania, and as accompanist for the Charioteers vocal group. Listen to how Billie comes in on *Me*, changing down like a crack driver in a thoroughbred racing car negotiating a hairpin bend, Lester following her all the way. But which one is the driver? It doesn't matter a damn. Solos: Young (four bars), Holiday (Clayton obbligato), Ed Hall, Clayton, James Sherman, Holiday (Young thirty-two-bar obbligato).

Me, Myself and I Are All in Love with You #2

Lester's intro is practically identical to take #1, Buck again is muted in his obbligato and open in his solo, and the other soloists differ only slightly. But Lester wanders away from Billie at the start of her second chorus and proceeds to teach us a lesson in the art of jazz improvisation. Solos: As #1.

A Sailboat in the Moonlight

My dearest memory of this song stems from watching the Edna Ferber–George S. Kaufman movie *Stage Door*. Starving actress Andrea Leeds, who looked as though she'd been eating alum, climbs a staircase while a companion trills *Sailboat* in the background, then plunges to her death through a window. I always felt she'd heard this version and couldn't stand the comparison. Lester's first obbligato conjures up a picture of him lying in a boat while the night wind ripples his saxophone keys. Solos: Clayton, Holiday (Young thirty-two-bar obbligato), Sherman, Clayton, Young (eight bars), Holiday (Young sixteen-bar obbligato).

Born to Love

This must have been a poor seller on 78. We assembled four copies in various stages of decay, plus a test pressing from a badly pitted master, selected the cleanest passages on each, spliced, edited, and finally came up with a complete take. Not a note is missing. The tune is not too inspired, but Lady and Prez give it their old one-two, turning it into a knockout! Solos: Sherman, Holiday (Sherman obbligato, Young thirty-two-bar obbligato), Clayton, Holiday (Young sixteen-bar obbligato).

Without Your Love #1

This session provided some of the greatest obbligato playing in the history of jazz. Lester's accompaniment here is delicate in the extreme, seemingly whispering consolations to Billie's lament. Solos: Young (four bars), Holiday (Young thirty-two-bar obbligato), Sherman, Clayton, Holiday (Young sixteen-bar obbligato).

Without Your Love #2

Very similar to take #1. However, Lester's obbligato seems to hum along with Billie, while Buck holds a sustained note at the end of his solo as opposed to the little flurry on take #1. James

Sherman sounds very like Teddy. That's probably why they used him. Solos: As #1.

JO JONES: "Lester Young was not a conversationalist. He spoke through his instrument."

Technical Note

Nothing illuminates the capriciousness of early recording techniques more than a project of this nature. In assembling the titles that make up the albums in *The Lester Young Story*, we drew on original shellac 78s, laminated reissues, sixteen-inch glass- and metal-based acetates, vinyl test pressings, ten-inch and twelve-inch LPs, and quarter-, half-, and full-track tapes, each with their own peculiar sound qualities. As we progressed chronologically, we found that the recording balance varied considerably from session to session and even from master to master. Eventually, we could almost plot the events that led up to Billie stepping back a few paces from the mike, or why the trumpet section was regrouped between takes #1 and #2. It became obvious that many of the unissued performances had been rejected because of technical problems rather than musicians' errors. Lester, especially, had a habit of producing certain sound frequencies on his horn that caused the needles on the recording gauges to practically burst through their glass. Test pressings, which should have provided us with the best of all possible transfers, were often virtually unusable, owing to the masters having buckled and corroded over the years. In some cases, unissued metal parts had been destroyed and we had to borrow less than perfect tape copies from generous collectors.

Engineer Doug Pomeroy, faced with this Pandora's box of sounds and surfaces, went way beyond the call of duty to get the best possible results: taking tapes home to listen to them in his spare time; keeping copious notes on each track; finding the right frequencies to tone down wear and distortion. The result is that he has enhanced the original sound without betraying the work of the engineers of nearly forty years ago. I should like to take this opportunity to pay tribute to his professionalism and dedication.

My thanks, also, to the following collectors who helped to make this project possible: Bob Altshuler, Jeff Atterton, John Hammond, John Kendall, Dan Morgenstern, Hank O'Neal, Brian Peerless. Special thanks are due to the staff of the Archives Division, CBS Records; Mary Prioli, Institute of Jazz Studies, Rutgers University; and to Jerry Valburn, who loaned us the only known copies of certain items.

Special thanks to Chris Albertson for making available to me rare, taped interviews with Lester Young.

(1976)

316

ART HODES

One of the great pianists and proselytizers of and for the Chicago school of jazz beginning in the late 1920s, **Art Hodes** was a warm, deeply blues-rooted player. He was an active teacher and disc jockey in his later years as well and did quite a bit of writing for a number of magazines, in which his epigrammatic, conversational style conveys a wonderful flavor of the times.

Pure Blues

Jimmy and Mama Yancey
(Atlantic 1283)

January '50 ... Pee Wee Russell, Chippie Hill, and myself, plus George Brunis, Fred Moore, Lee Collins; an eleven-week gig at the Blue Note, Chicago. When we closed, Chippie couldn't wait to get back to New York. A week later the news hit me; Chippie had been killed; automobile accident. And now it was "burial time" ... back in Chicago ... South Side. As I looked around the parlor ... faces ... her people. Where were the many fans; people she'd made happy ... what a drag. Then two people, directly in front of me, turned around ... a man and a woman ... Mama and Papa Yancey ... yeah, everybody spoke of 'em as Mama and Papa ... they turned around and looked at me, and I felt better...then we spotted young John Schenck...the only other white face in the room...a real jazz fan...he collected musicians...ran sessions ...heck, it wasn't two months before this that Chippie and I had done a gig for Schenck...the Yanceys were there. They sure liked Chippie...they were together a lot.

Course I'd heard of Yancey before this...Gene Williams of *Jazz Information* played some of his records for me...and Dan Qualey had recorded Jimmy on his Solo Art label. I'd heard his playin'...and I knew somethin' about the guy...he worked as a groundskeeper for the White Sox baseball team...Comiskey Park, Chicago...Nope, he didn't play piano for a living. As the story goes, in his youth, Jimmy was one hell of a dancer...made it all the way to the top...I mean you can't go much farther than a Command Performance before the Royal House of England. Why he quit dancin'? I don't know...never asked the man. I never got to know him then, in Chicago...and I was there up to '38. Guess I met Yancey in '47...Phil Featheringill introduced us ..."Art, this is Jimmy Yancey"...What you really noticed was the twinkle in his eye; good humor...and he wasn't movin' in any hurry. We shook hands, sat down, and chatted...the usual musician's talk...piano players we both knew; the South Side; barbecue ribs...all this over a drink or two. Then I got a hankering to see him dance...and I kept after him...well, you know (and this really describes him), he wasn't gettin' up off that chair... so, just a 'sittin' there he started movin' his feet; swingin' lightly; tappin'...and, man, that cat was makin' more sense...and more rhythm...than many a drummer I'd had to work with, who like to run me out of the music business.

Seymour's, a record shop on Wabash Ave. Upstairs, a cubbyhole room; dusty; small; a beat-up piano, well out of tune. Saturday afternoon frolic...jam session...this particular "hey rube" was special...photog's...maybe pictures in *Life*...or was it *Look*...the best of the local "le jazz hot" were there...the

Yanceys, George Zack, Floyd O'Brien, Bill Moore, Pfeiffer; maybe twenty musicians ... and about as many customers ... who cared ... you worried about your dough after it was over ... Mama sang ... soft, quiet like ... Jimmy played ... you don't notice him; you feel him ... he's always "in there" ... starts and ends in the same tempo; even, easygoin' blues ... it's a good kick just bein' in the room. When it's your turn to play, you don't "cut him" ... you don't try ... Jimmy never laid down that kind of sound ... the way you feel is you're glad he played before you did ... you feel like you're in the right place.

Rupneck's was jammed ... and a Wednesday nite ... raining, to boot ... it was our "one year" celebration. My notice was in ... a month from now I'd hit the road. We'd invited everybody ... a lot of musicians dropped in ... so did the Yanceys ... the drinks flowed and we had our "jolly's" ... Jimmy played and Mama sang ... That was about the last time I "caught 'em" ... You ask them to perform and they did ... I never heard them say no ...

The chapel was "full up" ... Mr. Preacher talked ... who can remember what he said ... no doubt the line in *Didn't He Ramble* was spoken ... "He was a good man" ... Dry sobs; wet eyes ... The principal character wasn't talking ... Jimmy Yancey had passed on. He played to a full house; standing room only ... no segregation ... a mixed audience ... The boys who drank with him; played the jam sessions with him, were there ... a very unusual send-off ... these boys who played it "hot" stood up and played it soft and mellow ... played Hymns ... When it was over, we filed out into the daytime air ... a depressed group that sought solace in everyday chatter that didn't quite "come off." The drive to the cemetery ... the burial; and during the lowering of the casket, the musicians played *High Society*.

(1958)

DUKE ELLINGTON AND STANLEY DANCE

Duke Ellington was, of course, jazz's greatest composer and bandleader. His unique sensibility came through in all aspects of his personal style, not least in his writing; his autobiography, **Music Is My Mistress**, is the **Moby-Dick** of jazz writing, a giant grab bag of various miniature forms in an utterly distinct voice.

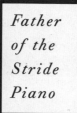

Father of the Stride Piano

James P. Johnson
(Columbia CL 1780)

My first encounter with James was through the piano rolls, the Q.R.S. rolls. There was a drummer in Washington who told me about them, took me home with him, and played me *Carolina Shout.* He said I ought to learn it. So how was I going to do it, I wanted to know. He showed me the way. We slowed the machine and then I could follow the keys going down. I learned it!

And how I learned it! I nursed it, rehearsed it . . . Yes, this was the most solid foundation for me. I got hold of some of his other rolls, and they helped with styling, but *Carolina Shout* became my party piece.

Then James came to Washington to play Convention Hall. It holds maybe four or five thousand people. I was always a great listener. I'm taller on one side than the other from leaning over the piano, listening. This time I listened all night long. After a while, my local following started agitating.

"You got to get up there and play that piece," they said. "Go on! Get up there and cut him!"

So, you know, I had to get on up there and play it.

"Hey, you play that good," James said. We were friends then, and I wanted the privilege of showing him around town, showing him the spots, introducing him to my pals, the best bootleggers, and so on. That, naturally, meant more leaning on the piano. Afterward, we were fast friends, and James never forgot.

Later, when I showed up in New York, I found him there, and I met Lippy, too. Lippy was his dear friend, his pal—his agent, you'd have said, except he never took that 10 percent. James was doing pretty good. He'd written the show *Running Wild*—not the tune but the show—and that's where *Charleston* was born. So he wasn't hungry. But he never lost contact with his foundations, with the real, wonderful people in Harlem. Harlem had its own rich, special folklore, totally unrelated to the South or anywhere else. It's gone now, but it was tremendous then.

So there in that atmosphere I became one of the close disciples of the James P. Johnson style. Some nights we'd wind up—James, Fats Waller, Sonny Greer, and I—and go down to Mexico's to hear The Lion. I was working and would buy a drink. "Ninety-nine" we called it, because it wasn't quite 100 proof. Tricky Sam had likely stayed up all night to help make it. Tricky was Mexico's official taster. So we would sit around, and during intermission I'd move over to the piano. Then it would be Fats. Perhaps he'd play *Ivie*. (He dedicated that to Ivie Anderson, I think.) Afterward, he'd look over his shoulder jovially at James and call, "Come on, take the next chorus!" Before you knew it, James had played about thirty choruses, each one different, each one with a different theme.

By then The Lion would be stirred up. James had moved into his territory and was challenging. "Get up and I'll show you how it should be done," he'd say. Then, one after the other, over and over again they'd play, and it seemed as though you never heard the same note twice.

James, for me, was more than the beginning. He went right on up to the greatest. You know, he ordinarily played the most, and in competition a little bit more. You couldn't say he cut The Lion. It was never to the blood. With those two giants it was always a sporting event. Neither cut the other. They were above that. They had too much respect for each other. They played some impossible things, but it was like a game.

Other times, Lippy and the bunch would get together, get James cornered, find a taxi, or maybe walk over to someone's house, and ring the bell. This would be 3 or 4 A.M. People stuck their heads out of windows, ready to throw a pot (flowerpot, maybe).

"Who's that down there?" they'd growl.

"This is Lippy," the answer would be. "I got James with me."

Those doors flew open. Lights switched on. Cupboards emptied, and everyone took a little taste. Then it was me, or maybe Fats, who sat down to warm up the piano. After that, James took over.

Then you got real invention—magic, sheer magic.

James he was to his friends—just James, not Jimmy, nor James P.

There never was another.

—*Duke Ellington*

322

James P. Johnson has never been accorded his due, yet it is not too much to claim that his was the first major influence on jazz piano. An enduring influence via the music of Fats Waller, Duke Ellington, and Count Basie, it may even be heard upon occasion in the work of Thelonious Monk.

Johnson was born in New Brunswick, New Jersey, in 1894, and there he received some elementary piano lessons from his mother. From her, too, he inherited a feeling for country and set dances. Hymns in church and parade bands on the street were among his other remembered musical experiences before the family moved to Jersey City in 1902. There he heard early ragtime, popular songs played with "strong rhythm and syncopated vamps," and piano styles from the South and West. It was not until 1908, when they moved again, this time to New York, that he heard real ragtime—and symphony concerts. He took lessons from a teacher, Bruto Gianinni, who corrected his fingering and taught him harmony. This tuition usefully supplemented the absolute pitch that was his birthright and the sense of style he was rapidly acquiring from his study of other pianists like Luckey Roberts and Abba Labba.

Jazz in the New Orleans idiom hadn't reached New York yet, but ragtime was played everywhere and pianists maintained a very high standard. Because they usually played alone, they had developed "the orchestral piano—full, round, big, widespread chords and tenths—a heavy bass moving against the right hand." In order to accompany entertainers properly, they also learned to play songs in all keys, and this further increased their versatility. The glamorous life of the "ticklers," as the pianists were called, appealed to Johnson, and he soon resolved to follow it himself. Quite apart from his professional opportunities, the tickler also had a social importance. Nearly every home had a piano before World War I, but not every home had a pianist. The well-equipped player could therefore go from party to party through the night, always sure of a welcome, food, and liquor.

In the spring of 1913, Johnson started working in the Jungles, the Negro section of New York's Hell's Kitchen, and later he played at Barron Wilkins' in Harlem. Within a short time he was recognized as one of the best ticklers in the city, and all kinds of avenues opened to him.

He began cutting piano rolls for Aeolian in 1916, and for Q.R.S. a few years afterward. He led a five-piece band onstage in a Broadway show. His compositions were accepted for publication (he sold the first two for twenty-five dollars each). He went on the road as musical director of the *Smart Set* revue. And in 1921 his first records as a piano soloist were issued.

Thus, about the time most detailed jazz stories begin, Johnson was already a successful and well-schooled musician of considerable and diversified experience. The transition from ragtime to jazz, as the former waned in popularity, was no problem for him. He had heard Jelly Roll Morton and an exponent of the walking, Texas, boogie-woogie bass years before. The blues had steadily grown in favor at the expense of the rags, and the Original Dixieland Jazz Band had arrived, "imitating," as he told Tom Davin, "the New Orleans style never heard in New York before."

Johnson was now master of the superb "stride" piano style. No question of origins or synthesis can affect the fact that it was a style completely compatible with the spirit of jazz. Alternating a chord in the middle of the keyboard with a single note, octave, or tenth in the lower register, his powerful left hand produced an exciting drive and momentum. Against this was set a stimulating treble part, executed with that grace and dexterity which had been the ragtime tickler's pride. Johnson and this music made a lasting impression on Art Tatum as early as 1923.

The twenties were the busiest of times for "The Father of the Stride Piano." He wrote popular songs of lasting merit like *Old-Fashioned Love* and *If I Could Be with You,* and he wrote music for all kinds of shows. One of the latter, *Plantation Days,* was so successful that he went on a European tour with it. In Hollywood, he did the score for a musical short starring Bessie Smith. There were playing engagements, too, uptown and downtown, and jam sessions, and parlor socials, and house-rent parties.

When the Depression came, he went into a kind of semiretirement, not an easy transition after so much success. "Radio and films changed things," he told Rudi Blesh, "and the Negro lost out." At home, he spent much of his time in satisfying an old desire to write concert music. A long choral work, *Yamecraw,* had been the basis for the Bessie Smith movie. His *Harlem Symphony,* written in 1932, received several performances in the United States and abroad. A piano concerto, *Jasmine,* and an elaborate concert treatment of *St. Louis Blues* were also completed, and he worked steadily at his most ambitious project, a symphony portraying the story of jazz.

Toward the end of the thirties, he was brought back into the limelight by means of records and the *Spirituals to Swing Concerts* at Carnegie Hall, but a partial stroke in 1940 again limited his activities. He nevertheless recorded extensively during the first half of the decade, worked in Greenwich Village in 1945, and wrote the music for a show called *Sugar Hill* in 1949. But after a further stroke in 1951, he was bedridden until his death in 1955.

Ten of the performances in this collection, all previously unissued in the United States, were recorded by John Hammond in 1939. (They were rejected at the time as being "uncommercial," an accusation which often really meant "too good," as John knew.) Five of these were made with a small band which included Henry Allen, J. C. Higginbotham, Gene Sedric, and Sidney Catlett, the remainder being piano solos. Five more solos date from the hectic twenties, and there is a duet with Clarence Williams from 1930.

They thoroughly demonstrate Johnson's rich musical resources as composer and performer. The opener is his striding version of Edgar Sampson's Swing Era favorite *If Dreams Come True* and *Carolina Shout* and *The Mule Walk* are examples of his translations of old-country dance tunes. Here his beautiful, crying blues, enhanced by a fine sense of dynamics and a touch that always draws a melodious quality from the piano, are fully expressed. They are not "primitive" performances, and yet his superior technique and conception in no way inhibit feeling. In all of them, his extraordinary gift for melodic variation is evident. With the band, he is invaluable as a soloist and as a member of the rhythm section. Like Fats Waller's, Duke Ellington's, or Count Basie's, his accompaniment is assured, imaginative and inspiring. The theme statement in *Hungry Blues* clearly reveals his penchant for a singing style, and for beauty of sound and texture. (This song, incidentally, was from his one-act opera, *De Organizer,* for which Langston Hughes wrote the libretto.) His voice is heard in some humorous banter with Clarence Williams in *How Could I Be Blue?,* and the way he ends it, a little impatiently, may serve as a reminder that of his many gifts his ability as a pianist was the greatest.

"Aw, c'mon, let's play piano!" he says.

—*Stanley Dance*
(1962)

DANNY BARKER

New Orleans-born guitarist **Danny Barker** played or recorded with everyone from New Orleans trumpeter Bunk Johnson to Charlie Parker; for much of the 1930s and 1940s he was a member of the Cab Calloway big band. A world-class raconteur, his books **Bourbon Street Black** and **A Life in Jazz** contain some of the best and most uninhibited jazz storytelling available.

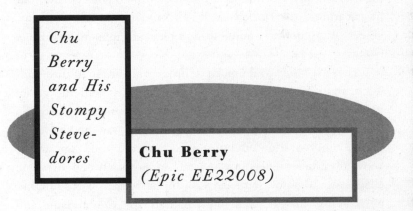

Chu Berry and His Stompy Stevedores

Chu Berry
(Epic EE22008)

Chu was one of the truly great giants of jazz—proven by paying the hard, cold, cruel dues of a jazzman.

He was one of the many of hundreds of jazz musicians who journeyed to the apple. "Big Apple!"—New York City—Harlem—the solid stone jungle. Musicians and performers came to New York from all over the United States because the country was in the grip of Depression. Music-playing for a living was in a sad condition. Money was scarce and jazz lovers could not support clubs, cabarets, ballrooms, and places of entertainment, so musicians came to New York City seeking fame and fortune. On the radio from New York City came the music of Duke Ellington, Cab Calloway, and Fletcher Henderson. On records the great sounds of Louis Armstrong and McKinney's Cotton Pickers.

When the musicians arrived in the big city, they went straight to the Band Box and the Rhythm Club, two meeting places—combination clubs and gambling houses. Both of these places had pianos, kept in tune, and an abundance of first-rate pianists who were continuously seated at the pianos twenty-four hours around the clock, and they would oblige any musician, singer, or group who wanted to start playing, jamming, or cutting contests.

These sessions could make or break a musician. At these sessions you showed your ability, talent, artistry, and the critics passed on the verdict. The competition was centered mostly on trumpets and tenor saxes. Coleman Hawkins was the king, boss of the tenor—acknowledged and acclaimed "King" the whole world over. In sessions Mr. Hawkins had heroically conquered all challengers. But now here arrived Chu Berry and scores of other great tenor players, and they battled for the acclaim and Hawkins' throne. There was Ben Webster, Lester Young, Herschel Evans, Don Byas, Dick Wilson, Bud Freeman, Georgie Auld, Pazuza (Stafford Simon), Jimmy Wright (who would always open the battles—warm up the scene), Joe Garland, Greely Walton, Cecil Scott, Sammy (Snake) Davis, Spider, Cass McCord, Teddy McRae, Elmer Williams, Bingie Madison, Johnny Russell, Joe Beatus (Theodore McCord).

When a band came to town to the big city, the critics stirred up a session, usually on a Monday night at the Victoria or Brittwood's or the Hollywood Big Apple or another small cabaret.

There was the constant prowling of Chu Berry and Roy Eldridge—in and out of joints—looking for contests and battles—Chu and Roy—Roy looking for trumpets and Chu after the scalps of tenor players. These two managed many exciting and historic battles—and gradually the contests dwindled down to a handful of competitors. I withstood many hours of these sessions—"It was dog eat dog." No place for the weakhearted. Here the men were divided from the boys. Chu's name and acclaim soared to the skies of Harlem and the music world. He and Roy cut many recordings for Commodore records. There is one tenor player who humorously stands out in my memory. Jimmy Wright—a handsome New York-born tenor player. He was always there with his tenor sax at his side as the gladiators sat around or stood at the bars—booming. The official instigators would yell loudly, "Jimmy Wright, start the fireworks," and Jimmy Wright would mount the small bandstands and start wailing on *Liza* or *Body and Soul* or *Stardust*—or *I've Got Rhythm*.

Chu Berry was there playing with Teddy Hill's Savoy Ballroom Orchestra, a fine swing band, and nightly his admirers gathered in front of him at the bandstand. Chu's acclaim was earned step by step, inch by inch—his name became famous—on the streets the people fondly greeted him; owners of clubs and joints welcomed him. You always saw the two with their horns under their arms, Roy Eldridge and Chu Berry.

In the thirties, New York was loaded with musicians. Some good, some great, some old, many young. You came to the big town. To Harlem with your instrument and the first impression you made was it. You were instantly classified—given a rating—once you were heard. And there were masters on every instrument. There were severe critics all about who classified your ability if great—good—so-so, or just a blower—nothing special—and you soon found out your rating by who hired you. There were many bands—dozens—and after a while you found out what class you were in—and it was a hard system for the moment of truth. Giants socialized with giants. Lobs with lobs. It was New

York City—the greatest in the world. You either upset New York or it upset you. It was sharp, keen competition. You either have it or you don't. If you have greatness, you had better keep alert—a young mind and forever on your guard because there is the new breed constantly snapping at your legs—keep your guard up. There's little sympathy for a loser in New York City. Most funeral services are at night because people are very busy during the day.

In the case of Leon (Chu) Berry, he fought all the way never stepping back one inch. He was a master of the tenor saxophone. I watched and listened to him play beautifully all types of songs—with great deep inner feeling with great facility and technique—speed, topped with a beautiful tone—and he never once stopped practicing and experimenting.

One of the most exciting nights I experienced in jazz happened in Harlem at a place called Puss Johnson's. Puss was a drummer out of Norfolk, Virginia, who opened a nightclub—strictly on his muscle—no license—no nothing—just paid off the right police people. This place was fairly large and musicians patronized it. He encouraged sessions like most joint owners—it meant great free music and large crowds of music lovers. It was a common sight to see any night in Harlem a large group of musicians, entertainers, and friends after midnight walking on Seventh Avenue, Lenox Avenue, or one of the side streets. The musicians with their horns—going to a club, cabaret, or joint down in a basement. The answer was if you asked what was happening, "Oh, we're going to so-and-so's place and jam. Two cats are going to settle who's the best." That was how the musicians made their reputations—in the twenties, thirties, and forties. No press agent or publicist. You made your name of fame the slow, hard way by proving your talent—under fire. There was no big buildup in the press and news media. Rarely did the news columnists write up musicians—especially jazz. Coleman Hawkins had gone to Europe and stayed for some years, and in his absence a dozen or more great tenor sax men sprouted up out of the concrete pavements of Harlem—Chu Berry and his men battled and fought in sessions for recognition.

I had joined Cab Calloway's Cotton Club Orchestra, which was the highest-paid band in the land (colored band). Cab worked constantly more than any other band—solid bookings—Chu Berry recommended me. I was real chummy with him and Roy Eldridge. They both liked my rhythm playing. Like a tornado, the news opened that Coleman Hawkins had arrived from Europe and was back in Harlem. For a couple of weeks, nobody saw Hawk at the usual spots. There were arguments that he was not in town. He was scared to come out and play before the public. It was said that he had stayed in Europe too long, had become rusty on his horn; corny, behind the times. The Harlem critics and instigators yelled. "Where is he?" "Well, find him." So Hawk was found and the news spread that he was coming to Puss Johnson's joint Monday night. Well that Monday night Puss' joint was packed to the rafters. Jimmy Wright took charge of the bandstand, blowing his tenor. All the famous musicians who were off were there sitting about, waiting for the entrance of the Mighty Hawk—Lester Young, Ben Webster, Don Byas, Bud Freeman—all tenor sax men of note. Chu Berry was restless on the Cotton Club bandstand. The phone was kept busy calling Puss' joint—"Is the Hawk there?"—"Is the Hawk there?"—"Has the Hawk arrived yet?" Finally the answer was—"Yes, the Great Bean is here, sitting at a special reserved table directly in front of the bandstand." At 3 A.M. after the last show half of Cab's band disappeared out of the club in cabs—uptown to Harlem. When we entered, you couldn't see anything for the smoke of nervous cigarette smokers. After about ten minutes, my vision became clear and I could see what was happening in Puss' joint. There was an electric tenseness about the place—a tenor player was blowing a slow, soft ballad and the packed, jammed club was quiet and orderly. Many famous jazz musicians were standing—glasses in their hands—talking softly. I squeezed through near the band-stand to get a look at the Hawk and there sat the Hawk looking into the eyes of a very beautiful woman. She was shocking, strange-looking—an Oriental beauty. She was olive-colored with long black hair and a silk dress with bold leopard designs—she had extra-large black eyes. She made the glamorous Harlem chicks look like yard dogs. She and Hawk sat whispering softly, as if alone—indifferent to the eyeballs of the gawkers. She and Hawk knew they were upsetting the crowd.

Then I heard: "There's Chu Berry!" "There's Chu Berry!" "There's Chu Berry!" These words echoed until all lips spoke them—and there was neck-straining to see Chu Berry.

Chu pushed his way through the crowd to Hawk's table. Both Hawk and the exciting-looking woman arose and shook hands with Chu—they smiled and chatted and Chu left and went up on the bandstand. Hawk and the woman looked up, watching the action on the stand. There was a change of musicians to relieve the ones playing on the stand. Up came Big Sid Catlett, Billy Kyle, John Kirby, Ben Webster, Lester Young, Don Byas, and Leo Paul—who was playing with Fred Waring and came to Harlem often—to jam. The place became very quiet—soft whiskies and tinkling glass noises. Then Big Sid started a fast fright drum rhythm going—a tune started. I recognized it as *Cherokee*. Then the voices of the crowd: *"Cherokee! Cherokee! Cherokee!"* That music was something to hear—*Cherokee* went on and on. I looked at Hawk and the woman as they talked seriously and softly. Hawk with a straight face looked at each of the tenor players as they took turns wailing—Chu—Ben—Dan—Lester—after each blowed a dozen or more choruses there was great applause—finally the *Cherokee* fracas ended—and there started a chant—

"We want Haw-kins!
We want Haw-kins!"

Puss Johnson approached Hawkins' table and talked to Hawk with all eyes watching. Then he spoke loud—"Hawk will play another night when he has his horn." There were sighs of disappointment from the large crowd—a couple of nights later Hawk came with his horn—and introduced his sensational version of *Body and Soul,* reclaiming his greatness and the respect of all—all tenor players copied that solo note for note.

Chu Berry was considered next to Hawkins in greatness and he earned that honor the hard way—by always being willing, ready, and able to stand on the bandstand among the truly great giants of jazz—bravely with his horn at his side. He was constantly looking for action. On the road traveling with Cab Calloway's band after the long, monotonous four or five shows daily seven days a week, he, Milt Hinton, and Dizzy Gillespie would find small clubs in the different cities and go there and join with the local musicians. At the theater the local musicians crowded. His, Hinton's, Dizzy's dressing rooms—talking music. His life was music first, last and always. I shared the dressing rooms generally with him, Jonah, Tyree. When in New York City he was kept busy recording with small groups under various leaders. I was surprised one day when he said seriously that Freddy Martin was a great tenor player. Freddy Martin had a hotel society band and never played jazzy in the frantic Harlem sense—mostly adaptations of great classical music. Chu answered my questioning of Freddy Martin, saying, "That man has a great big even tone and is a master technician."

The last time I saw Chu alive he was getting in a car going to Canada from Ohio. He asked me if I wanted to ride with the group in the car instead of the big Greyhound bus. It was after a dance and I was tired and could stretch out on the bus—Chu and the group left ahead of the bus—a half hour later the bus stopped on the highway. There were many night red flares on the road—an accident. The bus emptied to see what had happened. There was the car. The front smashed in, and on the roadside

Chu lay unconscious. The ambulance sped up. We followed to a small hospital in this small town. They laid Chu on a bed—and I heard the attendant say, "We can't get a doctor until tomorrow morning, 7 A.M." I looked at my wristwatch—it was 3 A.M. We boarded the bus and sped off to Toronto, Canada.

(1969)

CHARLES MINGUS

One of the great composers, bandleaders, and bass-ists of the past fifty years, **Charles Mingus** was a strong and unforgettable personality as well. He liked to write his own liner notes, too. The present set appeared as a large-format insert in the original LP issue of **Let My Children Hear Music** and was transcribed from a conversation with producer Teo Macero.

Let My Children Hear Music

Charles Mingus
(Columbia KC 31039)

Each jazz musician, when he takes a horn in his hand—trumpet, bass, saxophone, drums—whatever instrument he plays—each *soloist*, that is, when he begins to ad-lib on a given composition with a title and improvise a new creative melody—this man is taking the place of a composer. He is saying, "Listen, I am going to give you a new complete idea with a new set of chord changes. I am going to give you a new melodic conception on a tune you are familiar with. I am a composer." That's what he is saying.

I have noticed that there are many kinds of composers in this so-called jazz. For instance, there are musicians who simply take rhythmic patterns and very spare notes—very limited invention, melodically—and play in a soulful swinging way. Some people in the audience, when asked what they think about jazz, say, "I just go by the feeling. I go by the feeling the guy gives me." Now, whether there is feeling or not depends upon what your environment or your association is or whatever you may have in common with the player. If you feel empathy for his personal outlook, you naturally feel him musically more than some other environmental and musical opposite who is, in a way, beyond you.

I, myself, came to enjoy the players who didn't only just swing but who invented new rhythmic patterns, along with new melodic concepts. And those people are Art Tatum, Bud Powell, Max Roach, Sonny Rollins, Lester Young, Dizzy Gillespie, and Charles Parker, who is the greatest genius of all to me because he changed the whole era around. But there is no need to compare composers. If you like Beethoven, Bach, or Brahms, that's okay. They were all pencil composers. I always wanted to be a spontaneous composer. I thought I was, although no one's mentioned that. I mean, critics or musicians. Now, what I'm getting at is that I know I'm a composer. I marvel at composition, at people who are able to take diatonic scales, chromatics, twelve-tone scales, or even quarter-tone scales. I admire anyone who can come up with something original. But not originality alone, because there can be originality in stupidity, with no musical description of any emotion or any beauty the man has seen, or any kind of life he has lived. For instance, a man says he played with feeling. Now he can play with feeling and have no melodic concept at all. That's often what happens in jazz: I have found very little value left after the average guy takes his first eight bars—not to mention two or three choruses, because then it just becomes repetition, riffs and patterns, instead of spontaneous creativity. I could never get Bird to play over two choruses. Now, kids play fifty thousand if you let them. Who is that good?

Today, things are at the other extreme. Everything is supposed to be invented, the guys never repeat anything at all and probably couldn't. They don't even write down their own tunes, they just make them up as they sit on the bandstand. It's all right, I don't question it. I know and hear what they are doing. But the validity remains to be seen—what comes, what is left, after you hear the melody and after you hear the solo. Unless you just want to hear the feeling, as they say.

When I was a kid and Coleman Hawkins played a solo or Illinois Jacquet created *Flyin' Home,* they (and all the musicians) memorized their solos and played them back for the audience, because the audience had heard them on records. Today I question whether most musicians can even repeat their solos after they've played them once on record. In classical music, for example, people go to hear Janos Starker play Kodaly. They don't go to hear him improvise a Kodaly, they go to hear how he played it on record and how it was written. Jazz was at one time the same way. You played your ad-lib solo, you created it, and if it was worthwhile, then you played it in front of the public again.

Now, on this record there is a tune which is an improvised solo and which I am very proud of. I am proud because to me it has the expression of what I feel, and it shows changes in tempo and changes in mode, yet the variations on the theme still fit into one composition. (It is not like some music I hear where the musician plays eight bars and then the next eight bars sound like he is playing another tune.) I would say the composition is on the whole as structured as a written piece of music. For the six or seven minutes it was played (originally on piano), the solo was within the category of one feeling, or rather, several feelings expressed as one. I'm not sure whether every musician who improvises can do this. I think I do it better on bass, although most people in the past did not understand the range I used to play (nowadays, most all bass players use this range when they solo—the full scope of the bass), because they didn't really listen, they thought I was just playing high to play high, rather than realizing that my composition began someplace and developed to another. I have never struggled to be accepted as a great bassist—I imagine I could have been if I had seen my available musical goal there. If people really knew the qualification of a good bass player, they would flip—because I know thirty or forty bass players who have the technique that I have.* Whether or not they are as inventive is something else because when you study the instrument, it calls for a technique that jazz has not even begun to express yet, with the bow or with pizzicato. The full-developed bass player masters harmonics with a sense—I don't mean just scraping the bow across and making squeak sounds, I mean he can play compositions in harmonics. There are a million bowings that could and probably do duplicate a horn better. For instance, my dream has been to put basses, or maybe two basses in a reed section, in place of the baritone saxophone. I never had the chance so I could never say how it really sounds, it is only in my mind that I can say I hear it and it would work better than most baritone saxes. I had a classical student who was in the symphony in Minneapolis. He used to study through the mail and, for his lessons, I would write things for him and he would retape them and send them back. That was when I realized how much more could be done, musically, by using the bass with the bow, by utilizing all the possibilities of this instrument.

Back to the record: The music on this record is involved with my trying to say what the hell I am here for. And similar ideas. Another one is: Let my children hear music—for God's sake—they have had enough noise. But mainly I am saying: Do you really know Mingus, you critics? Here is a piece I wrote in 1939 and I

---

*Which, incidentally, brings to mind another thought: Along with the jazz hump music and nigger contests, there has never been a contest to decide who is the king of the trumpet in the symphony. Or who is the best violin soloist—Jascha Heifetz, Yehudi Menuhin, Isaac Stern, Salvatore Accardo? Or which is the best string quartet of the year—Budapest or Julliard?

wrote it like this because I thought in 1939 I would probably get it recorded someday. But when you have to wait thirty years to get one piece played—what do you think happens to a composer who is sincere and loves to write and has to wait thirty years to have someone play a piece of his music? That was when I was energetic and wrote all the time. Music was my life. Had I been born in a different country or had I been born white, I am sure I would have expressed my ideas long ago. Maybe they wouldn't have been as good, because when people are born free—I can't imagine it, but I've got a feeling that if it's so easy for you, the struggle and the initiative are not as strong as they are for a person who has to struggle and therefore has more to say.

Part of the reason I am a composer is that I studied composition with Lloyd Reese. Lloyd Reese taught Eric Dolphy; Harry Carney also studied with him and so did Ben Webster and Buddy Collette, to name a few. Art Tatum highly recommended him. When Art found out I was studying with Lloyd, he asked me to come and play for him. Lloyd Reese was a master musician, he knew jazz and all the fundamentals of music from the beginning. (He used to be the first alto player in Les Hite's band.) And he could play anything. I remember he turned a record on to me one time. (In my era the record stores weren't crowded with the Beatles' records or rock'n'roll or hillbilly. They had a few hillbilly and a few records they called rhythm & blues. But it wasn't a big market then. The record stores were mainly for white people. They had classical music. I remember Richard Strauss, Debussy, Ravel, Bach, Beethoven. I remember my favorites: Debussy, Stravinsky, and I liked Richard Strauss very much—the one who wrote *Death and Transfiguration*. In any case, I remember one day when I came to Lloyd's house, he said: "What is this?" and he played a record. I didn't know the title at the time, but he said: "What do you think is going on in this particular movement right there?" And I said: "I don't know, man, but there's a whole lotta shit going on. There's too much to figure out."

The timpani was playing and the basses were playing and the piano was playing a percussional sound with the bass—you could hardly hear the piano—and the flutes were playing syncopated chop rhythms, the trumpets were playing cock valves, and this cat said: "Well, here it is," and he took a C^7 chord—I remember it started on the third, and he played E, G, B♭, and D natural, and he said: "This is what the clarinets are doing..." and he began to decipher down what was going on. He said: "Here's the French horn part" and it came in on G, B♭, D, F an octave down and ended A natural, which clashed against the B♭, the clarinets were playing in the E, G, B♭, D natural line, and it made a beautiful sound. I said: "Whaaa? What is that?"

So I'm saying briefly that people don't know what a black man (it's nice to say black man)—people don't know what it took to make a jazz musician. In my young days, we were raised more on classical music than on any other kind. It was the only music we were exposed to, other than the church choir. I wasn't raised in a nightclub. I wasn't raised in a whorehouse (there wasn't any music in them, anyway—in the bars). Today I don't know how they train kids musically. But my point about Reese is that if you told the average person Lloyd Reese took the music of Stravinsky off a record, he would say you were crazy. There are millions of musicians, however, who have the capability of hearing and reproducing what they hear. It wasn't called ear training; I don't know what he called it. He would just say: "Now you take the trumpet part. Now, what's the French horn doing?" It was to show you structure, I imagine.

As I was saying, each jazz musician is supposed to be a composer. Whether he is or not, I don't know. I don't listen to that many people. If I did, I probably wouldn't play half as much to satisfy myself. As a youth, I read a book by Debussy and he said that as soon as he finished a composition he had to forget it because it got in the way of his doing anything else new and different. And I believed him. I used to work with Tatum, and Tatum knew every tune written, including the classics, and I think it got in the way of his composition, because he wasn't a Bud Powell. He wasn't as melodically inventive as Bud. He was technically flashy and he knew so much music and so much theory that he couldn't come up with anything wrong; it was just exercising his theory. But as far as making that original melodic concept, as Bird and Bud did, Art didn't do this for me in a linear sense. I would say he did it more in a chordal—structure sense. Bud and Bird to me should go down as composers, even though they worked within a structured context using *other* people's compositions. For instance, they did things like *All the Things You Are* and *What Is This Thing Called Love.* Their solos are new classical compositions within the structured form they used. It is too bad for us that they didn't compose the whole piece instead of using other people's tunes to work within. If they had, they would have been put in the same class as Bartók and Debussy—to anyone who knows. Bud wrote a few things and so did Bird. But they were still within the simple chord changes you were used to—either the blues (which shows how great they really were, to be able to create—with new and good melodic structures—on such simple chord progressions). In other words, if they had created anything complex, I am sure they could have upset the world.

For instance, Bird called me on the phone one day and said: "How does this sound?" and he was playing—ad-libbing—to the *Berceuse,* or *Lullaby,* section of Stravinsky's *Firebird Suite*! I imagine he had been doing it all through the record, but he just happened to call me at that time and that was the section he was playing his ad lib solo on, and it sounded beautiful. It gave me an idea about what is wrong with present-day symphonies: they don't have anything going on that captures what the symphony is itself, after written. I'd like to write a symphony, myself, on this form—the old Western form of classical music—I'd like to write a suite of three or four hours and have a solo in spots that is like Charlie Parker, with Bird in mind, playing ad-lib.

I think the music on this record is serious in every sense. I say, Let my children have music. I said it earlier. For God's sake, rid this society of some of the noise so that those who have ears will be able to use them someplace listening to good music. When I say good, I don't mean that today's music is bad because it is loud. I mean the structures have paid no attention to the past history of music. Nothing is simple. It's as if people came to Manhattan and acted like it was still full of trees and grass and Indians instead of concrete and tall buildings. It's like a tailor cutting clothes without knowing the design. It's like living in a vacuum and not paying attention to anything that came before you. What's worse is that critics take a guy who only plays in the key of C and call him a genius, when they should say those guys are a bitch in C natural. Pop music is still another story. Even tune structures are stolen. The music I've heard from the late pop groups (many of which are from England) seems to stem from a mixture of many different American composers and American music. *I Found a New Baby. Nature Boy. Ain't Necessarily So.* I hear these tunes, certain tunes, all through the Beatles' music, for instance. I don't know if they just surround themselves with this kind of music and compose from it. But it doesn't come out ringing true to me as English composition.

For instance, Schillinger used to say that you could take a sheet of music, turn it upside down—after you wrote a certain movement—eight or ten bars—copy it upside down, then copy it backward, from the end of the page back, turn the page over, and copy it backward and upside down. This would give you eighty bars or more of the same mood without working for it. It's the same as taking a tape recorder melody and splicing it up several thousand different ways. To me, that's not spiritual music. It leaves the feeling and emotion out. It seems to me that it should come from the heart, even though it's composed.

I think it is evident when a person is stealing or copying a form of music which is not his own. Other musicians recognize it, but I don't think it is important enough to them to say anything about it. Why, at least, doesn't the public, or don't the critics point it out? I heard a lot of Bird's solos in the music of this past and present rock music era. The names are not important. But what they do, more or less, is just take a melody created by a jazz soloist and put words to it. They add words to a solo with a few of the notes left out. That is what it sounds like to me and others I've discussed it with.

As I say: Let my children have music. Jazz—the way it has been handled in the past—stifles them so that they believe only in the trumpet, trombone, saxophone, maybe a flute now and then, or a clarinet. (Not too many of our "bad"—that is great—people go for the clarinet. Probably because there is not much work available for clarinetists, except for those who play in the studios.) But it is not enough. I think it is time our children were raised to think they can play bassoon, oboe, English horn, French horn, full percussion, violin, cello. The results would be— well, the philharmonic would not be the only answer for us then. If we so-called jazz musicians who are the composers, the spontaneous composers, started including these instruments in our music, it would open everything up, it would get rid of prejudice because the musicianship would be so high in caliber that the symphony couldn't refuse us.

In fact, who wants to be in the symphony anyway, nowadays? If you stop and take note of what jazz has done, and the kind of musicianship which has developed from each instrument (take the trumpet: Louis Armstrong, King Oliver, Maynard Ferguson, Cat Anderson, or the pyrotechniques of Dizzy Gillespie; you never hear that kind of high-note playing in symphonic works), it becomes obvious that it has made each player a virtuoso. That is probably why most European musicians now choose to be jazz musicians rather than classical players because they are always proving that the instrument can do more than is possible. I mean, the range has doubled in octaves. For instance, Stravinsky wrote a piece for a high trumpet. He used a special trumpet—a piccolo trumpet—to play high, but Cat Anderson played off the piano with an ordinary trumpet—played higher than the piano goes, higher than piccolos. So do Maynard Ferguson, Snooky Young, Ernie Royal, Louis Armstrong, King Oliver, Freddie Webster, Dizzy Gillespie, Fats Navarro, Clifford Brown, Hobart Dotson, Kenny Dorham.

There are many other instruments besides the trumpet which jazz musicians have made do the impossible. And they can play, for hours on end, technical, involved, difficult, educated lines that have melodic sense. They are all virtuosi. The same goes for string bass. The same goes for saxophone, although it is not used much in symphony. But anything Milhaud has done in classical music, McPherson and Bird, alone, do with ease as well as human warmth and beauty. Tommy Dorsey, for example, raised the range of the trombone two octaves. Britt Woodman raised it three. And take Jimmy Knepper. One of his solos was taken off a record of mine and written out for classical trombone in my ballet. The trombone player could barely play it. He said it was one of the most technical exercises he had ever attempted to play. And he was just playing the notes—not the embellishments or the sound that Jimmy was getting.

That about covers it.

Let my children have music! Let them hear live music. Not noise. *My* children! You do what you want with your own!

(1972)

344

BILL EVANS

Bill Evans was one of the major piano stylists to appear in the 1950s. His quiet, extremely intelligent, and precise approach is echoed in his writing. His notes to Miles Davis' **Kind of Blue** may be the most widely read liner notes in jazz history; the notes to the Webster–Zawinul **Soulmates** album contain some very valuable remarks on the meaning of "freedom" in the arts.

Kind of Blue

Miles Davis
(Columbia CS 8163)

There is a Japanese visual art in which the artist is forced to be spontaneous. He must paint on a thin stretched parchment with a special brush and black water paint in such a way that an unnatural or interrupted stroke will destroy the line or break through the parchment. Erasures or changes are impossible. These artists must practice a particular discipline, that of allowing the idea to express itself in communication with their hands in such a direct way that deliberation cannot interfere.

The resulting pictures lack the complex composition and textures of ordinary painting, but it is said that those who see well find something captured that escapes explanation.

This conviction that direct deed is the most meaningful reflection, I believe, has prompted the evolution of the extremely severe and unique disciplines of the jazz or improvising musician.

Group improvisation is a further challenge. Aside from the weighty technical problem of collective coherent thinking, there is the very human, even social, need for sympathy from all members to bend for the common result. This most difficult problem, I think, is beautifully met and solved on this recording.

As the painter needs his framework of parchment, the improvising musical group needs its framework in time. Miles Davis presents here frameworks which are exquisite in their simplicity and yet contain all that is necessary to stimulate performance with a sure reference to the primary conception.

Miles conceived these settings only hours before the recording dates and arrived with sketches which indicated to the group what was to be played. Therefore, you will hear something close to pure spontaneity in these performances. The group had never played these pieces prior to the recordings and I think without exception the first complete performance of each was a "take."

Although it is not uncommon for a jazz musician to be expected to improvise on new material at a recording session, the character of these pieces represents a particular challenge.

Briefly, the formal character of the five settings are:
So What is a simple figure based on sixteen measures of one scale, eight of another and eight more of the first, following a piano and bass introduction in free rhythmic style. *Freddie Freeloader* is a twelve-measure blues form given new personality by effective melodic and rhythmic simplicity. *Blue in Green* is a ten-measure circular form following a four-measure introduction, and played by soloists in various augmentation and diminution

of time values. *Flamenco Sketches* is a six-eight twelve-measure blues form that produces its mood through only a few modal changes and Miles Davis' free melodic conception. *All Blues* is a series of five scales, each to be played as long as the soloist wishes until he has completed the series.

(1959)

Soul-mates

Ben Webster and
Joe Zawinul
(Riverside RLP 9476)

As the music on this record poured into my ears, a Ben Webster portion prompted me to realize a fortunate historical coincidence: that the emergence and evolution of jazz has paralleled the invention and continued improvement of sound recording. It is not difficult to see that although musical notation is a device sufficient to preserve, record, and propagate music as traditionally composed in Western culture, there could be no conceivable system of notation that would allow a true and faithful recreation of the music of interpretive performers. The great composers as we know them may have been forced to many compromises in style because of the necessity of notating in such a way that the interpretive link could be used to preserve their music for future generations.

I was led to these thoughts, and to the others that follow here, as the magnificent maturity of Webster's music impressed itself on my mind. The great emotional scope revealed by a craft couched in simplicity is an accomplishment not easily measured, and those who do not react to anything but the spectacular or complex deserve to miss the deep satisfactions that can be gained from such an honest and mature artist.

This comment also applies to the work of Joe Zawinul and of the other players here, for each is a proven jazz performer of the first rank. All are capable of contributing in creative sympathy to the whole, as well as having the ability to serve as a lead voice. It seems to me admirable that jazz as an art and a discipline demands of its practitioners sufficient maturity to do both these things: to be a sensitive follower, as well as an authoritative leader. This spontaneous interplay of four or five individual creative voices is unique in musical performance today. Unlike composed music, which is the reflection of one personality, jazz performance is a constant document of a social situation.

The ideal and the accomplished fact of jazz thus far has been that of a group in harmony, and it is my personal hope that the impetus for group improvisation will never die out. Of course, a group expressing itself without regard for the quality of feelings or craft involved *can* still be considered the expression of a social situation, and some would argue that it is "truer art" or "free expression." But "free expression" as such exists most perfectly in infants, and their irresponsible and disorganized behavior can hardly be called art. I suspect that a deliberate seeking for lack of consciousness is apt to be the result of a fear of consciousness. It is peculiar that musicians who have developed to a degree in their craft by very conscious discipline would suddenly abandon this procedure—unless the truth is that they have thought too little and too late. I think no freedom is worthwhile that is not the result of responsible dedication. Furthermore, freedom of expression does not have to be sought. It is the natural outcome of disciplined work. I fear that those who seek it as a separate goal must end in an area of feelings so subjective as to be unfit for accomplished harmonious group performance and perhaps uninteresting to anyone but the individual performer himself.

The foregoing is certainly *not* a problem facing the performers on this LP; I'm sure it came into my mind because the music heard here is such a strong example of the "right" kind of freedom. But one might at first think that these musicians would face another kind of problem—that in some cases the differences in their ages and the varying eras out of which they have grown would create a disparity in style or craft that might preclude effective, mutually stimulating performance. Actually, however, these experienced and dedicated musicians have drawn their craft alike from the same basic traditions. All of them can, and at some time probably have, performed happily and effectively with jazzmen of all eras. Stylistic differences are transcended by a common intuitive understanding of certain challenges of their craft that are accepted by all—an understanding so pure that the boundaries between "strict" and "free" need never be spoken out loud.

This initial essential insight possessed by a person who directs himself toward the goal of becoming a jazz performer can be described as an entirely affirmative grasp of the basic challenges of his craft. It is based on a view of the trunk of jazz tradition as something that stands apart from specific "styles." To me, the only satisfying craft is one that stays in healthy relationship to this trunk and seeks to understand itself so well that it can reflect (with the least possible distraction on the part of style) the expressive desires of the individual's talent. A new branch that grows firmly from the trunk and sprouts higher than any other branch is something of value to all. The stoutest of these can eventually be recognized as further extensions of the trunk.

... Perhaps I should apologize for the lack of specific, detailed reference to the musicians or the selections played here. But the players are certainly well known, and the music speaks for itself more directly than any descriptive attempts I might make. So if these notes strike you as digressions, please excuse them and accept them as my highly respectful personal response to this demonstration of mature art by master jazz performers.

(1963)

350

DICK WELLSTOOD

A true eclectic, pianist **Dick Wellstood** was best known for his powerful stride playing, but he incorporated elements from the entire range of jazz. As a writer, Wellstood was almost shockingly good, with a funny, brilliantly allusive, and at times poetic style. This short appreciation of Earl Hines should raise a few eyebrows.

Quintes-
sential
Continued

Earl Hines
(Chiaroscuro CR 120)

Earl Hines— An Appreciation

Behold Earl Hines, spinner of yarns, big-handed virtuoso of the black dance, con man *extraordinaire,* purveyor of hot sauce.

Behold Earl Hines, Jive King, boss of the sloppy run, the dragged thumb, the uneven tremolo, Minstreal of the Unworthy Emotion, King of Freedom.

Democratic Transcendent, his twitchy, spitting style uses every cheesy trick in the piano-bar catalog to create moving cathedrals, masterpieces of change, great trains of tension and relaxation, multidimensional solos that often seem to be *about* themselves or about other solos—"See, *here* I might have played some boogie-woo-

gie, or put this accent *there,* or this run here, that chord there ...
or maybe a little stride for you beautiful people in the audience..." Earl Hines, Your Musical Host, serving up the hot sauce.

For all the complexity in his playing, Hines exercises fairly
simple harmonic vocabulary, and in any event his peculiar stut-
tering rhythmic sense gives his phrasing such force as to make
harmonic analysis almost meaningless. The dissonances he uses
are more the result of his fascination with the overtones of the
piano than of any concern with elaborate harmonic substitutions.
Accented single notes making the upper strings ring, or open
fifths or octaves sounded a tone or semi-tone apart (either will
do) at opposite ends of the keyboard are to him among the most
beautiful of sounds.

His is the music of Change, based on the rhythms of the
body in a graceful way unique to the older Jazz players. This may
be why he is more successful as a soloist than as a trio pianist.
The trio's oscarine petercision, a crutch for many, is a cage for
Hines. Its need for relentless accuracy and predictable responses
only betrays the tiny imperfections of freedom in his playing;
when he is playing alone, these imperfections meld into a sweet
flexible instrument of expression.

Hines is not a "stride" pianist. His rhythm is too straight
four-four, too free. He does not possess the magisterial dignity of
James P. Johnson, the aristocratic detachment of Art Tatum, the
patience of Donald Lambert, the phlegmatic unflappability necessary to maintain the momentum of stride. Hines needs silence
in the bass, room to let the flowers grow, space to unroll his
showers of broken runs containing (miraculously) the melody
within, his grace-noted octaves ("That's the way we make the piano *sing!*"–Eubie Blake), and his wandering, Irish endings.

His is Freedom in Discipline, infinite choice in a limited
sphere, the tension of Will vs. Material—his is human creativity.
Behold Earl Hines, King of Beasts!

(1973)

352

ANDREW WHITE

Washington, D.C.-based saxophonist **Andrew White** is best known for his exhaustive study and transcription of the solos of John Coltrane. His notes to this 1978 Coltrane reissue contain many independent-minded insights into the saxophonist's work and into jazz in general.

On a Misty Night

John Coltrane
(Prestige P-24084)

The first time I heard Coltrane was late in 1956 on a Miles Davis recording. His second break on *Dear Old Stockholm* was and still is the one frozen moment in music history for me. I was just getting into jazz, and even though I had already transcribed solos by Charlie Parker, Miles Davis, Jackie McLean, Horace Silver, and several others, Coltrane was something else. It was certainly the most unorthodox sound I had ever heard, and my saxophone teacher even said, "Ha! Ha! That guy is playing with his top lip on the mouthpiece." Well, I tried that on alto and it sounded a little bit like Coltrane but it was not natural. I was so intrigued that I had to write that solo down. So I did and *saw* what was happening.

353

I don't think Coltrane had any choice other than the sound that he came up with. I don't know if he was conscious of his unique situation but as a saxophone player delving into the depths of linear delineation, textural innovation, density of phraseology, and standard bebop inflection, he had to have a sound that would round out all of these other academic qualities of his music. Something unique. Otherwise, with a "normal" sound he would have sounded like he was running etudes.

Coltrane was an evolutionary artist and a craftsman. In my ten-volume publication *The Works of John Coltrane,* which consists of 421 transcribed saxophone solos recorded by Coltrane both as a leader and as a sideman, I divide his creative efforts into four loosely defined periods: 1955 through mid-1957, mid-1957 through 1959, 1960 through the end of 1964, and 1965 until his death on July 17, 1967. The music on this two-record set comes from the middle of the first period, the first two sides—originally the *Tenor Conclave* album—having been recorded early in September 1956 and the rest less than three months later. (The catalog number for the Coltrane solos from *Tenor Conclave* is Volume 6, Number 1; the solos on Sides 3 and 4—originally the *Mating Call* album—are Volume 4, Number 1.)

As was the custom in those days, the *Conclave* date was more or less a blowing session, with very informally put-together material and solo sequence. During this time, Coltrane was in and out of the Miles Davis band, also doing freelance work as a leader and sideman, and recording for several other record labels as well as for Prestige. His solos are freewheeling and spontaneous but do show significant signs of the level of ingenuity to be displayed in his later recordings. The November 1956 material that makes up Sides 3 and 4 here consists of six originals by composer-pianist Tadd Dameron. This would appear to have been Dameron's date, and was originally issued under his name, although any quartet session made up of one horn and rhythm section is apt to be dominated by the horn player. (It's particularly likely when he is *this* strong a soloist, while Dameron—one of the great arrangers of early modern jazz—plays in an unforceful style generally referred to as "arranger's piano.") However, Coltrane deserves much credit for being able to play solos as lyrical, as complementary to Dameron, and as personal as these. They project his image as a serious and sympathetic improviser, with a minimal amount of the self-indulgence that would later become a very noticeable part of his style.

The most dominant trait of Coltrane's music during this period was what I call his post-bebop lyricism. The concept of the "laid-back tenor player" (such men as Gene Ammons and Dexter Gordon were the most influential examples) is very apparent in his playing throughout, but particularly on these first two sides, undoubtedly because of his familiarity with the material and the informality of the session. It should be noted that during this period Coltrane was just budding on the jazz scene; national recognition of his ability as an improviser still lay ahead. Actually, he was pretty much playing in standard bebop style until he joined Miles Davis in 1955. The time spent with Miles, who many musicians accurately called the "star-maker," was the starting point of the Coltrane legacy. Miles had a way of putting bands together with musicians who were as diverse in their playing as they were in their personal life-styles. But some sixth sense seemed to give him the ability to bring the best out of everybody. In an interview many years later, Coltrane recalled that he was pretty much content to sound like anybody else until he joined the Davis band, that Miles had the ability to relax you while keeping you professional at the same time. He could also have pointed out that when Miles left the bandstand Trane *had to play*—he was the only horn left.

It was this constant professional pressure to produce that sparked the level of ingenuity in Coltrane's playing that would soon set him apart from the rest of the tenor players and mark him as the foremost saxophone player of the sixties, a crystallizer of the bebop era, and the so-called "Father of the Avant-Garde" (although, as is noted a bit later in this piece, this is a description with which I definitely disagree).

Trane was a very diligent and studious player. I do not, however, accept the popular belief that he was a "genius." I have already been put down quite a bit for saying this. But as someone who has transcribed as many Coltrane solos as I have, and is quite able to document his statements, I feel qualified to take this position. Besides, I am in no way seeking to diminish his importance—the vast amount of work I have put into transcription of his work should make that clear. It's simply that I would describe John Coltrane as an extremely gifted player who matched his talent with equal amounts of hard work and of self-indulgence. The combination of these latter two elements is what goes to make a total artist, not one or the other. And I feel that Coltrane expressed his very high level of diligence when he modestly said (during an interview with critic Frank Kofsky) that he always wanted to play a piece of material or a concept "better" or at least "different" the next time it came around.

To many people, Coltrane was an enigma. He is perplexing because his contributions to several different areas of jazz were so substantial that it is difficult to acknowledge that the uniqueness of each of his periods should be thought of as something quite separate and distinct from the others. Yet at the same time one cannot objectively deal with one period of his career without acknowledging those before and after it, because there is one aspect of his playing which never left any of his music. That was the bebop inflection.

Over the years before and since his death, Coltrane and his numerous imitators and followers have been responsible for many new directions in jazz, pop, and rock music, some more valid than others. But invariably the success of any new direction that spun off from Coltrane has been linked to the total Coltrane legacy—very much including elements from the mid-fifties period represented here. The groove, the swing, and the assertive bebop inflection are all essentials of the Coltrane style that have to be acknowledged in new directions. As Elvin Jones said to me as recently as August 1977: "After all, you can't get any more basic than John."

Although the point is hardly ever emphasized, the swing element of Coltrane's bebop influence never left his music and his musical language and sense of texture never took a really *free* form. I consider the title of "Father of the Avant-Garde" to be totally unwarranted. Avant-gardists tend to work from more sophisticated systems and use a much more liberal discipline than he did. In saying this, I am not taking sides either for or against the avant-gardists but merely seeking to draw attention to the fact that his work exemplifies the tried-and-true school of evolution rather than the radical type of departure made at the turn of the century by such composers as Schoenberg, Webern, and Bartók.

Coltrane never actually experienced such a radical departure. The rules and influence of the bebop period he had gone through were too strong to allow it. Perhaps some kind of compromise could have been made between these two approaches. But—just as in a business conflict the winner is going to be the one with the most resources to back up his venture—I don't feel that in this case Coltrane had a musical background substantial enough to afford radical change. Therefore, in his quest for newer ground, evolution took its course.

This is not to say that Coltrane was lacking in musical background according to the European standards which have been arbitrarily imposed on jazz and jazz musicians, but that his musical orientation was "different." Ironically, it is precisely this "difference" which is called style by many acclaimed jazz critics and aficionados. Style, in the European sense, usually implies usage and/or techniques, whether or not they have been learned or acquired in the standard academic sense of scholastic orientation. Because Coltrane, like so many other jazz musicians of the fifties, experienced an unorthodox education in the fundamentals of music, their approach to music should have only been judged by those unorthodox standards. It is one of the greatest injustices in the history of jazz to say that Miles Davis "can't play the trumpet," Thelonious Monk "can't play the piano," Philly Joe Jones "can't tune his drums," and John Coltrane sounds as if he is "playing with his top lip on the mouthpiece." Perhaps these assertions are correct according to strict European standards, but none of these artists are European, or had that kind of academic training. And, ironically, all of them are highly respected by a great many Europeans for their personal styles as well as their uniqueness and unorthodox ways.

The growth of jazz education programs in this country and abroad means that many people are being newly exposed to jazz. This is good up to a point, because so much jazz is academic (even though unorthodox). However, in bringing jazz to the classroom the romance and controversy surrounding the personal lives of musicians can lead to distractions. Like many others, John Coltrane did have a somewhat controversial life-style during the period represented musically on these four sides. While this would certainly make for provocative conversation, what does that have to do with the virtue of his music? In my opinion, very little. Excessive dwelling on the romance distorts the true virtue of jazz and the entire area of improvisation. When you get down to bare facts, it doesn't matter how "high" you get or how drunk, but how well you know the chord changes.

The music of John Coltrane and the other musicians involved on these four sides is an integral part of the testament of the bebop style. This is a sample of what was happening during that time in the story of jazz in general and of Trane in particular. The music should be judged according to the informality of the session and the studio, not by the Carnegie Hall standards of a Horowitz concert. It should be judged by the standards of the medium in which it is presented—vinyl, not manuscript. It should be judged in its own vernacular—improvisation, not the "thorough-composition" of a Beethoven. Above all, it should be judged according to the groove. Is it cookin'? *It's burnin'.*

(1978)

GUNTHER SCHULLER

Composer, conductor, and educator **Gunther Schuller** is one of the jazz world's preeminent citizens. Never limited by stylistic blinders, Schuller has written authoritatively about Ornette Coleman as well as King Oliver, and everything in between. His monumental studies **Early Jazz** and **The Swing Era** are landmarks of jazz thought and scholarship.

Ornette!

Ornette Coleman
(Atlantic 1378)

Well over a century ago (in 1830, to be exact), the musical élite of Paris first encountered the strange music of a twenty-seven-year-old composer named Hector Berlioz. The encounter was not a mutually agreeable one, for the Parisian public and musical professionals did not take kindly to Monsieur Berlioz's art. They accused him of not knowing his harmony, of having no sense of melody, of producing horrible dissonant sounds in his orchestration, of using conventional instruments in weird, hideously new ways, of writing a music that defied rhyme or reason, and ultimately condemned him as a "deranged madman."

The story, of course, doesn't end there. Some twenty years later public and musicians alike began to find some sense and logic in the "madman's ravings," and today the music of Berlioz figures consistently on orchestral concert programs.

The annals of music history are filled with similar instances of total public apathy and the temporary failure of the innovator's contemporaries to comprehend his creative efforts. One need only cite a few other cases: Schubert, who died of poverty and hunger, the bulk of his music unperformed and ignored; Beethoven, whose late music *still* baffles present-day "music lovers"; Mahler, Schoenberg, and Webern, who for long periods of their life were accorded epithets similar to those received by Berlioz, with some degree of comprehension of their music coming only *after* their death, and even then with holdouts most notably among musicians, whose prejudices are often bolstered by a little-but-not-enough knowledge; Lester Young, whose new sound and concept of the tenor saxophone was found unacceptable by fellow musicians for nearly a decade; Charlie Parker, who was laughed off the stand as a young man, later considered merely a weird "legend" by the relatively few who even knew of his existence, and whose music, like "late Beethoven," is still largely misunderstood (witness his countless imitators and the "false pretenders" to his throne); Thelonious Monk, who had to wait a decade or more for a belated sanctioning by his fellow musicians and the acceptance of his music by jazz audiences.

So much for historical fact and the old truism that history constantly repeats itself. In the process, time and time again, the well-entrenched authorities find self-righteous justifications and rationales with which to deride "the newcomer," little realizing, in their blissful ignorance, that the burden of artistic proof is as much on them as on the innovator.

One need not belabor the point. Ornette Coleman's music is part of the same historical process, and it has suffered some or all of the accusations enumerated above in the case of Berlioz.

But then as now, the end of the story has not yet been written. The freedoms Ornette Coleman's music has unlocked may yet be recognized as the triumphant breakthrough they in fact constitute.

What has this quietly intense man wrought to generate such violently divergent opinions? Are his concepts of melody, of tone, of musical form and continuity so radical as to justify the controversy enveloping his music? The answer lies in the music itself, obviously—although that is precisely the place where very few would seem to look, substituting instead their own "emotional" reactions as sufficient evidence for their claims.

Ornette Coleman's proposition is a very simple one: Release me from the bondage of long outdated harmonic and formal conventions, and I will take you away from the wallpaperlike clichés of my contemporaries and let you hear a world of sound which you have never heard before, which is free, and which is beholden only to its *own* innermost logic and discipline.

The scoffers, of course, reply that you can't have jazz without harmony and form, that anarchy is the inevitable result. Aside from the fact that one man's "anarchy" is another man's "freedom" (*vide* politics), it only needs to be pointed out that "classical" music started to do away with eight-bar phrases way back in the 1780s and with unalterably pre-fixed forms some sixty to eighty years ago. It has survived rather well despite the loss of those supposed guarantors of musical pedigree. There is no question that jazz will survive such "radical" changes as well. And since to date, no one has seriously questioned Ornette Coleman's claim to being a jazz musician, the day may yet come when he will find full acceptance among the "nouveau hippies" and jazz cognoscenti.

In the meantime, performances such as those recorded here give ample proof of the validity of Ornette Coleman's musical vision—a vision which embraces as many of the traditional bases of music making as one has a right to expect. That Ornette chooses

362

to work with a more fragmented, externally disrupted kind of continuity is *his* right, as is his tendency to exploit the more unusual timbres of his instrument, or his emphasis on melody and counterpoint over harmony. In fact, far from being a "poor melodist," Ornette is conceptually almost *all melody*, since harmony is given a decidedly secondary dependent role in his music.

All these qualities are amply represented on the four pieces recorded here. In addition, with the inclusion of long drum and bowed bass solos (*T.&T.* and *C.&D.*, respectively) and two examples of Ornette's ability to operate within a simpler, more traditional style (the theme of *R.P.D.D.* and his solo on *C.&D.*), there is perhaps an even greater variety in style and format than on previous Coleman Quartet recordings.

R.P.D.D., given over entirely to Ornette, is a fine example of how his solos and themes (compositions) are no more than two sides of the same coin. Like the theme of *C.&D.*, with its short motive treated sequentially, only to be answered by a tonality-disrupting phrase of rising fourths, his solo on *R.P.D.D.*, in expanded form, follows the same general pattern. Little motives are attacked from every conceivable angle, tried sequentially in numerous ways until they yield a motivic springboard for a new and contrasting idea, which will in turn be develped similarly, only to yield to yet another link in the chain of musical thought, and so on until the entire statement has been made. We can also hear Ornette's ability to exploit the unusual tonal-timbral characteristics of the alto. In the purposely split tones, harmonics, and abrasively gutteral low-register sounds, there lies a "beauty" of the same sort that we accept readily enough in Armstrong's gravel-voiced vocalism or Nanton's legendary trombone growls. Furthermore, these sonority investigations (as with Sonny Rollins) have an inevitability about them that removes them from the merely experimental.

Then there are Don Cherry's featherweight solos, twisted

and tortured, yet with an underlying touch of humor, and curiously unresolved and suspended.

Blackwell's subtly propulsive drumming is, by virtue of its omnipresence, too easily taken for granted. It is therefore a special pleasure to have his remarkable solo effort, *T.&T.* Starting with the decidedly "Latin" feeling of Ornette's theme, Blackwell gradually transforms the piece into one of the purest examples of African drumming in jazz. Tremendously pulsating, through a deft combination of repetition and variation, he generates the deep earthy feeling and pattern-conscious continuity of his forebears' art of drumming.

A final word about the late Scott LaFaro, who, had he lived, would certainly have become one of the great bass players (jazz *and* classical) of our century. The full range of his astounding abilities is exemplified in these four performances. While Scotty never quite found the unique three-way groove of providing the beat, harmonic foundation, and melodic counterpoint to the "horns" possessed by his predecessor, Charlie Haden, he did evolve a highly personal solution to the requirements of Ornette's music, still preserving its truly three-level counterpoint (horn, drums, bass). Within this concept, Scotty's role was slightly more independent of the "horns," less harmonically tied to them, and smoother in its continuity. Toward these ends, his lively, springy beat and elastic technique were eminently suited; and good examples of these qualities abound on this record: the *ostinato* figure under Don Cherry's splintered lines at the beginning of *W.R.U.;* a little later his driving low-register bass line (shortly before Ornette's entrance); the twisting sitarlike glissandos and double-stops of his own solo on *W.R.U.;* and his richly beautiful bowed tone on *C.&D.* The latter solo is of special interest, since it is the kind of playing which is still extremely rare in jazz, and because it displays the wide range of his imagination and technical skills, as well as his knowledge of the solo bass' role in contemporary nonjazz music. The *C.&D.* solo reflects, for example, Scotty's fascination with the bass part of Milhaud's rarely heard chamber orchestra work, *L'homme et Son Desir.*

But the ultimate measure of success in this music lies in the ability of these four musicians to give their manifold talents over to one single cooperative effort: the realization of a dream about music which Ornette Coleman continues to have and to cherish.

ORNETTE COLEMAN

One of the most influential musicians of the past forty years, saxophonist **Ornette Coleman**'s work changed the face of jazz in the early 1960s with its emphasis on group improvisation and rhythmic and harmonic freedom. As a writer, as in everything else, **Coleman** has a style of his own; he is certainly one of the most thoughtful of all jazz musicians.

> *Change of the Century*
>
> **Ornette Coleman**
> *(Atlantic 1327)*

Some musicians say, if what I'm doing is right, they should never have gone to school.

I say, there is no single *right* way to play jazz. Some of the comments made about my music make me realize though that modern jazz, once so daring and revolutionary, has become, in many respects, a rather settled and conventional thing. The members of my group and I are now attempting a breakthrough to a new, freer conception of jazz, one that departs from all that is "standard" and cliché in "modern" jazz.

Perhaps the most important new element in our music is our conception of *free* group improvisation. The idea of group improvisation, in itself, is not at all new; it played a big role in New Orleans' early bands. The big bands of the swing period changed all that. Today, still, the individual is either swallowed up in a group situation, or else he is out front soloing, with none of the other horns doing anything but calmly awaiting their turn for *their* solos. Even in some of the trios and quartets, which permit quite a bit of group improvisation, the final effect is one that is imposed beforehand by the arranger. One knows pretty much what to expect.

When our group plays, before we start out to play, we do not have any idea what the end result will be. Each player is free to contribute what he feels in the music at any given moment. We do not begin with a preconceived notion as to what kind of effect we will achieve. When we record, sometimes I can hardly believe that what I hear when the tape is played back to me is the playing of my group. I am so busy and absorbed when I play that I am not aware of what I'm doing at the time I'm doing it.

I don't tell the members of my group what to do. I want them to play what they hear in the piece for themselves. I let everyone express himself just as he wants to. The musicians have complete freedom, and so, of course, our final results depend entirely on the musicianship, emotional makeup, and taste of the individual members. Ours is at all times a group effort and it is only because we have the rapport we do that our music takes on the shape that it does. A strong personality with a star complex would take away from the effectiveness of our group, no matter how brilliantly he played.

With my music, as is the case with some of my friends who are painters, I often have people come to me and say, "I like it but I don't understand it." Many people apparently don't trust their reactions to art or to music unless there is a verbal *explanation* for it. In music, the only thing that matters is whether you *feel* it or not. You can't intellectualize music; to reduce it analytically often is to reduce it to nothing very important. It is only in terms of emotional response that I can judge whether what we are doing is successful or not. If you are touched in some way, then you are *in* with me. I love to play for people, and how they react affects my playing.

A question often asked of me is why I play a plastic alto. I bought it originally because I needed a new horn badly, and I felt I could not afford a new brass instrument. The plastic horn is less expensive, and I said to myself, "Better a new horn than one that leaks." After living with the plastic horn, I felt it begin to take on my emotion. The tone is breathier than the brass instrument, but I came to like the sound, and I found the flow of music to be more compact. I don't intend ever to buy another brass horn. On this plastic horn, I feel as if I am continually creating my own sound.

Now to the music. They are all originals. Each is quite different from the other, but in a certain sense there really is no start or finish to any of my compositions. There is a continuity of expression, certain continually evolving strands of thought that link all my compositions together. Maybe it's something like the paintings of Jackson Pollock.

Ramblin' is basically a blues, but it has a modern, more independent melodic line than older blues have, of course. I do not feel so confined to the blues form as do so many other jazz musicians. Blues are definite emotional statements. Some emotional situations can only be told as blues.

Free is well explained by the title. Our *free* group improvising is well demonstrated here. Each member goes his own way and still adds tellingly to the group endeavor. There was no predetermined chordal or time pattern. I think we got a spontaneous, freewheeling thing going here.

Face of the Bass begins as a vehicle for our bassist. Charlie Haden is from Missouri and he has a lot of heart. It is unusual to come across someone as young as he is and find that he has such a complete grasp of the "modern" bass: melodically independent and nonchordal.

Forerunner shows the interchangeability and flexibility of the component parts of the group. I like the way the melody here often runs through the rhythm instruments, with the melody instruments—the horns—providing rhythm accents (the traditional function of drums and bass).

Bird Food has echoes of the style of Charlie Parker. Bird would have understood us. He would have approved our aspiring to something beyond what we inherited. Oddly enough, the idolization of Bird, people wanting to play just like him and not make their own soul search, has finally come to be an impediment to progress in jazz.

Una Muy Bonita, in Spanish, means "a very pretty girl." I had no one in particular in mind. It is perhaps a little lighter in mood than some of our other pieces. It has a relaxed feeling and a more settled rhythm—and yes, I suppose, a "prettier" melody.

Change of the Century expresses our feeling that we have to make breaks with a lot of jazz's recent past, just as the boppers did with swing and traditional jazz. We want to incorporate more musical materials and theoretical ideas—from the classical world, as well as jazz and folk—into our work to create a broader base for the new music we are creating.

Every member of the group made an important and distinctly personal contribution to this album, which I think is the best we have made so far.

(As told to Gary Kramer)

ABOUT THE EDITOR

Tom Piazza is the author of the short story collection *Blues and Trouble* and *The Guide to Classic Recorded Jazz*. A former jazz pianist, he has written liner notes for a variety of jazz record labels and articles about jazz and other American music for *The New York Times, The Atlantic Monthly, The Village Voice,* and many other periodicals. A graduate of the Iowa Writers' Workshop, he is the recipient of a 1995–96 James Michener Award for fiction. He lives in New Orleans, where he is at work on a novel.

9695